Showdown at the 1964 Democratic Convention

Showdown at the 1964 Democratic Convention

Lyndon Johnson, Mississippi and Civil Rights

JOHN C. SKIPPER

McFarland & Company, Inc., Publishers
Jefferson, North Carolina, and London

LIBRARY OF CONGRESS ONLINE CATALOG DATA

Skipper, John C., 1945–
    Showdown at the 1964 Democratic Convention :
Lyndon Johnson, Mississippi and civil rights /
John C. Skipper.
        p.   cm.
    Includes bibliographical references and index.

    ISBN 978-0-7864-6161-5
    softcover : acid free paper ∞

    1. Democratic National Convention (1964 : Atlantic City,
N.J.)   2. Johnson, Lyndon B. (Lyndon Baines), 1908–1973.
3. Civil rights movements— United States— History— 20th
century.   4. United States— Politics and government—
1963–1969.   I. Title.
JK2313 1964 .S55 2012
324.2736 — dc23   2012008464

BRITISH LIBRARY CATALOGUING DATA ARE AVAILABLE

On the cover: *inset* Aaron Henry, chair of the Mississippi Freedom
Democratic Party delegation, reading from a document while
seated before the Credentials Committee at the 1964 Democratic
National Convention, Atlantic City, New Jersey (Library of Con-
gress); *background* interior of Convention Hall, looking toward
the speaker's platform, 1964 Democratic National Convention
(Lyndon Baines Johnson Library & Museum, photograph by
Cecil Stoughton)

Manufactured in the United States of America

McFarland & Company, Inc., Publishers
  Box 611, Jefferson, North Carolina 28640
    www.mcfarlandpub.com

For Arian Schuessler

Table of Contents

Preface   1

Introduction   5

  1. The Movement   11

  2. Robert Moses   24

  3. Lyndon Johnson   41

  4. A Nation Awakened   55

  5. The Republican Revolution   67

  6. The Journey   74

  7. Political Espionage   83

  8. Showdown   96

  9. Compromises and Consternation   112

10. Into the Lion's Den   124

11. A Compromise and a Lynching   134

12. Power, Protest and Politics   151

13. The Forces of Human Decency   159

14. Turning Points   164

15. Political Espionage Documented   175

Epilogue   179

Chapter Notes   193

Bibliography   203

Index   207

Preface

Benjamin Disraeli, the 19th century British prime minister, once said, "Power has one duty — to secure the social welfare of the people." In the summer of 1964, three examples of power came together in Atlantic City, New Jersey, each having the potential to shake the moorings of traditional American democracy.

One was the power of domination exercised by white, southern bigots who controlled the destinies of poor Negroes who lived in their midst and were denied, many times forcibly, the basic rights of citizens in a democratic society, such as the right to vote. This kind of prejudice manifested itself in such things as the belief by many that God was a segregationist and proved it by putting the blacks in Africa.

In Mississippi, many black citizens grew up thinking they did not have the right to vote. They didn't learn it in any textbook or classroom. They learned it by personal experience or by what they witnessed — white men with shotguns standing at the courthouse door, if not threatening at least menacing black citizens who tried to register to vote. If black citizens managed to get through the harassment and into the courthouse, they often had to deal with registrars of voting who administered literacy tests to them that were not only not given to white citizens but contained questions that the wisest of whites would have had trouble answering. To the black man, the law of the land was whatever the Ku Klux Klan and other white supremacists said it was. It was power by domination.

Another one of the forces at work was the quest for power. Young, ambitious black citizens realized their only hope for a better life was to challenge those whose oppression was smothering them. They had help when Robert Moses, a black, Harvard-educated schoolteacher from New York, traveled to Mississippi to see if he could make a difference. Largely through his efforts, poor, ignorant Negroes began to realize that individually they could do nothing, but together, with good organization and specific goals, they could change things—or die trying—and that death for the cause was more honorable than blandly accepting what was wrong.

What emerged was a mass movement to teach uneducated blacks about the principles of democracy: that they had the right to vote and in order to vote they must register; and that it was through voting that change takes place in a democracy in what is often called "power of the people."

Hundreds of northern white sympathizers, many of them recruited from college campuses, came to Mississippi in the summer of 1964 to teach, to encourage, and to help their black brethren register to vote. A new political party emerged, the Mississippi Freedom Democratic Party (MFDP), to challenge the racist and often violent ways of what was called the regular Mississippi Democrats—white males who excluded blacks from their politics.

One of the results of white supremacy was the exclusion of blacks from participating in the delegate selection to the Democratic National Convention that was to take place in August 1964 in Atlantic City. The Mississippi Freedom Democratic Party held a convention and elected its own slate of delegates. They went to Atlantic City to appeal to the Democratic Party's Credentials Committee to be seated instead of the all-white "regular Democrats."

The force of the "quest for power" sought to go toe-to-toe with the "power of domination" on the floor of the convention before a national television audience. The Freedom Democrats felt certain they would succeed because President Lyndon B. Johnson, who was sure to be nominated, was the man who signed the most sweeping civil rights bill in the history of the country and who led a political party that prided itself on helping the downtrodden.

But those two agents of power were up against a third force, one that was methodical, conniving, manipulative, secretive and domineering. It was the United States government, headed by a president who was sympathetic to the civil rights movement but wanted no trouble at the convention and certainly no trouble that could cause a walkout by delegates from southern states who were likely to stay home on election day in November if Johnson and the Democratic Party caved in to the wishes of blacks.

So in addition to the "power of domination" and the "quest of power," the third force, political power, took over and overmatched all the rest. That is a lesson from the summer of '64, the lesson of what political power can do to the best or worst of intentions in American life.

It is perhaps best exemplified by a conversation Secretary of Defense Robert McNamara had with Joseph Califano, who at that time worked in the Defense Department. Johnson wanted to push his anti-poverty program through Congress. Southern Democrats balked because Adam Yarmolinsky, deputy director of the program, was of Russian descent and also was a proponent of integration of military facilities. The politicians wanted Yarmolinsky out if Johnson wanted to get his anti-poverty program passed. Yarmolinsky was relieved of his duties and the bill passed.

Later, Johnson was asked at a press conference if Yarmolinsky had in fact been fired and Johnson denied it. Califano was disheartened that the president had lied to the press and to the American people. McNamara told Califano that if he was concerned about the president's lies, he was missing the big picture — that "power is not for the squeamish," that the greater good is defined by the president and however he defines it supercedes everything else. "None of us is important," said McNamara. "Everyone's expendable."[1]

It is McNamara's explanation of how government power works, that it is used for the greater good as defined by the president — and nothing else matters — that is the cornerstone on which this book is written. To understand that principle — not to agree with it necessarily, but to understand it — will help the reader put into perspective what happened and why it happened in the summer of '64. The context of McNamara's remarks are included in chapter 7.

The author is indebted to the resources available at the Lyndon Baines Johnson Library and Museum at Austin, Texas, for providing invaluable, indisputable research materials, including thousands of tape recordings of President Johnson's telephone conversations and photographs that are available for public consumption both at the library and online. The John F. Kennedy Presidential Library and Museum in Boston, Massachusetts, and its online services were also helpful.

Another valuable source of information were taped interviews with many figures in the civil rights movement that were part of *Eyes on the Prize*, a 14-hour documentary broadcast in 1987 by the Public Broadcasting System (PBS). Individual interviews from the series are available online and have been published in a book by the same title.

Personal interviews with people involved in the movement helped the author breathe life into the multitude of facts, figures and written documents that give important but passive validity to the subject matter.

Former vice president Walter Mondale, who in 1964 was the attorney general of Minnesota and who played a pivotal role in the showdown in Atlantic City, was extremely gracious in the giving of his time to grant an interview with the author, whom he had never met, in order to provide his perspective on what happened.

The author also wishes to thank Patti Miller, a white woman who has devoted her life to the advancement of civil rights causes. In 1964 she was a college student in Iowa and went to Mississippi to take part in the movement. Hers is an important aspect of the total narrative because she represents hundreds of college students who embodied the relentless spirit of youth in the worthy challenge of wanting to right a wrong, to make a difference in the world they lived in.

The late Martin Yoseloff was an author and friend, who, through his writings and teachings, provided vivid examples of how to avoid sentences that were like "living rooms with too much furniture" and how others needed "more red corpuscles," and who seemingly never spoke or wrote a sentence that didn't have pace and rhythm. Yoseloff died in 1997 but his teachings remain motivational.

Ted Savas is an author and publisher who instilled a "Yes, you can" attitude in me years ago that I have learned was not a threat but a prod and is best employed by the recipient with earnest humility.

A special thank you to a special group of encouragers— JoAnn Lower, Rita Bigger, Carol Rosenthal, Thorvald Sorensen, Sharon Koenigsfeld, Karl Horn, Fred Newton, John Culbertson, Stephanie Seemuth and Janet Kuhlmeier.

Michael Grandon, Bob Link and Arian Schuessler form a trilogy of patience and understanding because these three men, more than any others, have the distinction of hearing this book before they had a chance to read it. Their fate was cast because of their greatly appreciated indulgence in listening to the author for more than a year as he told them "what I'm working on."

The same would hold for family — wife Sandi at home, and daughters Stephanie Clark, Suzanne Skipper and Jennifer Skipper, scattered in different parts of the country but all a part of the whole, all who realize that their husband and father does what he does in the wholesome pursuit of searching for the greater good.

Introduction

One of the keys to understanding many events in world history is to answer a single question that encompasses everything in a single word: Why?

Why did terrorist attacks occur in the United States on September 11, 2001? Why did President Harry Truman order the atomic bomb to be dropped on Hiroshima in 1945? Why did the Japanese bomb Pearl Harbor four years earlier? Why did the stock market crash in 1929? Why did John Wilkes Booth assassinate Abraham Lincoln, and why did Thomas Jefferson write the Declaration of Independence, and why did Washington cross the Delaware?

The answer to each of these questions can be followed by another "why?" and each subsequent answer by yet another "why?" because the recording of history, and more important, the understanding of it, necessitates asking and answering the question over and over again.

The same is true of human achievement. Why did Mozart take up music and Picasso painting? Why did Thomas Edison start tinkering with electricity and Henry Ford with motors? Why did Orville and Wilbur Wright try to fly an airplane and Henry David Thoreau go into the woods to think? Why did Robert Frost write poetry and Frank Lloyd Wright take up architecture?

Motivation. It has always been a powerful force in shaping destiny. To understand what prompts man to do what he does is to answer the "why" question and provides a perspective — a lens — through which to see the world a little more clearly.

It is a way to look at six days in Atlantic City, New Jersey, in August of 1964 and to explain how American politics and the civil rights movement clashed at the Democratic National Convention, how the United States government felt compelled to spy on its own people for purely political purposes and how the political landscape of the country was changed for generations to come.

For one week in Atlantic City, two formidable forces collided in what one observer described as the morality of politics versus the politics of morality; another said it was the challenge of harmonizing legal problems with moral obligations.

It is necessary to view the broad picture first, to see three entities that chugged along like locomotives, fueled by fiery and relentless pride, each on a different track, coming from different directions but headed for an inevitable collision that was certain to have casualties.

On one track was the Mississippi delegation to the convention, a group of white segregationist men, duly elected not only through the laws of the state but through tradition that meant black citizens were not allowed even to participate in the process, much less be elected as delegates.

A second force to be reckoned with was an upstart group of citizens, most of them black, who decided to organize and form their own political party, the Mississippi Freedom Democratic Party, elect their own delegates to the convention, and then go to Atlantic City en masse and demand to be seated in place of the all-white delegation.

Also whistling into Atlantic City for those six days in August was the most powerful engine of all, the government of the United States, personified by a sitting president who wanted no trouble at the convention and was willing to use the strong arm of the government to make sure his wishes were carried out.

The account of what happened in those six days can best be told by examining the motivations of the central characters in the real-life drama that ensued.

There was Lyndon Baines Johnson, 36th president of the United States, who was catapulted into the presidency through the assassination of John F. Kennedy nine months earlier. Johnson was the consummate juggler of multiple agendas, which included a sincere desire to bring about social change, to earn the adulation of the people, and to secure a lasting legacy in history for himself that would give him distinction beyond just being the "accidental president" who carried out the programs of his more youthful, debonair predecessor.

There was Hubert Humphrey, the affable United States senator from Minnesota, who wanted to be president someday and, more immediately, wanted to be Johnson's vice president in 1964 as a stepping stone to his ultimate goal. Humphrey, a former mayor of Minneapolis and a longtime champion of civil rights for all Americans, would be given a challenge in those six days in Atlantic City that would make or break his political career — and he knew it.

There was Walter F. Mondale, attorney general of Minnesota and at age 36 a youngster in hardball politics. He was assigned to be a member of the Credentials Committee at the convention, a routine job that was tantamount to checking IDs of delegates before the convention began — making sure, in effect, that everyone who entered was a dues-paying member of the club, as one might picture happening at a national gathering of Kiwanis. However, within hours of the first meeting of the Credentials Committee, Mondale would be given another assignment, this one putting him in a position that would not only affect his career but those of Humphrey and Johnson as well, and have a profound impact on the Democratic Party and the civil rights movement in America.

There was Robert P. "Bob" Moses, a 29-year-old, New York–bred, Harvard-educated black man who traveled to Mississippi one summer to try to do what he could to right some wrongs. He ended up staying for years and created a game plan in which he and his followers would have a confrontation with the most powerful forces in the United States government.

There was Fannie Lou Hamer, a poor, black, uneducated, Mississippi sharecropper — the opposite of Bob Moses in so many ways. And yet, more than anyone else, she became the symbol of black oppression in America and someone the president of the United States did not want to tangle with.

There was Joseph Rauh, a wealthy, white, Washington, D.C., attorney, who, over the years, had an on-again, off-again relationship with Lyndon Johnson. He was an ardent supporter of Hubert Humphrey and a champion of liberal causes, including the civil rights movement. Rauh, more than any other individual in the Atlantic City debacle, found himself caught in the cross hairs of a controversy that resulted in his being loathed by the government forces he was up against and not trusted by the very people he had put his reputation on the line to help.

There was Walter Reuther, president of the United Auto Workers, who was an ally of Lyndon Johnson, a supporter of Hubert Humphrey, a financial contributor to the civil rights movement and whose corporate lawyer was Rauh. Because of these relationships, he was in a unique position to be a deal maker. Reuther eventually broke away from labor negotiations in Detroit and flew to Atlantic City to help his friend, the president, avoid public embarrassment at a convention he thought should be honoring him. Reuther would bring to the table what he would call a compromise but what in fact was an ultimatum.

There were Mickey Schwerner and Andrew Goodman, two idealistic, well-educated and energetic young white men from New York, and James Chaney, a black laborer from Mississippi, who struck up, if not a friendship, a kinship, that led to their brutal murders — a turning point in what the nation as a whole thought the civil rights movement in the South was all about.

There were the leaders of the major civil rights organizations of the day, among them the Rev. Martin Luther King, Jr., of the Southern Christian Leadership Conference; John Lewis of the Student Nonviolent Coordinating Committee; and Ralph Wilkins of the National Association for the Advancement of Colored People — all black leaders having the same goals but far different approaches on how to reach them.

There was Robert F. Kennedy, brother of the slain president and attorney general of the United States who was a powerful force in American politics because of his surname, because of the sympathy the American people had for him and his family, and because of his own personal ambitions. Johnson was obsessive in his distrust of him, and Kennedy avoided dealing with the president as much as possible.

And there was J. Edgar Hoover, director of the Federal Bureau of Investigation for 40 years, in fact, its only director, who was the personification of law enforcement in America, who worked tirelessly at keeping the image of the FBI squeaky clean, and who was a racist who scoffed at hiring black employees and thought much of the civil rights movement in America was Communist inspired. He despised both Martin Luther King and Robert Kennedy.

It is understanding the motivation of each of these people — understanding why they did what they did in the summer of 1964 — that at least helps explain why the Democratic National Convention and its surroundings were the setting for a huge domestic spying operation ordered by the president, carried out by a reluctant Hoover ("Lyndon is way out of line"[1]) and done for purely political purposes.

There is yet another element that shapes this episode in American history, the element of "compromise" — something that is often portrayed as a solution to a problem so that everybody goes home with something to brag about as Lyndon Johnson described it. And yet, when the compromise turns out to be the white man telling the black man what has been decided, it's not a compromise at all to the black man. It's business as usual, it's sitting in the back of the bus again, it's being denied access, it's not having a voice — and it's not something he's going to go home and brag about.

The following describes what turned out to be a series of turning points in American history, all because of six days in Atlantic City in 1964. It is documented by hundreds of tape recordings of telephone conversations of President Johnson, all archived at the LBJ Presidential Library in Austin, Texas. Johnson used the telephone as both a political tool and a weapon and had enough telephones installed so as to have one within arm's length of wherever he might be in the White House. In addition, his preoccupation with preserving his place in history prompted him to install recording devices so that future historians would be able to listen in while that history was being made. Because of that, those same historians as well as scholars and interested citizens are able to better understand how the struggle for civil rights clashed with political might in the summer of 1964.

It helps answer that first basic question: "Why?"

CHAPTER 1

The Movement

It was the spring of 1964, the season of the British invasion of the American music culture. The Beatles, four singers from Liverpool, occupied the top five spots on *Billboard*'s "Top 40" with "Can't Buy Me Love," "Twist and Shout," "She Loves Me," "I Want to Hold Your Hand," and "Please Please Me."

Americans, recovering from the collective grief over the assassination of President John F. Kennedy six months earlier, were busy working, raising their families, buying McDonald's hamburgers for 15 cents each, filling their gas tanks for 27 cents a gallon, buying their cigarettes for 50 cents a pack and mailing their letters after affixing six-cent stamps to them. The movie *Goldfinger*, with its hero James Bond, would captivate audiences from coast to coast.

In February, a young, brash boxer named Cassius Clay knocked out Sonny Liston to become the heavyweight champion of the world. In March, the first Ford Mustang rolled off the assembly lines in Detroit, and later that same month, the quiz show *Jeopardy* debuted on NBC. In April, Shea Stadium, the nation's newest Major League baseball park, opened in New York and, a few weeks later, the New York World's Fair got under way. On May 2, Senator Barry Goldwater of Arizona won the Republican presidential primary in Texas, another step on his way to winning his party's nomination in July. In August, President Lyndon Johnson was nominated by Democrats, a little over a month after he signed the civil rights act aimed at ending segregation throughout the United States.

Beneath the surface of all the activities that signaled a vibrant, progressive America, and despite passage of the most comprehensive civil rights legislation in American history, thousands of Negroes, primarily in the South, feared for their lives if they even tried to have a piece of the lifestyles enjoyed by white America. Nowhere was that truer than in Mississippi. "Mississippi was a police state, pure and simple," according to civil rights activist Victoria Gray Adams. "Totally isolated from every-thing.... It was truly a closed society — the law enforcement agencies, the government, for all practical purposes, not accountable to anyone."[1]

By 1964, the civil rights movement was part of the American fabric, with massive demonstrations and the emergence over the years of leaders such as the Rev. Martin Luther King, head of the Southern Christian Leadership Conference (SCLC); Roy Wilkins, president of the National Association for the Advancement of Colored People (NAACP); James Farmer, leader of the Congress of Racial Equality (CORE); and others. Americans north of the Mason-Dixon Line knew of discrimination in the South primarily from news accounts of demonstrations that became violent or when thousands of people took part, such as the March on Washington in 1963.

But few in the North knew what was occurring every day somewhere in Mississippi. They didn't know about Ivanhoe Donaldson being confronted by a police officer as he stopped for gas and was told to get in the squad car whereupon the officer drew his gun, cocked it, put the barrel in Donaldson's mouth, and said, "I'm going to kill you, nigger." Donaldson's life was spared when the officer's partner intervened.

Similarly, few knew about the time Donaldson had gone to Michigan, and picked up a truckload of groceries to be distributed to poor people in Mississippi. Upon his return to the state, he was arrested by a white police officer, charged with possession of narcotics, and held in jail for five days without family or friends knowing where he was.[2]

It went unnoticed in most of the country when the Rev. George Lee, a black man in Humphreys County, was killed by white extremists because of his efforts to get black people to register to vote; or when Lamar Smith was shot to death on a courthouse lawn in Brookhaven. Though the shooting was witnessed by dozens of people, the killer went free because nobody would admit to seeing a white man shoot a black man.

Most of the nation was unaware that Emmett Till, a 14-year-old black boy on vacation from Chicago, was kidnapped, beaten, shot to death and dumped in a river near Money, Mississippi, because he had reportedly flirted with a white woman in a store. An all-white jury found his killers innocent of the murder.

There were no headlines in the North when Mack Charles Parker, 23, accused of raping a white woman in Poplarville, was dragged from his jail cell by a white mob three days before his trial, and was beaten, shot to death and his body tossed into the Pearl River.

Little notice was given to the death of Herbert Lee, a black man killed by a state legislator in Liberty for helping blacks register to vote, and to the shooting death of Louis Allen, who witnessed Lee's murder.

There was hardly a mention in the press when Corporal Roman

Ducksworth, Jr., a military officer stationed in Maryland, on leave to visit his sick wife, was ordered off a bus in Taylorsville and shot dead by a white police officer who mistook him for a "freedom rider" testing bus segregation laws.[3]

The killing of black Americans was an unspoken part of the culture of the segregationist South, not just limited to Mississippi. John Earl Reese, a 16-year-old black youngster in Mayflower, Texas, was gunned down in a restaurant with shots fired through the windows by angry whites. Willie Edwards, Jr., a truck driver, was on his way to work in Montgomery, Alabama, when Ku Klux Klansmen forced him out of his truck and ordered him at gunpoint to jump off a bridge into the Alabama River. Edwards drowned. William Lewis Moore, a white mailman from Baltimore, was shot and killed in Attalia, Alabama, while on a one-man crusade against segregation.[4]

Civil rights and American politics had been intertwined for nearly two decades. In 1948, President Harry Truman ordered the desegregation of the nation's armed services, ending the practice of blacks having separate living conditions from their white counterparts. At the Democratic National Convention in Philadelphia that year, Hubert Humphrey, mayor of Minneapolis, gave an impassioned speech pleading for a civil rights plank in the party's platform.

Humphrey made reference to the convention's keynote speaker, Alben Barkley, who had spoken of Thomas Jefferson. Barkley said, "He did not proclaim that all the white or the black or the red or the yellow men are equal; that all Christian or Jewish men are equal; that all Protestant and Catholic men are equal; that all rich and poor men are equal; that all good and bad men are equal. What he proclaimed was that all men are equal; and the equality which he proclaimed was the equality in the right to enjoy the blessings of free government in which they may participate and to which they have given their support."

Building on that, Humphrey told the delegates, "My friends, to those who say we are rushing this issue of civil rights, I say to them we are 172 years late. To those who say this civil rights program is an infringement on state's rights, I say this: The time has arrived in America for the Democratic Party to get out of the shadow of state's rights and to walk forthrightly into the bright sunshine of human rights."[5]

The plank was adopted but not without political cost. Southern Democrats rebelled, several of them leaving the convention floor while Humphrey was speaking. They formed the Dixiecrat Party with a slogan of "Segregation Forever." South Carolina governor Strom Thurmond ran as the Dixiecrats' candidate for president. In November, Thurmond and the Dixiecrats lost but sent a message that segregation was alive and well in the South by carrying South Carolina, Mississippi, Louisiana and Alabama in the general election. That same year, Humphrey was elected to the U.S. Senate from Minnesota, as was Lyndon Johnson from Texas.[6]

In 1954, politics, justice and civil rights reached a milestone when the United States Supreme Court, in a case known as *Brown v. the Board of Education*, issued a ruling in which it said schools in America were to be desegregated "with all deliberate speed." The case was particularly significant because through the court's ruling, the government of the United States, not just a political party, had taken a strong, uncompromising stand against segregation. The case involved a black child, Linda Brown, in Topeka, Kansas, who had to go to an all-black school miles from where she lived because she was not allowed to go to an all-white school closer to her home.[7]

In December of 1955, Rosa Parks refused to take a seat in the back of a city bus in Montgomery, Alabama, and was arrested for violating a city ordinance. Her arrest drew nationwide attention and led to a year-long boycott by blacks of the Montgomery bus system. The next year, the Supreme Court issued a ruling in which it said any local ordinance mandating segregation was unconstitutional. But in that same year, 77 southern House members and every southern senator except for three signed a document called the "Southern Manifesto" in which they vowed to defy the Supreme Court's school desegregation order.

The manifesto, which became part of the Congressional Record of the 84th Congress, said the Supreme Court ruling in *Brown v. Board of Education* flew in the face of the state's rights provisions of the Constitution. In making their case, signators of the manifesto referred to "the increasing gravity of the situation following the decision of the Supreme Court in the so-called segregation cases, and the peculiar stress in sections of the country where this decision has

Governor Strom Thurmond of South Carolina, a segregationist, ran as an independent for president in 1948 after Democrats approved a civil rights plank in their party platform (Library of Congress).

created many difficulties, unknown and unappreciated, perhaps, in other parts of the country." They went on to say:

> We regard the decisions of the Supreme Court in the school cases as a clear abuse of judicial power. It climaxes a trend in the Federal Judiciary undertaking to legislate, in derogation of the authority of Congress, and to encroach upon the reserved rights of the States and the people.... This unwarranted exercise of power by the court, contrary to the Constitution, is creating chaos and confusion in the States principally affected.
>
> It is destroying the amicable relations between the white and Negro races that have been created through 90 years of patient effort by the good people of both races. It has planted hatred and suspicion where there has been heretofore friendship and understanding. Without regard to the consent of the governed, outside mediators are threatening immediate and revolutionary changes in our public school systems. If done, this is certain to destroy the system of public education in some of the States....
>
> We commend the motives of those States which have declared the intention to resist forced integration by any lawful means.... We pledge ourselves to use all lawful means to bring about a reversal of this decision which is contrary to the Constitution and to prevent the use of force in its implementation.[8]

In addition to the 77 House members, the manifesto was signed by Senators James Eastland and John Stennis of Mississippi, Russell Long and Allen Ellender of Louisiana, J. William Fulbright and John McClellan of Arkansas, Harry F. Byrd and A. Willis Robertson of Virginia, Lister Hill and John Sparkman of Alabama, Strom Thurmond and Olin Johnston of South Carolina, Sam Ervin and W. Kerr Scott of North Carolina, George Smathers and Spessard Holland of Florida, Richard Russell and Walter F. George of Georgia, and Price Daniel of Texas.[9]

Three southern senators who declined to sign the manifesto were Albert Gore Sr. and Estes Kefauver of Tennessee — and Lyndon Johnson of Texas, all of whom had future presidential aspirations. Their political support was already solid in the South. By not signing the manifesto, they hoped to gain the favor of white, liberal voters in the North.

"The civil rights movement," wrote historian Nick Kotz, "was transforming mid-twentieth century America, building political pressure for change. John Kennedy and Lyndon Johnson — indeed any Democrat aspiring to run for national office — would now need to respond to the rising tide of black protest to inequalities that belied the nation's most cherished ideals if they hoped to be elected."[10]

It was a delicate tightrope act for ambitious southern politicians like Johnson who had to strike a balance between satisfying the needs and rights of black Americans without losing the powerful voting bloc of southern seg-regationists. He was put to the test again in 1957 when he helped pass a civil rights act that created a U.S. Commission on Civil Rights and created a civil rights division in the Justice Department. The new elements were symbols of change and marked the first civil rights legislation since Reconstruction.

Johnson backed the bill, despite being called a turncoat by some of his fellow southern senators, but he still had aspirations of being president someday and needed to have something to show for himself on civil rights. By now he was part of the Senate leadership and was virtually assured of re-election.

As the civil rights movement grew and the government got more involved, segregationists became more organized. As new laws were passed and new enforcement departments created within the government, White Citizen Councils were forming in the South and Ku Klux Klan membership was increasing.

The black community had an organized establishment in the National Association for the Advancement of Colored People (NAACP) headed by Roy Wilkins. The NAACP, which had the largest membership of any black group and a strong and stable structure, had fought its battles for equality through vigorous lobbying and by filing lawsuits. Wilkins had a back-ground in journalism and was a reporter and later managing editor of the *Kansas City Call*, a black-owned newspaper. He joined the staff of the NAACP in 1931, edited its official publication for several years and became executive director in 1955.

Another primarily black organization, the National Urban League, led by Whitney Young, focused its attention on attempting to end dis-crimination in employment and to lobbying for better jobs for black Amer-icans. Young, a Kentucky native who earned a master's degree at the University of Minnesota, worked at several Urban League chapter offices and then became dean of the School of Social Work at the University of Atlanta in 1954. In 1961, he became executive director of the National Urban League and called for a "Domestic Marshall Plan" in which black men and women would receive preferential treatment in jobs, education and housing to make up for centuries of abuse.

Yet another organization, the Congress of Racial Equality (CORE), headed by James Farmer, also worked to end discrimination. Of all the black leaders of the day, Farmer was perhaps the smartest. As a youngster he was a brilliant student who entered Wiley College in Marshall, Texas, at age 14 and graduated when he was 18. While there, he was a member of a national championship debate team. He graduated from the Howard University School of Religion. It was there that he developed a philosophy of "nonviolent resistance."

During the time that the black community in Montgomery, Alabama, boycotted the city bus system, a young minister named Martin Luther King, Jr., emerged as the leader of the Montgomery Improvement Association. King, son of a Baptist pastor in Atlanta, had come to Montgomery to get some pastoral experience at the Dexter Avenue Baptist Church and had planned on returning to Atlanta to help with his father's ministry.

The success of the bus boycott energized King and he contacted other black ministers throughout the South to use a new force in the fight for equality—community action. On February 10, 1957, 97 people, mostly black ministers, formed the Southern Christian Leadership Conference (SCLC) and elected King as its first president.

Organized black groups were now planning and participating in more demonstrations throughout the South, emphasizing nonviolence. Some drew national attention. On February 1, 1960, Ezell A. Blair, Jr., David Richmond, Joseph McNeil and Franklin McCain, four black students at North Carolina A&T University in Greensboro, sat down at a lunch counter in Greensboro and were refused service. When they refused to leave, police arrested them.

Word spread about the lunch counter sit-in in Greensboro and it spawned similar sit-ins throughout the South. On April 15, about ten weeks after the Greensboro sit-in, a group of about 200 black students met at Shaw University in Raleigh, North Carolina, and formed the Student Nonviolent Coordinating Committee (SNCC), united in purpose but otherwise independent from the other civil rights groups. SNCC, led by John Lewis, became a powerful force in keeping segregation and discrimination in the forefront and forced them to inevitably become political issues.[11]

Lewis, a 21-year-old college student at American Baptist Theological Seminary in Nashville, Tennessee, said the organized efforts by black people to end discrimination brought a new word into the civil rights lexicon; it had become a "movement." Years later, he wrote: "That term 'movement' was beginning to look as if it might actually apply to American society at large, to the nation's attitude about and response to the struggle for racial equality. Three years earlier, the first civil rights bill since Reconstruction had passed and now another was being discussed.... Whoever ran for president was going to have to deal with this issue."[12]

The intertwining of presidential politics and civil rights took an unusual twist on October 19 when blacks conducted a sit-in at Rich's, one of Atlanta's leading department stores. By this time, King had resigned his position at Dexter Baptist Church in Montgomery and had returned to Atlanta to be a pastor at his father's church, Ebeneezer Baptist Church. He took part in the sit-in and spent his first night in a jail cell for being an activist. When it was discovered his arrest violated his terms of probation for a traffic violation a few weeks earlier, authorities kept him in custody for a week.

His arrest drew nationwide attention. On October 26, presidential candidate John F. Kennedy called Coretta King, Martin Luther King's wife, to express his concern about the situation. The next day, Kennedy's brother, Robert F. Kennedy, called a county judge in DeKalb County and persuaded the judge to release King on $1,000 bond.

Whether the Kennedys' motives were based on moral outrage or political expediency is not known. What is known is that the Democratic National Committee spread the word about how John and Robert Kennedy had come to the aid of the civil rights worker, hoping the news of their involvement would win support of black Americans. A week later, Kennedy was elected president over Richard Nixon by a razor-thin margin.[13]

On May 4, 1961, a little more than three months after Kennedy was inaugurated, CORE and SNCC formed two teams whose purpose was to integrate the Greyhound and Trailways bus systems. Thirteen Freedom Riders boarded buses in Washington, D.C., and traveled south through Virginia, North and South Carolina, Mississippi, Alabama and Louisiana, to arrive in New Orleans on May 17. They were accosted by angry whites in a waiting room in Rock Hill, South Carolina. In Anniston, Alabama, a fire bomb was thrown through a bus window. But the biggest trouble occurred in Montgomery where gangs of whites wielding baseball bats and other weapons stormed the bus depot and attacked those waiting inside. Lewis, the SNCC leader, was knocked unconscious.

"They were all around me," said Lewis. "Someone grabbed my briefcase which I had been holding in my right hand since stepping off the bus. I pulled back but it was ripped from my fingers. At that instant, I felt a thud against my head. I could feel my knees collapse and then nothing. I was unconscious." He learned later he had been struck on the skull with a wooden Coca-Cola crate.

Also knocked unconscious was John Siegenthaler, a white assistant to Robert Kennedy, now attorney general of the United States. Siegenthaler had been dispatched to Montgomery to observe what was happening and report back to Kennedy. Eventually, Montgomery police arrived and broke up the disturbance. Lewis said he learned later that police officers were outside the depot and did not enter until the white mob had done its damage. That night, the battered bus patrons met at a church. Once again, an angry mob appeared but was dispersed by federal marshals sent to the scene by Robert Kennedy. The government was now officially involved with the bloodshed of the movement.[14]

By 1963, racial demonstrations and civil unrest had woven tightly into the fabric of American society. On Good Friday, King was arrested and jailed in Birmingham for violating a court order prohibiting him from taking part in demonstrations. In his jail cell, he read a report in the Birmingham newspaper of white clergymen who empathized with the plight of blacks but urged them to have patience.

King was moved to write a response. In it, he said, "When you have seen vicious mobs lynch your mothers and fathers at will and drown your sisters and brothers at whim; when you have seen hate-filled policemen curse, kick and even kill your black brothers and sisters; when you see the vast majority of your 20 million Negro brothers smothering in an airtight cage of poverty in the midst of an affluent society; when you suddenly find your tongue twisted and your speech stammering as you seek to explain to your six-year-old daughter why she can't go to the public amusement park that has just been advertised on television, and see tears welling up in her eyes when she is told that Funtown is closed to colored children ... when you are forever fighting a degenerating sense of nobodyness, then you will understand why we find it difficult to wait."[15]

King believed Birmingham was the most segregated city in America. He thought it could be the setting that would draw the attention of much of America to the plight of the black person in a segregated society. So he continued to organize demonstrations there. Birmingham's police commissioner was a former sportscaster and now career politician, Theophilus "Bull" Connor, an outspoken segregationist. In May, Connor's response to a demonstration in downtown Birmingham sent a message across the country that was a turning point in the quest for fair treatment of black Americans. Connor ordered police and firefighters to use police dogs and powerful firehoses against the black demonstrators, a scene witnessed by millions in televised news reports.[16]

On June 11, 1963, a few days after Alabama governor George Wallace helped block black students from enrolling at the University of Alabama, Kennedy addressed the nation from the White House. He said in part:

> My fellow Americans, this is a problem which faces us all — in every city of the north as well as the south. Today there are Negroes unemployed, two or three times as many as compared to whites; inadequate education, moving into larger cities unable to find work, young people in particular out of work, without hope, denied equal rights, denied the opportunity to eat at a restaurant or lunch counter or go to a theater, denied the right to a decent education, denied almost today the right to attend a state university even though qualified.
>
> It seems to me these are matters that concern us all, not merely presidents or congressmen or governors but every citizen of the United States. This is one country. It has become one country because all of us and all the people who came here had an equal chance to develop their talents.

President Kennedy addresses the nation in June 1963 urging an end to racial discrimination. A few hours after his speech, civil rights leader Medgar Evers was gunned down in Mississippi (John F. Kennedy Library).

> We cannot say to ten percent of the population that you can't have
> that right, that your children cannot have the chance to develop what-
> ever talents they have, that the only way they are going to get their
> rights is to go to the streets and demonstrate. I think we owe them and
> we owe ourselves a better country than that.[17]

Shortly after midnight on June 12, just a few hours after Kennedy
had addressed the nation from the White House, Medgar Evers, state
field director for the NAACP in Mississippi, was gunned down in the
driveway of his home after attending a meeting to discuss NAACP activities. He held in his hands T-shirts bearing the message "Jim Crow Must
Die."

His death, at the hands of white supremacists, drew national attention
but was just the latest incident in Mississippi — no worse than the kidnap-
ping and killing of Emmett Till, the 14-year-old boy who was accused of
flirting with a white woman in 1955; or Herbert Lee, a civil rights activist
gunned down by an angry state legislator in 1961; or Army Corporal Roman
Ducksworth, ordered off a bus by an angry mob and fatally shot in 1962.

When Victoria Gray Adams, a civil rights leader, described Mississippi
as a "police state," she was not only referring to the restrictions put on
blacks, such as not allowing them to register to vote, but also to police
brutality against blacks and their penchant for turning their backs while
whites beat blacks or burned their homes, or how the police took their
time showing up at scenes where blacks were being attacked.

On May 28, 1963, two weeks before Kennedy spoke to the nation,
students from Tougaloo College in Jackson, Mississippi, staged a sit-in at
the segregated lunch counter at a Woolworth store when a white mob surrounded them. Anne Moody, one of the demonstrators, said she was
snatched from her stool and dragged by her hair toward a door. She managed to get free and returned to the lunch counter where demonstrators
were being taunted and, in some cases, beaten. They had been trained to
remain nonviolent so they absorbed what was happening to them as best
they could.

"There were now four of us," Moody recalled, "two whites and two
Negroes, all women. The mob started smearing us with catsup, mustard,
sugar, pies and everything on the counter. Soon Joan and I were joined
by John Salter but the moment he sat down, he was hit on the jaw by what
appeared to be brass knuckles. Blood rushed from his face and someone
threw salt into the open wound."[18]

A few days after Kennedy spoke to the nation, he sent sweeping civil
rights legislation to Congress, which, when enacted, was intended to make
integration the law of the land — all of the land, including Mississippi.

On November 22, 1963, Kennedy was assassinated while riding in a

A somber Lyndon Johnson takes the oath of office, flanked by wife Lady Bird and Jackie Kennedy, after President John F. Kennedy was assassinated in Dallas on November 22, 1963 (LBJ Library).

motorcade in Dallas, Texas. Vice President Lyndon Johnson ascended to the presidency, a man almost the polar opposite of the popular president he succeeded. Kennedy was part of the latest generation of a rich and powerful eastern establishment family. The son of a multimillionaire and former U.S. ambassador to England, Kennedy was Harvard educated, a World War II hero and winner of a Pulitzer Prize for literature. Johnson grew up in a small town in Texas, taught school for a while before going to Washington where he gained the reputation as being a brash politician, a master of behind-the-scenes maneuvering with a single goal — to get what he wanted. What he wanted was power and influence and achieved both. As Senate majority leader, he told a colleague how much President Eisenhower needed him. "Ike couldn't pass the Lord's Prayer in Congress without me," he said.[19]

As a leader in the Senate, Johnson had helped push through the Civil Rights Act of 1957; that was minor compared to what Kennedy had proposed. But Kennedy was gone and the fate of the civil rights movement was now in the hands of a man who was born and raised in the South and whose political cronies, men who had mentored him, such as Senator Richard Russell of Georgia, were lifelong segregationists.

Kennedy's eloquence was in stark contrast to Johnson's crudeness.

Senator Lyndon Johnson (third from left) smiles as he takes part in a bill-signing ceremony by President Eisenhower in 1955. Johnson boasted that Eisenhower couldn't get the Lord's Prayer through Congress without his help (LBJ Library).

Whereas Kennedy sought to raise the country's moral conscience in appealing for integration, Johnson often called it the politics of necessity.

And he had a unique perspective, one far removed from anything Kennedy had experienced. James Farmer, head of the Congress of Racial Equality (CORE), knew Johnson never did anything without a pragmatic motive. So he asked him what his motive was in pushing for civil rights.

Johnson told him a story about Zephyr Wright, the Johnsons' black cook. When she traveled in the South, she was often denied access to restrooms. She would have to "go squat in the middle of a field to pee," he said.

He told the same story to Senator John Stennis of Mississippi, an ardent and vocal segregationist. "That's wrong," Johnson said, "and there ought to be something to change that. And it seems to me if the people in Mississippi don't change it voluntarily, that it's just going to be necessary to change it by law."[20]

CHAPTER 2

Robert Moses

In 1964, the average black person in Mississippi earned $1,500 a year at whatever jobs were either beneath the dignity of white people or, at best, jobs white people would allow them to have. This meant that about 90 percent of blacks lived below the poverty level. Ninety-three percent of the black population never finished high school; there were chores in the cotton fields and plantations that needed their attention.

Only 20,000, about 5 percent of Mississippi's 435,000 black citizens over the age of 21, were registered to vote — and in some counties, none were registered.[1] Blacks who tried to register were often met at the courthouse door by armed white citizens or gun-toting sheriff's deputies and police officers who blocked the doorways, threatening them with arrests or violence if they proceeded. In some counties, if blacks registered to vote or even tried to, their names were published in the local newspapers, making them targets of abuse and victims of violence.

One hundred and one years after Abraham Lincoln freed the slaves, ten years after the Supreme Court ordered schools integrated "with all deliberate speed," seven years after Congress passed the first civil rights bill since Reconstruction, the white man's law — segregation — was the law in most parts of Mississippi.

Senator James Eastland, a wealthy plantation owner, urged his fellow Mississippians to defy Supreme Court rulings on integration. In 1955, he gave a speech to an audience that included the Mississippi governor, a congressman and state legislators in which he said, "The Supreme Court of the United States, in the false name of law and justice, has perpetrated a monstrous crime. The anti-segregation decisions were dishonest decisions. They were dictated by political pressure groups bent upon the destruction of the American form of government and the mongrelization of the white race." It was not the only time Eastland referred to blacks as "mongrels." He was still in the Senate in 1964 and still a racist as was his Senate counterpart, John Stennis.[2]

Many blacks in Mississippi had been fighting discrimination for years. They participated in marches, demonstrations, sit-ins and did what they could to buck the establishment, always with the knowledge that retaliation could come in the form of murders, beatings, arrests and having their homes, businesses and churches firebombed. What they needed, perhaps without realizing it, was someone and something to galvanize their efforts, to synchronize all of their individual efforts into one concerted effort — to create a giant waterfall fed by many tiny streams.

It all started to come together when Robert Parris Moses, a 25-year-old black schoolteacher from New York, came to Mississippi in 1960 to see what he could do to help the civil rights movement. No one could have known then that his efforts would culminate four years later in a confrontation that would involve the president of the United States, create havoc at a national political convention and change the political landscape of the Democratic Party.

Bob Moses and Lyndon Johnson were worlds apart geographically, ethnically and culturally, but in their two worlds both realized that none of their goals could be realized without political power. Johnson had it and wanted to keep it. Moses saw it as the only real way black people in Mississippi could attain the rights to which they were entitled.

Moses was a native of Harlem, the son of a janitor, who displayed early in his life a penchant for problem solving and deep thinking.

Senator James Eastland of Mississippi said the Supreme Court's desegregation ruling was a "monstrous crime." He often referred to blacks as "mongrels" (U.S. Senate photograph).

He scored high enough on a battery of tests to be admitted to Stuyvesant, a high school for gifted students, where, among other things, he was president of his senior class and captain of the baseball team.

He was one of three black students at Hamilton College in upstate New York where the color of his skin prevented him from belonging to a fraternity. He developed a deep interest in philosophy and passive resistance, and went on to earn a master's degree in philosophy from Harvard University.

He also had a love of mathematics and got a job teaching high school math at Horace Mann, a private school in New York. It was during this time that he became interested in the civil rights movement in Mississippi. He decided to get involved with the Student Nonviolent Coordinating Committee.

Moses had been inspired to come to the South when he saw news reports of the lunch counter sit-in in Greensboro and other similar demonstrations. What struck him was the passion and determination of hundreds, perhaps thousands, of young people to do what they could to right some wrongs.

"Before, the Negro in the South had always looked on the defensive, cringing," said Moses. "This time they were taking the initiative. They were kids my age and I knew this had something to do with my own life." He was motivated to come to Mississippi to see what he could do to help.[3]

One of the first people he met was Amzie Moore, a postal worker and civil rights activist in Cleveland, Mississippi, who told him the marches and sit-ins had their place, but in Mississippi the biggest problem was blacks being denied the right to vote, being threatened if they even tried to register. Moore believed the key to social and economic equality was to become a political force, strong enough to topple the power structure that smothered the black community. He

Robert Moses, a Harvard-educated schoolteacher from New York, came to Mississippi to be part of the civil rights movement and became the catalyst for the Mississippi Freedom Democrats' attempt to be seated at the Democratic National Convention (Library of Congress).

told Moses about how blacks had been murdered for just trying to register to vote. "Shooting has replaced lynching in Mississippi," he said.

Moses listened to Moore's voice of experience and began planning voter registration drives. At first, he worked alone, going door to door in McComb, a tiny community on the western edge of the state. By day, he tried to convince local blacks to go register to vote and could tell immediately how scared they were to even try. By night, he stayed in the homes of local activists, putting his life and theirs in danger. He suffered many beatings at the hands of angry whites and by police officers.

He soon discovered that Mississippi was a closed society to the black man and opening it up would take a massive effort. He was prepared to mobilize students, black and white, from the North and South to help with voter registration drives. Moore was right, he thought. Voter registration was the necessary first step toward achieving leverage to upset the white power base.

Years later, he reflected on his first days in Mississippi. "When I went to Mississippi in 1960 ... trying to get people to come to an initial SNCC meeting, the only person I met in the whole state who was actually willing to embrace the students (SNCC) and what they stood for was Amzie. I think he saw in the students what had been lacking ... some kind of deep commitment that no matter what the cost, people were going to get this done."[4]

Moore said there was good reason for poor, black Mississippi residents to distrust the Harvard-educated schoolteacher. "I felt like if a man was educated, there wasn't much you could tell him. This had been the case in the South. Bob was altogether different. When I found out he was honestly seeking to help, then, in any way I could, I was willing to help," said Moore.[5]

Moses, a quiet, soft-spoken bespectacled man, brought organizational skills, passion, commitment and intensity to the movement, and he warned those who joined the effort that it should be a cause they were willing to die for — and for many, it was. Herbert Lee, a 52-year-old father of nine in Amite County, was gunned down by a state legislator in 1961 as he tried to get blacks to register to vote. Lewis Allen, who had witnessed the shooting, was also shot to death days before he was to testify before a grand jury. The violence, like the movement itself, would continue for years.[6]

State government officials defended segregation as fervently as Mississippi's two senators. Gov. Ross Barnett said, "The Good Lord was the original segregationist. He put the Negro in Africa, separated him from all other races."[7]

Paul Johnson, who succeeded Barnett as governor, often referred to the NAACP as "niggers, apes, alligators, coons and possums." He was perplexed as to how to handle the situation of demonstrators, some white and from the North, others native black Mississippians, all with the intent of changing the status quo of segregation. He told an interviewer in 1964 that if all "they" did was meet and hold peaceful demonstrations, there would be no trouble. (The word "they" signaled the governor's distrust and distaste for the intruders.)

Governor Johnson asked: What if they evoked the anger of the Ku Klux Klan and other white supremist groups? The governor said he only had 250 state troopers at his disposal so there wouldn't be much he could do to prevent or stop violence. He did not address the possibility of law enforcement officers initiating the violence, which had been the case in several instances.[8]

Meanwhile, Moses was winning over doubters in the Mississippi black community. His commitment was obvious and stronger than his fears. On August 17, 1962, several carloads of young, white extremists ambushed SNCC volunteers and trashed their office in Greenville. Some workers fled to the roof, then jumped to another nearby rooftop and slid down a television antenna tower to evade the intruders. Moses, 40 miles away, heard about the violence and immediately drove to Greenville. He went into the ransacked office, made up a bed on the floor, and went to sleep. It was classic Moses—taking control of a situation by showing control rather than fear. The incident became legendary among those involved in the movement.

Word spread about the Moses "nap" and actions like that helped him develop a huge following. SNCC leader John Lewis said he was thought of as a "Jesus-figure, all knowing and all holy. That made him so uncomfortable, he felt like climbing

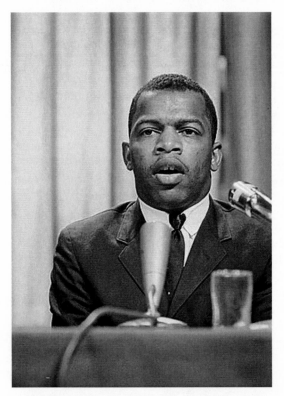

John Lewis, later to become a congressman, was president of the Student Nonviolent Coordinating Committee and suffered severe beatings because of his civil rights activities (Library of Congress).

out of his own skin. He always remained a true intellectual. He had a near-religious attitude toward autonomy and self-direction."[9]

"We were working in a context of Constitutional permissiveness," said Moses. "SNCC was permitted to work on voter registration. Terrorists were permitted to gun us down. Mississippi was permitted to lock us up. The Civil Rights Division of the Department of Justice was permitted to set us free. None of the above was required by the Constitution or, for that matter, forbidden."[10]

One of the keys to Moses gaining support for his efforts was his methodical approach to problem solving rather than acting purely on impulse or emotion. One volunteer in the movement observed, "In the same way one listens more attentively to a whisper, people were drawn to Bob — he was so unobtrusive that in his quiet, self-possessed stillness, he fixed additional attention on himself."

Cleveland Sellers, a SNCC volunteer in Mississippi, had much the same impression from the many days he worked with Moses. Sellers said, "There was something about him, the manner in which he carried himself, that seemed to draw all of us to him. He had been where we were going. And more important, he had emerged as the kind of person we wanted to be."[11]

Moses' work in Mississippi drew the attention of influential liberals in other parts of the country. Allard Lowenstein, a white college professor

Allard Lowenstein was a lawyer and former teacher who helped mobilize college students all over the country to come to Mississippi and help with Freedom Summer (Library of Congress).

and civil rights activist from New York, was one of them. Lowenstein, 35, was a graduate of the University of North Carolina where he had been president of the National Student Association. His teaching career included stints at Stanford University, North Carolina State University and City College of New York.

Lowenstein recruited hundreds of white college students and convinced them to join him in coming to Mississippi. His approach was much more aggressive than that of Moses, and the notion of a white man recruiting white people was met with some degree of suspicion and apprehension within the movement. Some black people, so accustomed to being shoved to the back, feared the same thing might happen in their own movement. Others, however, believed it was exactly the right element to get the attention of white people in other parts of the country to the despicable conditions in Mississippi.

Joseph Rauh, a white Washington, D.C., attorney, had been active in civil rights causes for 20 years and was well acquainted with Washington politicians, including Lyndon Johnson. He also championed the movement spearheaded by Moses and, in the months ahead, would be instrumental in seeing it through.

Rauh was with Humphrey at the Democratic convention in 1948 in which, as he put it, "we upset the machinery of the Democratic Party." He said in those days, the Democratic Party was as reactionary as the Republicans when it came to civil rights. Many people talked about it; nobody did anything about it. Then Humphrey gave his speech and "tied civil rights to the masthead of the Democratic Party."

Rauh recalled that it was 100 degrees in Philadelphia that day and 120 inside the convention hall. "But as we came out of that sweatshop, we all knew that we had forever changed the Democratic Party," he said. "We made the Democratic Party take a civil rights plank. We shifted the whole emphasis of the Democratic Party from a southern dominated party to a civil rights dominated party." It was the first time since Prohibition that a minority plank had been accepted into the party platform.[12]

Now, the Democratic Party was about to face a new challenge on an old issue, and Rauh and Humphrey would be deeply involved in it once again, but from different perspectives.

Rauh first met Bob Moses in March of 1964 at a meeting of the National Civil Liberties Clearinghouse, a civil rights think tank. Rauh was heading a panel discussion on voting rights when a young man stood up and told him he represented some people who were thinking about challenging Mississippi's "lily white delegation" at the Democratic National Convention. The young man was Bob Moses and he asked Rauh what he thought his group's chances of success would be.

Rauh said he told Moses he stood a good chance of stirring things up at what would probably otherwise be a fairly predictable convention. "That's where we first saw each other," said Rauh. "Apparently I liked him, he liked me and we started in partnership there."[13]

Eventually, a grand plan emerged that had several steps:

1. The volunteers would create "Freedom Schools" and "Freedom Houses" where blacks, young and old, would be educated about their Constitutional rights, the importance of voting, and how to register to vote.
2. A mock election would be held in which blacks throughout the state would nominate their own candidates for governor and other statewide offices. The election results wouldn't count, of course, but the act of voting would be a tremendous learning experience for blacks and would send a powerful message to segregationists that change was coming.
3. Blacks would hold county and district conventions and a state convention, performing the same functions that segregationists prevented them from participating in. They would elect their own slate of delegates to the Democratic National Convention to be held in August 1964 in Atlantic City, New Jersey.
4. The delegation would go to Atlantic City and demand to be seated instead of the delegation that had excluded them from the democratic process.

By now, SNCC, CORE, the SCLC and the NAACP had banded together in Mississippi to form an umbrella group called the Council of Federated Organizations (COFO).Though each organization brought its name to the coalition, most of them were heavily engaged in other priorities. CORE's efforts were aimed at northern events, such as making a presence at the New York World's Fair. The SCLC was busy with movements in St. Augustine, Florida, and other southern cities. The NAACP occupied itself with fighting discrimination in court cases and did not fully trust upstart, aggressive organizations such as SNCC and CORE. So SNCC was the primary force.[14]

In October of 1963, SNCC leaders met to discuss how to bring more attention to the movement to give it more momentum. They talked about how the presence of white supporters from the North had made an impact in demonstrations in Selma, Alabama. The events drew national media attention, and also, law enforcement officers seemed to be more restrained than they were when no white people were involved and there were no television cameras.

In November, the mock election was held. COFO volunteers set up polling places throughout the state and urged black citizens to participate. Their nominees were Aaron Henry, a druggist from Clarksdale and head of the state NAACP, for governor and the Rev. Ed King, a white chaplain at Tougaloo College in Jackson, which had an all-black student body, for lieutenant governor.

The Democratic candidate was Paul Johnson who reminded voters that, as lieutenant governor, he had stood in the doorway blocking James Meredith, a black man, from enrolling at the University of Mississippi. The Republican candidate was Rubel Phillips, also a staunch segregationist.

Moses managed the campaign. Henry went all over the state, speaking about the oppression of blacks. In many places, local police broke up the rallies and threatened to arrest Henry for disturbing the peace. He and Moses decided not to campaign in certain counties for fear of being shot.

Moses, Henry and King knew they would lose; that wasn't the point. COFO had set up voting precincts in churches, businesses and homes in black neighborhoods all over the state and had worked for months educating poor black people on the importance of voting, how to register and how to vote.

So the results, though meaningless on the face of them, had great meaning in the movement—for a black man and a white man had run together on the same ticket. More important, 80,000 blacks voted that day, most of them for the first time.

"The election had shown the country that Mississippi Negroes would vote if given the chance," Henry said later. "It was established that the sacrifices of the people and the labor of the civil rights movement were not in vain.... And perhaps most important, white college students from the North had seen what a significant role they could play in the Mississippi struggle."[15]

Within a week of the election, the SNCC staff met to discuss further the idea of involving young, white northerners even more in the movement. The idea was to create a summer project involving hundreds of white youth who would be recruited to come to Mississippi to set up Freedom Schools to educate blacks about their rights and to help them register to vote all over the state.

Fannie Lou Hamer, the sharp-tongued sharecropper from Ruleville, spoke in favor of it. She said the influx of whites would not only get the attention of the national press but also of the federal government, which had the reputation among many blacks as being slow to react to their troubles. Lawrence Guyot, a highly respected civil rights leader in the state, and David Dennis, head of CORE in Mississippi, agreed. They also believed that the presence of whites would encourage reluctant blacks by showing them they were not alone in the struggle for equal rights.

But many in the local movement disagreed. Ivanhoe Donaldson, Hol-

One of the great civil rights events of the early 1960s was the March on Washington in 1963. Here, demonstrators are getting organized. The tall, white man in the front row wearing a bow tie is Joseph Rauh who would represent the Freedom Democrats the next year at the Democratic National Convention (Library of Congress).

lis Watkins and Charlie Cobb believed the danger would increase because the white involvement would incite the Ku Klux Klan and other white extremist groups. They also expressed concern that enthusiastic, well-meaning, well-educated, well-to-do white kids might come in and take control, leaving menial tasks to the less-educated, less-sophisticated blacks they were trying to help.

By December, COFO personnel reached a tentative agreement to organize a limited summer project, perhaps recruiting 100 white youths, with the mission of educating black citizens on their right to vote and helping them to register. As talks continued, the scope of the project grew larger. At a meeting in Hattiesburg in January, a final decision was made to put together the summer project.

The movement was gaining momentum in other parts of the country as well. Led by Martin Luther King, John Lewis and other black leaders, a march on Washington was held on August 28, 1963, to bring attention to the goals of reaching racial equality and justice and freedom to get a good education, get good jobs and be treated decently.

More than 200,000 people spanned for miles around the Lincoln

Memorial to rally together, sing and hear inspirational speeches. Lewis spoke of a revolution taking place but the most memorable speech was delivered by King who told the masses gathered there and, via television, the rest of the nation, "I have a dream."

On April 26, 1964, the Mississippi Freedom Democratic Party was officially established at a meeting attended by several hundred blacks in Jackson.

The regular Democratic Party in Mississippi had adopted a policy in 1960 that segregation was the preferred and acceptable way of life and augmented it four years later by stating "separation of the races is necessary for the peace and tranquility of all of the people of Mississippi and the continuing good relation which has existed over the years."

To members of the newly formed Freedom Democratic Party meeting in Jackson, this meant "a Negro's belief in his own dignity and the U.S. Constitution makes him ineligible to participate in the political processes of Mississippi."[16]

Journalist Kay Miles said, the "MFDP provided them with a vehicle through which they could learn about the political system and see how its decisions affected them.... The party gave them a voice, a way to take collective action so they weren't challenging the system all by themselves."[17]

The new party stated its purpose forthrightly. "The Mississippi Freedom Democratic Party was conceived to give Negro citizens of Mississippi an experience in political democracy and to establish a channel through which all citizens, Negro and white, can actively support the programs and principles of the National Democratic Party."[18]

In its documents establishing its existence, party leaders quoted James W. Silver, in his book, *Mississippi: The Closed Society*, who wrote: "In the history of the United States, democracy has produced great leaders in great crises. Sad to say, the opposite has been true in Mississippi. There is little evidence that the society of the closed mind will ever possess the moral resources to reform itself."

In Washington, President Johnson was watching developments in Mississippi. He had been working feverishly to try to get his civil rights bill through Congress, but, as was his way, he meticulously measured the political consequences of the challenges he faced.

On April 9, a little more than two weeks before the Mississippi Freedom Democratic Party was established, Johnson discussed his Mississippi concerns with one of his old Senate cronies, Richard Russell of Georgia, a staunch segregationist but a man who had been one of Johnson's mentors in his early days in the Senate. In a phone conversation, Johnson said, "Now the governor of Mississippi wants to come up here and see me and I think that'll just cause a lot of talk about me trading out, selling out and everything else. But they tell me every Nigra family down there is buying a gun and that there's gonna be the damnedest shootings you ever saw on voter registration and they're sending 'em in buses by the hundreds from all over the country to help them register and they're gonna try to get 'em all registered in Mississippi and there's gonna be a bunch of killings."[19] Russell advised him to see Gov. Johnson but not until the congressional fight over the civil rights bill was over.[20]

The movement had momentum and was a cause for concern not only in Washington but even within the inner circles of black organizations that had been fighting for civil rights for years and now wondered whether this new wave of energy was emerging too quickly and with a bunch of enthusiastic but naïve amateurs.

"Bob Moses," according to historian David Levering Lewis, "was the indispensable implementer of a plan whose audacity troubled Martin Luther King Jr., exasperated NAACP officials and initially angered SNCC and CORE leaders." Hundreds of young Northern white students were set to invade territory in which CORE and SNCC volunteers, "toiling unsung in Mississippi backwater towns since the beginning of the decade, might find themselves upstaged even as they wet-nursed clueless sojourners."[21]

Helped by Lowenstein's connections, John Lewis and other SNCC leaders began speaking on college campuses throughout the country, telling of the plight of blacks in Mississippi, the plans for the summer project, and how anyone interested should fill out an application to become part of the movement. The application process was important because SNCC leaders didn't want a bunch of white kids coming down to Mississippi thinking it would be a cool summer job or a unique summer vacation. By early June, 1,200 applications had been received at the COFO headquarters in Jackson.

Two week-long training sessions were held in mid–June on the campus of Western College for Women in Oxford, Ohio. Originally, a second site, Berea College in Kentucky had been selected, but Berea backed out because of concerns of alumni and trustees. So on June 13, 1964, the first group of recruits, 300 of them, began training in Oxford. Their role would be to assist in voter registrations. On June 20, the second group arrived. Their mission would be to help establish and work in Freedom Schools.

The recruits heard from some of the nation's top civil rights leaders, including Farmer from CORE and Lewis from SNCC, as well activists heavily involved in the movement in Mississippi, such as Moses and Fannie Lou Hamer, the uneducated but streetwise sharecropper from Ruleville. They told the young people of the challenges and possible violence they would face in the fight for equality. Volunteers were schooled on the principles of nonviolence and how best to defend themselves against being struck with billy clubs and other forms of abuse.

One of the speakers, R. Jess Brown, a black lawyer from Jackson, knew firsthand what the young volunteers would be facing. Brown was the defense attorney for Mack Charles Parker, a young black man accused of rape who never got a chance to go to trial because a white mob dragged him from his jail cell and murdered him. Brown warned the young volunteers, "You're going to be classified into two groups in Mississippi — niggers and nigger lovers. And they're tougher on nigger lovers.[22]"

Another speaker that day was John Doar, a white Justice Department attorney, who had been dispatched to Mississippi by the government to monitor civil rights activities and to report his findings back to Washington. In that role, Doar was an observer, not a law enforcement officer, and while his presence was appreciated by some in the black community, others found it frustrating that his role was so limited in stopping what was going on.

Nonetheless, Doar found himself at the scene of many confrontations and, on one occasion, even acted as an intermediary, standing between protesters and club-wielding police officers. That occurred on a street in Jackson in June of 1963 after the shooting of Medgar Evers. A year earlier, Doar escorted James Meredith as he attempted to be the first black student to enroll at the University of Mississippi.

So his presence at Oxford, where the movement was about to take an important step, was greatly appreciated by black leaders. "He was our link to the federal government. He gave us reason not to give up on those in power. John Doar could reach Bobby Kennedy," said John Lewis.

Bob Moses said, "People we're working with are bombarded by all the forces in Mississippi telling them what they're doing is wrong. So what Doar and the people from the Justice Department are telling them, that what they're doing is right, is really important."[23]

Doar told the young volunteers at Oxford that day that their cause was just but any federal protection for them would be difficult. The Justice Department was filled with lawyers and investigators but there was no federal police department.

While some of the black SNCC volunteers were at first cool to the idea of rich white kids coming down to help and getting a lot of publicity for it, Moses and Lewis saw the symbolic and moral value of blacks and whites working together for the same cause — to show this wasn't a black issue or a white issue but an American issue.

The young, white volunteers were dedicated and enthusiastic but totally inexperienced in dealing with the hardships of those they were committed to helping. For many of them, for the first time in their young lives, they were coming face to face with poverty and ignorance and it was quite an adjustment.

"Many affluent children of the North were trying to relate to young

Patti Miller of Audubon, Iowa, stands on the front porch of the home where she stayed while taking part in Freedom Summer in Mississippi (courtesy Patti Miller).

people who were not only poor but black," wrote volunteer Tracy Sugarman. "Some were surprised by the cautious suspicion of the blacks and started to recognize that the partnership on which their lives might depend was going to take some major effort by each group."[24]

Historian Theodore White, who traveled to Mississippi to see firsthand what was taking place, said it was easy to find the SNCC office in Jackson because in front of it, a young black man and white man had a ball and were playing catch. It was not a scene you'd see anywhere else in Jackson, he noted.

Lewis said, "I always felt that it was important that white people be involved with us, that they bear witness not just from a distance but by standing beside us, suffering with us and, ultimately, succeeding with us."[25]

One of the young, white volunteers was Patti Miller, a 21-year-old student from Audubon, Iowa, who was a music major at Drake University in Des Moines. Two years earlier, she went to Mississippi with friends from the Wesley Foundation, a religious organization on campus, to get a firsthand glimpse of what life was like in the south. What she saw changed her life.

She said she was astounded to see separate facilities for blacks and whites and was tempted to go sit in the "colored section" of a bus terminal until others with her, older and wiser, convinced her to cool her emotions.

She returned to the comforts of Iowa and the cushy life as a student seeking a degree in music when she was reminded one day of her experience in the Deep South. "It was the simple brochure on a bulletin board at Drake that gave me an opportunity to do something with the passion I was feeling that something, indeed, needed to be done about segregation," she said. The brochure enticed students to get involved with the Mississippi Summer Project (later called Freedom Summer) and Patti wasted no time in applying, filled with youthful, idealistic yearnings to make a difference with little or no regard to the possible danger involved.

"My parents simply said, as they always did, that if it was something I felt I should do, they would support me," she said. "They were always incredibly supportive even though they may have had misgivings about my going into such a dangerous situation."

She took a bus to Jackson, Mississippi, for orientation and then went to Meridian. Her stay lasted a month. During that time, she lived with a black family and spent most of her time working at Meridian's Community Center, which also housed the COFO office. She helped oversee summer programs for children who spent their days at the center. The Community

Patti Miller and another volunteer work with black children in Mississippi in a reading program as part of the Freedom Summer activities (courtesy Patti Miller).

Centers and Freedom Schools were far from elaborate; most were makeshift, but most of them were well supplied with books donated for the cause.

Danger lurked every day. Patti helped distribute leaflets inviting citizens to attend the funeral of James Chaney, a black civil rights worker. She attended the funeral, which clearly labeled her in the eyes of some whites as a "nigger lover." She also attended a court hearing for a fellow volunteer, a white man from New York, and had to be hustled out a back door to safety when violence erupted.

> I never actually asked myself, "What in the world am I doing here?'—because I knew what I was doing there. And I believed so deeply in the cause that nothing could have taken me away.
>
> That is not to say, however, that I did not go through incredible upheaval—almost on a daily basis—because of the stress and the uncertainties we faced every day. The question I perhaps asked myself was "Can I survive this emotionally?" That was the most difficult part of the summer. Surviving emotionally."[26]

The violence or threat of it was constant with people involved in the movement being arrested on trumped-up charges and often beaten either by police or by angry whites with full knowledge of police. Blacks who registered to vote or who tried to register were victims of cruel retaliation. Crosses were burned on their lawns, gunshots ripped through the windows of their homes and businesses, or their dwellings were set on fire.

The violence punctuated the cause, as defined in the original papers of the Mississippi Freedom Democratic Party: "We are not allowed to function effectively in Mississippi's traditional Democratic Party; therefore, we must find another way to align ourselves with the National Democratic Party."[27]

The leaders of the movement had tried to follow the rules and procedures of the Democratic Party. They had tried to register to vote and were rebuffed and often threatened. They had tried to take part in precinct and county and state meetings and were turned away. After the Mississippi Freedom Democratic Party was formed in April, they nominated candidates to run in the state's primary elections— Fannie Lou Hamer for U.S. senator and Victoria Gray, John Houston and the Rev. John Cameron for the U.S. House. They knew all of their candidates would lose, but they wanted to show the national party that they had done everything in their power to be included in the process. Moses, Lewis and Henry were convinced that by taking their case and their cause to the Democratic National Convention in August, they would receive the fair and equal treatment they deserved.

Three powerful forces were headed for a collision in Atlantic City:

There was the regular Mississippi Democratic Party — segregationists who believed Negroes were "mongrels" and "coons," unfit to have the same rights as whites.

There was the Mississippi Freedom Democratic Party, whose members believed they had been deprived of their rights and were intent on pleading their cause at the Democratic National Convention.

And there was President Lyndon B. Johnson, far from Mississippi, but powerful and active. The native southerner who had pledged his administration to the cause of civil rights was not about to allow a bunch of unruly blacks disrupt a convention, embarrass the Democratic Party and anger segregationists from southern states who represented a huge political voting bloc for him. He was prepared to use his immense political clout to see that things went his way.

CHAPTER 3

Lyndon Johnson

When Lyndon Johnson ascended to the presidency because of the assassination of President Kennedy, it was one of the few times in his political career where his advancement was not part of a calculated strategy on his part. From the time the lanky lad from rural Texas arrived in Washington in 1931, he made a point of knowing who to hang out with so that eventually he would be able to elevate himself to where he would be the person that rising young politicians would need to befriend.

He was born on a farm in Stonewall, Gillespie County, Texas, on August 27, 1908, the first child of Sam and Rebekah Baines Johnson. His mother had come from a good upbringing, the daughter of Joseph Wilson Baines, a lawyer, educator, lay preacher, state legislator and at one time Texas secretary of state. Rebekah considered her father to be a model of decency, dignity and civic responsibility.

She grew up and attended Baylor University — one of the few women on campus, majoring in literature with dreams of becoming a great novelist some day. When her father took ill and died, Rebekah lost her hero, and she became withdrawn and lacking in ambition.

Through her father's connections in state government, she met Sam Johnson, a legislator and farmer, and married him in 1907. Their life together was far different than what Rebekah had been accustomed to in her father's home, where culture and good manners were part of her everyday life. Sam Johnson was crude, vulgar and domineering. He liked to get together with his beer-drinking buddies and swap stories into the middle of the night.

When Lyndon was born, Rebekah found in him the person with whom she could have a loving companion who would be devoted to her and would return her love. She taught him to read at an early age and how to play simple games that the two of them could enjoy together. She envisioned for him the good life that her father had. As Lyndon grew older, he learned that much was expected in return for that love.

Little Lyndon Johnson, age 3, standing at left in this family photograph, was not close to his father (back row in straw hat). His mother, standing directly in front of her husband, was loving but demanding (LBJ Library).

As an adult, Johnson spoke lovingly of his mother but hardly ever mentioned his father. He could remember his mother hugging him so tightly that it would hurt. Yet if he did not do what was expected of him, such as not practicing the violin like she thought he should, Rebekah would cut off the affection, sometimes to the point of not speaking to him for long periods of time.

Many of the characteristics of his parents became part of the Lyndon Johnson persona as an adult. He could be crude and vulgar like his father, and he could display great love and affection for someone — help them pay their bills or counsel them or get them a job, like a good father would treat a son — but withdraw that love abruptly if he did not receive the loyalty and affection he thought he deserved in return.[1]

Lyndon graduated from Southwest Texas State Teachers College at San Marcos (now Texas State University–St. Marcos) with a teaching degree in 1930. He was a high school teacher for three years, including time when he was still getting his degree.

In 1931, having already made some political connections in Texas, Johnson went to Washington as secretary to Congressman Richard Kleberg. He developed a love for politics and saw firsthand how traveling in the right circles and meeting the right people were two keys to success.

He became fascinated with the power and political prowess of Senator Huey Long, from the neighboring state of Louisiana. Long was a political heavyweight in his state, having served as governor and getting his programs through the legislature by cajoling and controlling and using a patronage system that had hundreds of people beholding to him for their livelihoods. Long wasn't afraid to take on power brokers when he was in Louisiana; therefore he became one. Now he was a senator and on display on the Senate floor for a youthful Lyndon Johnson to watch, every chance he got.

What most fascinated Johnson was how Long had amassed political power and then won adoration from his constituents by using that power to secure government services for them. Johnson not only wanted to accomplish great things but also yearned to be loved by the people as he imagined Long had been.[2] It was a combination of qualities that would both motivate Johnson and haunt him during the rest of his political career, including his dealing with civil rights issues during his presidency, such as the Mississippi Freedom Democratic Party's emergence. He saw perseverance, manipulation and arm-twisting as a way of attaining power; power as a way of doing good things for people; and doing good things for people as a way of attaining love and adulation. Johnson, historian Nick Kotz wrote, had "both an ego and insecurities as outsized as his extraordinary talent, an intense desire to be loved by everyone and a burning need to be in control of the action."[3]

Long seemed to be a perfect role model for the ambitious Johnson and, characteristically, he obsessed. He maneuvered to go to lunch with one of Huey's secretaries to learn more about him — what he ate, how he dressed, what time he arrived for work, his demeanor in the office. Johnson began wearing silk pajamas because he learned Long did.

In June of 1935, President Franklin D. Roosevelt signed an executive order creating the National Youth Administration (NYA), which was designed to create jobs for thousands of young people in the throws of the Great Depression. The executive order was signed on a Tuesday morning. On Tuesday afternoon, Johnson was on the phone with each member of the Texas congressional delegation proposing himself as the ideal person to head the program in Texas.

"It was characteristic of Johnson to react with celerity when he saw something he wanted," his biographer Doris Kearns Goodwin wrote. "His quickness gave him an immediate advantage over potential competitors. It was to assist him at many turning points.... In this instance, Johnson's opportunism resulted in his appointment ... as the youngest NYA director in the country."[4]

Johnson served in that capacity for two years and had hands-on experience in trying to help the downtrodden. His political career — a mixture of ego, passion, compassion and attaining and using power to accomplish things that would bring adulation to him — had its roots in the dusty backroads of Texas and his work with the National Youth Administration.

"However much Johnson craved power and used it to his

Huey Long, governor and then senator from Louisiana, was one of Lyndon Johnson's heroes because he knew how to achieve power, use the power to help people and receive the love and admiration of the people (Library of Congress).

own ends," according to Kotz, "he had always believed that the purpose of government was to benefit ordinary people. He pursued this goal as Texas director of the National Youth Administration ... and later as a full-fledged New Deal supporter in Congress."[5]

Johnson seized another political opportunity in 1937 when Congressman James P. Buchanan of Texas died. Johnson decided to be a candidate to fill Buchanan's term, and once again, his swiftness paid off. Buchanan's widow had intentions of running and would have been the favorite. But Johnson announced his candidacy just a few days after Buchanan's funeral. Seven other candidates jumped in the race. Mrs. Buchanan decided not to get in the fray.

He campaigned hard, stressing his loyalty to Franklin D. Roosevelt's programs. He saw in Roosevelt some of the same traits he had seen in Huey Long — the ability to use political power to not only help people but gain their affection. Johnson was elected to six terms in Congress.

After his first two terms, he became restless again, frustrated with a seniority system in the House that impeded his quest to move into leadership positions. In 1941, another death gave him another opportunity to improve his lot. U.S. Senator Morris Sheppard died and a special election was held to fill the vacancy. Just as he had in 1937, Johnson wasted no time in getting into the race.

But this time, he had much stiffer opposition — Wilbert "Pappy" O'Daniel, the governor of Texas. Johnson worked hard, traveling across the state making speeches and promises. On election night, it appeared that he had won. But the next day, when late returns were counted, O'Daniel was declared the victor by 1,311 votes. There were many allegations of vote fraud but Johnson decided not to challenge the results. He remained in the House of Representatives for seven more years.[6]

In 1948, he decided again to run for a U.S. Senate seat from Texas that became open, but it was a difficult decision because he already had a comfortable House seat. He could not run for both the House and Senate, and if he ran for the Senate and lost, he would lose everything. That was at first unthinkable — but the quest for more power and authority took over and Johnson decided to run. In the closest Senate race in Texas history, Johnson defeated his opponent, Coke Stevenson, by 87 votes out of more than 900,000 that were cast in a primary runoff.

Stevenson accused Johnson of vote fraud — stuffing the ballot boxes — and filed suit to have the election results overturned. The case went all the way to the U.S. Supreme Court, with Johnson's political future hanging in the balance. Johnson's defense attorney was Abe Fortas who contended the Supreme Court had no jurisdiction in a matter that amounted to counting or recounting votes in an election in Texas. There was no

Coke Stevenson lost to Lyndon Johnson in a close race for the U.S. Senate in 1948. He took his allegations of vote fraud all the way to the Supreme Court but lost. The election earned Johnson the nickname "Landslide Lyndon" (Texas State Library and Archives Commission).

constitutional authority to do that, he said, and the court agreed. It did not take up the case. So Johnson was able to climb to the next rung on the ladder of his political career, also winning the general election, but not without having to withstand the nickname of "Landslide Lyndon."

One of Johnson's campaign speeches that year provides insight into the tenor of the times and how Johnson calculated it politically. He said,

This civil rights program, about which you have heard so much, is a farce and a sham — an effort to set up a police state in the guise of liberty. I am opposed to that program. I fought it in Congress. It is a province of the state to run its own elections.

I am opposed to the anti-lynching bill because the federal government has no more business enacting a law against one kind of murder than another. I am against the FEPC [Fair Employment Practices Commission] because if a man can tell you whom you must hire, he can tell you whom you cannot employ. I have met this head-on.[7]

The "freshman class" in the Senate in January 1949 included Johnson; Hubert Humphrey, the former mayor of Minneapolis who gave the eloquent civil rights speech at the 1948 Democratic convention; Paul Douglas of Illinois, a professor of economics at the University of Chicago and a well-known scholar; Robert Kerr, former governor of Oklahoma; and Russell Long of Louisiana, son of one of Johnson's heroes, Huey Long.

The new senator from Texas was perhaps the least known of the newly elected ones, but he had developed a knack over the years of traveling in the right circles, meeting the right people, assessing strengths and weaknesses of his political friends as well as his enemies, and using all of this information to advance himself and his causes. Two of his mentors were Representative Sam Rayburn of Texas, a crafty politician who became Speaker of the House in 1940, and Senator Richard Russell of Georgia, a segregationist who was well versed in the protocols of getting things done on the Senate floor.

"Conversation for him," according to Doris Kearns Goodwin, "was always a medium through which he sought to impose his will as well as a source of information that helped him direct his energies toward desired goals.... And such information would serve his compelling inward need to neutralize the possibility of surprise."[8]

Within three years of his election to the Senate, his colleagues chose him as minority whip; within five years, as minority leader; and within seven years, as majority leader, a position he held until he became vice president in 1960. Johnson honed skills that helped him push legislation through the Senate and gave him the power he so desired.

His "people skills" had more to do with assessing how best to use others rather than a way of manifesting their friendship. "From facts, gossip, observation ... he shaped a mental portrait of every senator.... As Johnson's mental portraits of his colleagues became more complete, his political touch became finer."[9]

He knew the birthdays of his fellow senators, what their favorite meal was and how they handled their liquor. He knew when a senator's son or daughter was graduating from high school or college or if there was illness in the family. He knew their favorite sports teams and whether they preferred playing Scrabble or poker. And he knew what motivated or angered them. He knew how to help them, to flatter them, to use them.

When he doled out committee assignments to his Democratic colleagues, he kept careful track with pencil and paper of who got the assignments they requested, who had received special consideration and who had received favors in the past. To Johnson, these were more than just appointments—these were IOUs that he would collect on when the timing was right.

Johnson's ability to get people to see things his way was legendary in Washington, so much so that over the years its victims and observers gave it a name—the Johnson Treatment. It was effusive without necessarily being offensive. It was to cajole, to control. The most remarkable thing about the Johnson Treatment is that it seemed to come naturally and not part of some elaborate, well-thought-out game plan, which, in fact, it almost always was. Historian Marshall Frady described it as "a ferocious manner of persuasion that proceeded by a kind of progressive physical engulfment, wrapping one big arm around a colleague's shoulder with his other hand clenching his lapel.... Johnson would lower his face closer and closer to the subject's until the man would be bowed backward."[10]

If he was sitting with someone, the guest was often on a couch or comfortable cushioned chair with Johnson seated next to him in a higher chair so that he would in effect tower over his subject even when he was seated. He also had a manner of crossing his long leg so that it stretched across and in front of his subject, having the effect of caging him in until Johnson was through talking.

Rowland Evans and Robert Novak, Washington columnists, were both observers and recipients of the treatment. They said it could last ten minutes or four hours and it could happen anywhere—from high level offices in Washington to the swimming pool at the Johnson ranch in Texas. "Its tone could be supplication, accusation, cajolery, exuberance, scorn, tears, complaint, and the hint of threat.... Its velocity was breathtaking.... He moved in close, his face a scant millimeter from his target, his eyes widening and narrowing, his eyebrows rising and falling."[11]

Benjamin Bradlee, at one time a *Newsweek* staffer who later became executive editor of the *Washington Post*, described the physicality of the treatment. "You really felt like a St. Bernard had licked your face for an hour.... He never just shook hands with you. One hand was shaking your hand; the other was always someplace else, exploring you, examining you.... He'd be feeling up Katharine Graham and bumping Meg Greenfield on the boobs." But all the while, Bradlee said, Johnson would be talking, trying to make a point. Even when he knew he was stretching the truth,

Abe Fortas, President Johnson's attorney, friend and Supreme Court appointee, laughs as LBJ leans into him during a White House conversation. Johnson's penchant for making his point with people through close body contact was often called "The Johnson Treatment" (LBJ Library).

he'd do it with a little smile on his face. "It was just a miraculous performance," he said.[12]

Johnson's biographer and onetime staffer Doris Kearns Goodwin said he was the master of creating a feeling of intimacy, even with men, by the physical closeness of his presence. "In an empty room, he would stand or sit next to a man as if all that were available were a three-foot space.... The intimacy was all the more excusable because it seemed genuine and without menace. Yet it was the product of meticulous calculation. And it worked."[13]

Another tactic of the Johnson Treatment was to catch his subjects off guard, to create unsettling moments for them as if to show he could do anything he wanted to do in their presence because they were beholden to him. When he was Senate majority leader, it was not uncommon for him to be talking with men in the Capitol parking lot when he would stop, unzip his pants and urinate, without ever pausing in his conversation. Senate colleagues who happened to be beside him at a urinal told of how he bragged about the size of his penis, referring to it as "jumbo."[14]

His crudeness, while certainly an offshoot of his days back in rural Texas, was nonetheless part of the Treatment, of leaving his guests sometimes awestruck by his abandonment of common decency and yet remaining in complete control. He would sometimes be in the midst of a conversation when he felt the urge for a bowel movement. He would get up and motion to his unsuspecting guests to follow him whereupon he would go in a bathroom and relieve himself in their full view while still carrying on the conversation.

He took particular delight in doing this in the White House in the presence of staffers who were holdovers from the Kennedy administration, many of whom Johnson looked on with contempt. He enjoyed telling the story of a "Kennedyite who came into the bathroom with me and then found it utterly impossible to look at me while I sat there on the toilet.... For there he was, standing as far away from me as he possibly could, keeping his back to me the whole time, trying to carry on a conversation."[15]

His earthiness was not confined to just talking politics. In a conversation captured on the White House taping system, the president telephoned Joe Haggar, president of the Haggar clothing company in Dallas. Johnson wanted to personally place an order for six new pairs of slacks, custom made for his comfort. As Haggar listened intently to the instructions, probably carefully writing them down, Johnson told him to make the pockets a few inches deeper this time, because when he sat, his change and knife and other contents often fell out. Also, the president told Haggar, he wanted a couple of extra inches in the crotch "where your nuts hang," because the slacks he was wearing now were too tight and made him feel like he was "sitting on a wire fence."[16]

In December of 1963, not long after Johnson took office after the Kennedy assassination, he invited executives from the three major television networks— ABC, CBS and NBC — to the White House for a "get to know you" session with the new president. They had lunch with Johnson and then, to their amazement, he invited them to "skinny dip" with him in the White House swimming pool. "They splashed, all four naked to the skin, in the water."[17]

Robert Kennedy, who had stayed on as attorney general after his brother's assassination, told of the ritual of Johnson's associates being invited for a weekend at the LBJ ranch. Inevitably, at some time during the weekend, the guests would be invited to go out into the hinterlands of the ranch with Johnson and try their hand at shooting a deer. Johnson was an expert marksman and this was just one more way he could show his superiority over whomever it was that he was entertaining. Kennedy was appalled when he saw that Johnson had erected a concrete stand and took aim at his prey from an elevated position. "It wasn't hunting," he said. "It was slaughter."[18]

Robert Kennedy's reaction to Johnson as president was a direct reflection, without saying so specifically, of his interpretation of the Johnson Treatment. Kennedy said, "The president does not know how to use people's talents, to find the very best in them and put the best to work. But more than any other man, he knows how to ferret out and use people's weaknesses."[19]

Shortly after he had taken office as president, Johnson was concerned that a tax bill he supported was tied up in a committee. He determined that Senator Harry Byrd of Virginia could end the bottleneck. As the two of them left a Gridiron Dinner at a Washington hotel, Johnson invited Byrd back to the White House for a nightcap. Byrd resisted, saying it was late and maybe they could do it some other time. But the president insisted, telling Byrd it was important. Byrd relented and made the late-night trip to the White House. Hubert Humphrey was also invited.

When they got to the living room, Johnson instructed Humphrey to fix some drinks and to bring Byrd his favorite — "two fingers of bourbon." As the three men sat and enjoyed two or three drinks and engaged in small talk, Johnson told Byrd that before he left he should enjoy some time with his girlfriend. The president got up and went to the doorway of a nearby bedroom and called for his wife Lady Bird, shouting to her that her boyfriend was here. Mrs. Johnson, who had been sleeping, came out in a housecoat and sat next to Byrd on a couch. They exchanged pleasantries and shared some laughs.

After a while, the president said it was getting late and for Lady Bird to go back to bed. But he joked that any time he couldn't find Lady Bird,

Lady Bird Johnson helped her husband win a key legislative victory by flirting with a senator at the White House (LBJ Library).

he knew she might be with Byrd. They all laughed. Then Johnson walked over to where Byrd was sitting, leaned over to him with his face nearly touching Byrd's cheek, in typical Johnson style, in a stage whisper he told him that he needed his commitment to get that tax bill out of committee. Byrd promised he would not hold it up.

The president, knowing Byrd's strengths and weaknesses, had taken advantage of a tired man late at night, plying him with liquor, having a woman flirt with him and flatter him, and then extracting what he wanted from him. It is likely Johnson had the whole scenario in mind before he even went to the Gridiron Dinner that night. Humphrey witnessed the whole thing and called it a classic Johnson Treatment.

Humphrey described LBJ's methods as using facts "salacious as well as salutary, nothing escaping his observation and judgment, attending to every little detail, using virtually all he knew to bargain, persuade, pressure, punish or reward."[20]

Historian Theodore White, in describing how Johnson's personality played out, revealed a telling consequence of this powerful man who believed power was the key to achieving great things for people — and that achieving great things for people was the key to receiving their adoration. In observing the president in 1964, White wrote, "Of all men in public life, Lyndon Johnson is one of the most friendless. Those who come in contact with him are accepted generally as cronies or partners or supplicants, or men he can use — as servants. But of real friends he had few, for, above all else, he lacks the capacity for arousing warmth."[21]

Johnson was a crude, rude, complex individual who craved power and knew how to use it. But he was also the man who, as Senate majority leader, had helped put through the first Civil Rights bill since Reconstruction and, as president, got Congress to pass the most comprehensive civil rights bill in history in the spring and summer of 1964.

In Mississippi, Robert Moses, Aaron Henry, the Rev. Ed King, Fannie Lou Hamer and others were confident that Johnson and the party he led would bring them out of the deadly turmoil of white oppression once they brought their case to the Democratic National Convention in Atlantic City.

How could they miss? The president and his political party, the party of John Kennedy and Robert Kennedy and Hubert Humphrey, champions of civil rights, would do what was right for the black people of Mississippi while millions of people watched the noble deeds on their television screens. It was not only good government; it was good politics, they thought.

They had no way of knowing that in Washington, Johnson was intent on not letting anything get in the way of having a celebratory convention where he would not only receive the nomination of his party but the adulation of the public for bringing the country through extremely difficult times.

The civil rights bill had become the law of the land, the War on Poverty was under way and Johnson expected gratitude from the people he thought he had helped the most — the poor, black people in southern states. In addition, Johnson still faced a delicate balancing act — addressing the needs of the victims of segregation without antagonizing the segregationists who represented the largest voting bloc in the south.

A showdown in Atlantic City was inevitable.

But one incident, more than any other that year, put an exclamation point on the problems in Mississippi. It occurred just as Robert Moses's "Freedom Summer" project was getting under way, when hundreds of white, northern college students were heading south to help right a wrong. It involved three of those young people, two white and one black, and it involved an all-too-familiar sound in Mississippi — gunshots in the middle of the night.

CHAPTER 4

A Nation Awakened

June 21, 1964, was Father's Day in America, a day for family gatherings, picnics, picture taking, outdoor barbecues and, in most parts of the country, enjoying summer sunshine.

In New York, Jim Bunning, a pitcher for the Philadelphia Phillies and the father of seven, threw a perfect game on Father's Day — no hits, no runs, no errors, no base runners — against the New York Mets. With his instant celebrity status, he was hustled off to a television studio after the game where he made a guest appearance on *The Ed Sullivan Show,* a variety program in which one of the staples was introducing famous guests in the studio audience.

The pennant races were taking shape in Major League baseball with Bunning's Phillies leading the pack in the National League, while the New York Yankees, under first-year manager Yogi Berra, were holding forth in the American League, fending off a stiff challenge from the Chicago White Sox.

Later that night, many television viewers in America tuned into the popular CBS program *What's My Line?* in which a panel of questioners tried to guess the occupations of contestants. Each week, panel members were blindfolded when a mystery guest appeared, and they asked questions and tried to guess the guest's identity. On this night, the mystery guest was actor Frank Fontaine who played Crazy Guggenheim, a lovable drunk on the Jackie Gleason television show.

It was a time in the United States when advertising agencies were busy honing messages about the products they represented, so Americans were urged to become part of the "Pepsi generation," to "let their fingers do the walking" through the Yellow Pages of their telephone books, and they often heard the admonition "Please don't squeeze the Charmin" bathroom tissue from the fictitious but effective character Mr. Whipple.

As Bunning was throwing his perfect game in New York, President

Johnson was flying back to Washington from a trip to California, concerned about the escalating war involving U.S. troops in Vietnam, but also basking in the satisfaction of the civil rights bill finally being approved by Congress. Always mindful of political opportunities in the midst of duty, he contemplated signing the bill, surrounded by Republicans and Democrats, men and women, blacks and whites, on July 4.

The president was also keeping close tabs on the condition of Senator Edward "Ted" Kennedy, younger brother of the slain president and of Attorney General Robert Kennedy, who had been badly injured in the crash of a private plane two nights earlier.

In Mississippi, Robert Moses' "Freedom Summer" was about to get under way — using hundreds of volunteers to educate blacks on their constitutional rights and the importance of registering to vote. It was the first part of the plan that called for the oppressed black people of Mississippi to finally get the respect they deserved when their delegates took their seats at the Democratic National Convention.

The volunteers had gone through a week of training in Ohio, described as part education and part shock treatment — because trainers not only told them of the violence they might encounter but also engaged them in mock situations to demonstrate the hatred they were likely to face. On the last day of training, after hearing a pep talk from Moses, the students locked arms, sang freedom songs, then boarded buses and headed for Mississippi.

On Sunday, June 21, three of the volunteers got up and had an early breakfast in Meridian, Mississippi. Then they got into a 1963 Ford Fairlane station wagon owned by CORE and headed for Longdale, about 35 miles away, just outside of Philadelphia in Neshoba County, scene of a church bombing a few days earlier. Neshoba County was a stronghold of the Ku Klux Klan.

Michael "Mickey" Schwerner, 24, and his wife Rita had been working in Mississippi for six months. They left their New York home in January and drove their Volkswagen Beetle to Mississippi to help in the freedom movement. Mickey, a native of Brooklyn and a graduate of Cornell University, was described as jovial, fearless, and fiercely idealistic. He made friends easily in the black community. He gave residents rides in his Volkswagen and talked to them about their rights and the importance of registering to vote. They teased him about the goatee on his chin and his New York accent, but more important, they trusted him.

Rita Schwerner, a petite brunette, worked with children, reading to them, comforting them, befriending them. The Schwerners believed it was important to educate both adults and children — and that children were a key link to connecting them with adults. The Schwerners set up a

Freedom School in Meridian and it was not long before the couple, who were Jewish, were targeted by the Ku Klux Klan.[1]

One of the people Mickey Schwerner met in his travels was James Chaney, 21, a black man who had grown up in Meridian. He was uneducated and worked from time to time as a plasterer, but was considered by many who knew him to be a drifter. One day he stopped by the Schwerners' Freedom School in Meridian, met Mickey Schwerner and found him to be someone who seemed to understand his problems and wanted to help. Schwerner liked him and affectionately started calling the big black man "Bear."

In June, Chaney, accompanied by Schwerner and his wife, drove to the training grounds in Ohio to join others recruited from throughout the country to participate in Freedom Summer in Mississippi. There they met and befriended Andrew Goodman, a 20-year-old student from Queens College in New York.

Goodman, a second year anthropology student at Queens, grew up in a family in which his parents were wealthy, liberal and intellectual. The importance of social justice was not a new concept. Goodman had been exposed to it from the time he was a youngster, listening to his parents and their friends at the dinner table. He had been taught from an early age the importance of getting involved, of making a difference, so when he told his parents he wanted to go to Mississippi and be part of the movement, he had their blessing.

SNCC had scheduled Goodman to go to work in Vicksburg, but during their time in Ohio, Schwerner convinced him to come work with him at the Freedom House in Meridian and SNCC went along with the change of plans.[2]

At about 3 P.M., the trio left Longdale, where they had consoled and counseled victims of the church bombing, and headed back to Meridian. Chaney was driving with Schwerner next to him in the front seat and Goodman in back. Chaney was an ideal partner for Schwerner and Goodman and would be an ideal driver on their trips because he was a native and knew the territory much better than Schwerner, who had been in the state for six months, and Goodman who had spent one day in Mississippi. The three of them anticipated a productive summer together.

Just inside the city limits of Philadelphia, their car was pulled over by Neshoba County Deputy Sheriff Cecil Price, a Ku Klux Klansman, who accused them of speeding. They were easy prey for law officers, easy to spot, because a black man riding with two white men automatically meant they were "troublemakers" in that neck of the woods and Schwerner, "the Jew boy," sported the goatee that made him easily recognizable by law officers suspicious of him.

The three men were hustled into the Neshoba County Jail where they were held for seven hours. When they were finally released, Price escorted their car to the county line and told them to go on their way and never to come back. He knew they never would because as Price departed and the men continued their journey, a band of Ku Klux Klan members awaited. Mickey Schwerner, Andrew Goodman and James Chaney were never heard from again.

Before they left Meridian, the three made arrangements to call back to the SNCC headquarters in Meridian periodically to let everyone know they were safe. When they had not called by four o'clock that afternoon, their coworkers suspected the worst and contacted authorities and dispatched searchers of their own to look for them. By the next day, their disappearance was national news.

The brutal murders of young civil rights volunteers Andrew Goodman, James Chaney and Mickey Schwerner (left to right) brought national attention to the violence taking place in Mississippi (poster distributed by the FBI).

On Tuesday, President Johnson, acting through Attorney General Robert Kennedy and FBI Director J. Edgar Hoover, ordered more FBI agents be sent to Neshoba County to beef up the investigation.

These were difficult days for Hoover. He was known to be a racist who shunned hiring black FBI agents. The agency, formed in 1924 and with Hoover its only director, had only five black agents out of a work force of 5,000, and none of the five actually participated in investigations but were either drivers or office workers.

Hoover believed Martin Luther King and other black leaders were pawns of the Communist Party. That is perhaps one of the reasons the FBI's initial response to trouble in Mississippi was to

J. Edgar Hoover, the only director the FBI ever had, was reluctant to have agents investigating the crimes against blacks in Mississippi. When President Johnson wanted the FBI to conduct espionage on the Freedom Democrats in Atlantic City, Hoover said, "Lyndon's way out of line," but complied with LBJ's wishes.

send agents in as observers only. Their role had been to take copious notes and report back to the director.

An example of Hoover's racism is found in his response when Joseph Rauh asked to have the FBI investigate a death threat against Walter Reuther, who was white and head of the United Auto Workers union. Hoover's response, in effect, was that the FBI couldn't investigate every request for service it got, but the way he phrased it was telling. He said he wasn't going to send in the FBI "every time some nigger woman gets raped."

When violence escalated in Mississippi, Hoover was angered. "We simply can't wetnurse everybody who goes down to try to reform or re-educate the Negro population of the south," he said.[3]

Burke Marshall, a Justice Department official who worked closely with Hoover, said the FBI as an agency developed a mindset modeled by Hoover, one that was anti-civil rights probably because of Hoover's racism. But Marshall said another factor was Hoover's belief in how the FBI should operate under any circumstances— as purely an investigative agency.

"The way the investigative agency worked in his highly bureaucratic mind was that something happened that there was reason to believe that what happened violated a federal law — wasn't just wrong or unjust but violated some federal law that you could name." If the crime met those criteria, said Marshall, he would need a memo from someone in the Justice Department asking the FBI to make a full investigation, naming the federal law that had been broken. So if someone was shot or beaten in Mississippi, for example, that would be a violation of state law or city law but it would not be the FBI's business, according to Hoover. Marshall said Hoover believed "it's none of [our] business, not only to investigate it afterwards but it's sort of doubly none of our business to interfere with what's going on at the time since Bureau agents are not policemen, they're investigators."[4]

So, given his personal prejudices and the professional standards he adhered to, Hoover was reluctant to act swiftly to the civil rights disturbances in Mississippi but carried out the orders of the president.

Johnson saw the need for the FBI to move in full force to try to solve the mystery of the three missing civil rights workers. In a telephone conversation with House Speaker John McCormack, placed at 12:45 P.M. Tuesday, Johnson said he had Hoover put teams of FBI agents in Mississippi several weeks earlier to try to infiltrate the Klan and do whatever they could to head off trouble.

Johnson was upset with two New York congressmen, Ogden Reid, a Republican, and William Ryan, a Democrat, who had been calling the White House wanting to know what the president was doing about the killings of the civil rights workers, two of whom were from New York. Johnson thought the congressmen wanted to arrange for him to meet with the slain men's parents. LBJ thought that would be a bad precedent to set. Plus, he suspected the congressmen wanted to have their pictures taken at the White House for their own publicity. So he wanted McCormack to call Reid and Ryan and tell them what the White House was doing and for them to back off.

His conversation with McCormack gives insight into the government's stepped-up role in Mississippi:

> What we have done in Mississippi is this: About three weeks ago, I called in Edgar Hoover and told him to fill Mississippi — I can't say this publicly — load it down with FBI men, put 'em every place they can ... put 'em in the Klan and infiltrate it — we can't advertise this — but get all the informers we need so we can know what's going on and we can protect these kids as best we can.
>
> So he shipped the FBI in there and he's got 'em joining up everything and trying to get in a position where we can be helpful. When these kids didn't show night before last, yesterday we sent a new bunch of FBI in to supplement in numbers. We got the Defense Department to turn over the helicopters and turn over the facilities of the Naval Air Station to the FBI. And the FBI's using the helicopters to go over all the roads and fly over them and take pictures and try to locate these people.
>
> The FBI's got two big groups that have gone in at my request although I don't want to be appearing to direct this thing and appearing to be invading this state and taking the rights of the governor of the mayor. Nevertheless, I have quietly shown plenty of firmness and plenty of power. It's the only power I have. The marshals couldn't do much better. The marshals are not investigative by nature and can't locate anybody.

Johnson told McCormack he'd known the Freedom Movement was dangerous.

> "We don't recommend it, don't advise it, but they're going to do it anyway. So we're gonna give 'em as much protection as we can...."
> "They can't disappear forever, can they?" said McCormack.
> "No, unless they've killed them," said Johnson.[5]

Early that afternoon, Robert Kennedy left a message with Johnson, saying he thought the president should make a public statement about the disappearance of the three men and perhaps make arrangements to meet their parents. When Johnson returned Kennedy's call, the attorney general was out so Johnson talked with Nicholas Katzenbach, assistant attorney general.

"I'm afraid if I start house mothering each kid that's gone down there that doesn't show up, that we'll have this White House full of people every day asking for sympathy, and Congressmen too 'cause they want to come over and have their picture made and get on TV," he told Katzenbach.[6]

Johnson then called Marshall, whom he regarded as the top man in the Justice Department on civil rights, to get Marshall's opinion on how much involvement he should have with Mississippi officials. Marshall told him to call Senator James Eastland to get his opinion. If he contacted Governor Paul Johnson, he might take offense at the president stepping in on his territory. "We need to keep the governor helpful if we can," said Marshall.[7]

At 3:59 P.M., Johnson called Eastland at his home in Ruleville, Mississippi. They chatted for a few minutes about how the lack of rain was hurting the crops. Then the president asked Eastland for his assessment of the situation with the missing kids.

Eastland told him, "I don't believe there's three missing. I believe it's a publicity stunt. I don't think there's a damn thing to it. They were put in jail in Philadelphia right next to John Stennis's home county. There's no Ku Klux Klan or White Citizens Council in that area. If it happened in some other area, I'd pay more attention to it. I don't think there's anything to it."[8]

Six minutes later, the president received a call from Hoover. He told him the blue station wagon was found, engulfed in a swamp. It had been set on fire and was still smoldering. The heat was so intense that agents couldn't get close enough to see if there were any bodies inside. Eventually, they determined no one was in the car. Johnson asked Hoover if he should meet with the parents of the missing men. Hoover advised against it, saying that "there's going to be more cases like this down there" and meeting with the parents might set a precedent he would regret.

LBJ just got off the phone with Hoover when Eastland called back. Eastland said he had just talked with Mississippi governor Paul Johnson about the disappearances. "He says he expects them to turn up with bruises and claiming that somebody's whipped 'em. He doesn't believe a word of it."

Johnson told Eastland the burned car had been found. "Well, I know nothing about that," said Eastland.[9]

Moses, Lewis and other leaders of the movement were shocked and frustrated for many reasons. They grieved for Schwerner, Goodman and Chaney because they knew what the outcome of this episode would be. It was just a matter of time. Also, while they knew that violence would occur and had warned the volunteers at the Ohio training camp just a few days earlier, the disappearance of the three men occurred on the very day Freedom Summer had gotten under way.

Another factor gnawed at them — the national attention this case was getting. It was really no different than what had been happening for years in Mississippi — no different really from when Emmett Till, the 14-year-old, was shot down and dumped in a river; or when Mack Parker was dragged from a jail cell by an angry mob and he too was shot and tossed in a river; or when the state legislator shot to death Herbert Lee for trying to help blacks register to vote; or when Army Corporal Roman Ducksworth was pulled off a bus and murdered; or when black churches were fire-bombed; or when angry mobs beat black citizens while police watched.

Moses and Lewis and others knew what the difference was this time. "We had been absolutely correct in assuming that America would respond in a different way once white people began dying along side blacks," said Lewis. "It is a shame that national concern is aroused only after two white boys are missing."[10]

They noticed other inequities as well, some certainly unintended but hurtful nonetheless. The president, despite his earlier hesitation, did meet with Schwerner's parents and Goodman's mother at the White House in a session arranged by members of the New York congressional delegation. There was no such meeting with Chaney's parents, in part because nobody in Congress from Mississippi was sympathetic enough to lobby for a meeting with Johnson on their behalf.

Johnson signed the landmark Civil Rights Act on July 2 instead of July 4, thinking it would get more attention from the press and the public not distracted by the holiday. The bill was a tribute to John F. Kennedy, who had first proposed it, but was also a benchmark of the Johnson administration, something he hoped would be part of his legacy.

It outlawed segregation in businesses, such as theaters, restaurants and hotels; in public places, such as schools, libraries and swimming pools; and it prohibited discrimination in employment practices. It was a hard fought victory for Johnson who had to overcome roadblocks set up by segregationist House and Senate members as well winning the support of conservative northern Republicans.

The bill was tied up by opponents in the House Rules Committee who voted it out of committee only after supporters threatened to take it to the House floor without committee approval. In the Senate, the bill was stymied by the longest filibuster in Senate history and came to a vote only after Johnson pressured Senator Everett Dirksen, the influential Republican from Illinois, who pressured his fellow senators to get the job done.

As Johnson looked toward the Democratic National Convention six weeks away, two priorities surfaced. One, he wanted the case of the missing civil rights workers solved long before the convention started, and two, he wanted no trouble on the convention floor regarding the seating of the Mississippi delegation. There wasn't much he could do personally to solve the murders in Mississippi, but there was plenty he could do and would do to control what would happen on the convention floor.

On August 4, 44 days after Schwerner, Goodman and Chaney disappeared and 20 days before the Democratic convention was to begin, FBI agents, acting on a tip, discovered the bodies of the three men in an earthen dam in the swamplands of Neshoba County. All three had been shot to death.

There was some question as to who provided the lead that led to the discovery and if that person, as rumored, received a $30,000 reward for his or her efforts. For the next several weeks, white agitators in Neshoba County were on the lookout for any friend or neighbor who might be driving a new car or building a new home or going on a spending spree. Outside of Mississippi, Americans were gasping at what they were learning about the state. As historian Bruce Watson pointed out, "No one disagrees that the discovery of the bodies disgraced Mississippi in the nation's eyes."[11]

For the United States, situations were perilous abroad too, particularly in Southeast Asia, where three presidents, including Johnson, had committed U.S. troops to try to stop the spread of communism. Focus of much of the fighting was in the tiny entities of North and South Vietnam.

In early 1964, the U.S. Navy armed South Vietnam, a U.S. ally, with fast patrol boats known as PTFs and maintained the vessels in the northern part of South Vietnam. In covert Operation 34A, directed by American officials, the PTFs bombarded radar stations on the coast of enemy territory in North Vietnam and landed South Vietnamese troops to destroy bridges and other targets. But many of the missions failed because of faulty intelligence.

So military officials in Washington, with Johnson's approval, ordered the navy to conduct intelligence-gathering operations in the region. One of the destroyers gathering intelligence along the coast of North Vietnam was the USS *Maddox*. North Vietnamese intelligence had made the connection between the *Maddox* and Operation 34A. The patrol boats of 34A were too fast for North Vietnamese defenses but the slow-moving *Maddox* was a better target. On the afternoon of August 2, the North Vietnamese fired torpedoes at the *Maddox*, and the *Maddox* returned fire and got help from F-8 fighter jets from the aircraft carrier USS *Ticonderoga*. The *Maddox* steamed away to safety.

Johnson and his military advisers were taken aback by the North Vietnamese aggression and apparent fearlessness to the pressure the United States had applied with the PTF bombings. They directed the *Maddox* to return to its intelligence gathering and supplemented it with the destroyer USS *Turner Joy*. On August 4, American officials received reports of the U.S. ships being under attack.

Johnson was informed of the latest attack when he was meeting House members to discuss his anti-poverty program. He called a meeting of the National Security Council and congressional leaders to discuss a military response which resulted in his ordering the bombing of an area known as the Gulf of Tonkin, killing many North Vietnamese and damaging or sinking about 30 ships.[12]

It was at about 8 P.M., during the meeting with the National Security Council, that the president received a call from Cartha "Deke" DeLoach, assistant FBI director, informing him the bodies of the three civil rights volunteers had been found. That moment — when the president was discussing war strategy abroad and being briefed on a civil rights crisis at home — was a sterling example of the complexities facing President Johnson who hoped to cruise to a presidential nomination at a celebratory convention filled with adoring delegates in just two weeks.[13]

Three days later, the president sought and received the support of Congress on the Gulf of Tonkin Resolution. It gave the commander in chief the power "to employ all necessary measures to repel any armed attack against the forces of the United States and to prevent further aggression" in that area. The resolution was passed unanimously in the House and received all but two votes in the Senate.

Johnson used the power given to him through the Gulf of Tonkin Resolution to increase U.S. forces in Vietnam from 17,000 in 1964, to 184,000 in 1965, to more than 500,000 in 1968. It was to define his presidency as much or more than his accomplishments in civil rights.[14]

Later, the navy reported that the American military response was either based on false information provided to the White House or that it was misinterpreted. The navy said, "More recent analysis of the data and additional information gathered on the 4 August episode now makes it clear that North Vietnamese naval forces did not attack Maddox and Turner Joy that night in the summer of 1964."[15]

Meanwhile, in Jackson, the Mississippi Freedom Democratic Party followed through on the plan of action Robert Moses and others had drafted several months earlier. They had already set up their Freedom Schools and Freedom Houses; they had held their mock election; they had recruited hundreds of volunteers and put them through training sessions in Ohio; those volunteers were now educating the uneducated in Mississippi and conducting voter registration drives.

Freedom Democrats also attempted to participate in the Democratic Party's precinct, county and state conventions, knowing from past experience their members would be barred. So they held their own meetings all over the state. By making these efforts, they abided by all the protocols of the national Democratic Party, giving them the impetus to legally challenge the seating of the regular Democratic Party delegates at the national convention.

Now there was one more important step — holding their own state convention in which they would elect their own slate of delegates to go to Atlantic City. That convention was held in the Masonic Hall on Lynch Street in Jackson on August 6. The temperature outside was over 100. Inside, 2,500 exuberant attendees crowded elbow to elbow in an un-air-conditioned auditorium decked out in red, white and blue bunting and colorful balloons floating overhead. They found their seats beneath hand-written placards identifying their home counties— Amite, Neshoba, Sunflower, Talahatchie, Hinds...

They folded their programs and fanned themselves as they listened to one speaker after another — Lawrence Guyot, chairman of the Mississippi Freedom Democrats; Joe Rauh, the liberal, white lawyer from Washington; Fannie Lou Hamer, the fearless, sharecropper from Ruleville; John Lewis, the SNCC leader who had been through so many battles, many of them bloody; and the keynote speaker, Ella Baker, a veteran of civil rights movements who was ready to mobilize the next one.

Baker had been active in civil rights for 40 years and had an impressive track record. She worked in the offices of the NAACP and then helped Dr. Martin Luther King, Jr., start the Southern Christian Leadership Conference. Inspired by the student sit-in at the Woolworth store in Greensboro, North Carolina, in 1960, she went to North Carolina and helped the students organize what became the Student Nonviolent Coordinating Committee, mentoring young men such as John Lewis and Stokely Carmichael. Now she was in Jackson and she minced no words as she spoke of the Mississippi Freedom Democrats' noble mission.

Noting the discovery of the remains of Schwerner, Goodman and Chaney just two days earlier, Baker said, "The symbol of politics in Mississippi lies in those three bodies that were dug from the earth this week."

The audience applauded and shouted exhortations of approval as Baker defined the challenge that everyone in the auditorium had taken on — to be "let into America."[16]

She went on, "It is important that you go to the convention whether you are seated or not. It is even more important that you develop a political machinery in this state. The Mississippi Freedom Democratic Party will not end at the convention. This is only the beginning."[17]

By day's end, 68 delegates were elected to be the Mississippi Freedom Party's delegates to the Democratic National Convention in Atlantic City. As the state convention closed, the participants, hoarse, sweaty, tired and determined, joined hands and sang "We Shall Overcome."[18]

CHAPTER 5

The Republican Revolution

One of the senators who voted against the landmark civil rights bill was Barry Goldwater, the conservative Republican from Arizona, who maintained, "You can't legislate morality."

Later that month, Goldwater accepted his party's presidential nomination at a raucous Republican National Convention in San Francisco where liberal and moderate Republicans clashed openly with a conservative bloc, led by Goldwater, that took over the convention.

Goldwater, at 55 just a few months younger than President Johnson, was born in Phoenix, Arizona, on New Year's Day in 1909, the grandson of a Jewish immigrant who came to America and opened a department store in Prescott, Arizona. His son, Goldwater's father, later opened a branch of the family business in Phoenix. Barry was a freshman at the University of Arizona when his father died in 1929. He returned home to Phoenix to help run the family's store

Senator Barry Goldwater voted against the civil rights bill, one of many areas of disagreement the Republican presidential candidate had with President Johnson (U.S. Senate photograph).

and eventually became its general manager. He had a flair for gadgetry and gimmicks and for marketing his merchandise. An example was the store's "antsy pantsy" men's shorts, which were white with a design of red ants crawling all over the fabric. They were an instant hit.

But Goldwater also realized good business meant keeping employees satisfied. While he was general manager, he initiated a five-day work week and vastly improved his workers' fringe benefits. After a military stint that included service in World War II, he returned to Phoenix and got interested in politics. In 1949, he was elected to the Phoenix City Council.

Four years later, disenchanted with America's involvement in Korea, Goldwater ran for the Senate against Senator Ernest McFarland, the Senate's majority leader. It was a longshot, to be sure, but Goldwater, riding the coattails of President Dwight D. Eisenhower's popularity, won the Senate seat by 7,000 votes. He was re-elected to the Senate in 1958 and, in 1960, became chairman of the Republican Senatorial Campaign Committee. In this role, he crisscrossed the country, meeting with state party leaders and helping with individual Senate campaigns. He developed contacts, made friends and was well known and well respected within the party. It proved to be the launching pad for winning the Republican presidential nomination in 1964.

Goldwater's ultra-conservative views, which he explained in detail in his best-selling book *Conscience of a Conservative*, and his blunt, often piercing language, made people within his own party uncomfortable and his road to the nomination rocky. He lost the Republican primary in New Hampshire to Henry Cabot Lodge, a write-in candidate. Lodge was a former U.S. ambassador to the United Nations who was Richard Nixon's running mate in 1960.

Goldwater lost to New York governor Nelson Rockefeller, an unabashed liberal Republican, in Oregon. He achieved narrow victories in Illinois, Indiana and Nebraska. The clincher was a victory in California where Rockefeller had been heavily favored and after which Rockefeller dropped out of the race.

But discontent among moderates and liberals in the party continued and led to Pennsylvania governor William Scranton announcing his candidacy six weeks before the Republican convention. Scranton, 47, grandson of a congressman and whose ancestors founded the city of Scranton, Pennsylvania, was elected to Congress in 1960 and was dubbed by critics as a "Kennedy Republican" for his support of Kennedy programs such as the Peace Corps. He was elected governor in 1963, succeeding David Lawrence, a popular Democrat, who could not seek re-election because of state-mandated term limits.

Scranton was at first reluctant to be a candidate but entered late, hoping to be a moderate alternative to the Goldwater conservatism that was taking over the Republican Party. But his efforts were too little and too late.

President Johnson, who obsessed over identifying the opposition and plotting how to defeat it, had an obvious adversary in Goldwater, whose conservative principles and votes on civil rights and states rights appealed to the very voting base Johnson was fearful of losing — the segregationist South.

On the day he was nominated at the Cow Palace in San Francisco, a reporter talked with Goldwater at the Mark Hopkins Hotel where the Goldwater entourage was staying. He asked the senator if the Democrats had campaign fodder in the fact that 70 percent of Republican delegates had voted down a platform plank affirming the recently passed Civil Rights Act. Goldwater responded by calling LBJ "the biggest faker in the United States. He opposed civil rights until this year. Let them [Democrats] make an issue of it. He's the phoniest individual who ever came around."[1]

At the convention, when Rockefeller spoke and denounced extremism, he was booed so loudly that it drowned out his voice from the podium. What caused their ire was his statement that "the Republican Party fully respects the contribution of responsible criticism and defends the right of dissent in the democratic process. But we repudiate the efforts of irresponsible extremist groups such as the Communists, the Ku Klux Klan, the John Birch Society and others, to discredit our party by their efforts to infiltrate positions of responsibility in the party or to attach themselves to its candidates."

Many in the convention hall could not hear the words because of the raucous boos and shouting. His message

New York governor Nelson Rockefeller was shouted down as he tried to address delegates to the Republican National Convention in July of 1964 (Library of Congress).

was not lost on black citizens throughout the country who felt they had cause to worry if Goldwater was elected.

The convention was filled with rancor between the conservative and liberal wings of the party, all of whom wanted to have their say. Though Goldwater appeared to have the nomination well in hand before the gavel struck, opening the convention on July 13, he was nonetheless one of eight Republicans whose names were placed in nomination two days later.

The others were Scranton, Rockefeller, Lodge, Gov. George Romney of Michigan, Senator Margaret Chase Smith of Maine, Senator Hiram Fong of Hawaii and former congressman Walter Judd of Minnesota. Delegates sat through 33 nominating and seconding speeches, including Senator Everett Dirksen's nomination of Goldwater. He told the delegates that Goldwater was "a peddler's son who rose in politics because of his courage.

"It is the fashion of our critics to sneer at patriotism, to label positions of strength as extremism, to find other nations' points of view right more often than our own. Perhaps too long the bugles have sounded 'retreat' in our relations with other lands," said Dirksen. He assured the crowd that Goldwater's sure-handedness could retrieve American's self-respect.

Dirksen addressed Goldwater's vote against the civil rights bill, calling that vote an example of "that quality of moral courage which has won him the admiration of the citizens of this land."[2]

After all the speeches had been made, the roll call began at 10:13 Pacific Daylight Time, which meant it was after midnight in half the country. Goldwater won easily on the first ballot. On the next night, it was his turn to address the delegates.

"The Good Lord raised this mighty Republic," he said, "not to stagnate in the swamplands of collectivism, not to cringe before the bully of Communism."

Taking aim at big government and the Johnson administration, Goldwater said, "Our people have followed false prophets.... This party with its every action, every word, every breath and every heartbeat has but a single resolve, and that is freedom — freedom made orderly for this nation by a constitutional government; freedom under a government limited by the laws of nature and of Nature's God; freedom balanced so that order, lacking liberty, will not become the slavery of a prison cell; balanced so that liberty, lacking order, will not become the license of the mob and of the jungle."

He rattled off problems abroad such as the failed Bay of Pigs invasion in Cuba, the figurative and literal division represented by the Berlin Wall and the war in Vietnam. He then turned to domestic problems—violence in the streets, corruption in government, despair of the people.

"We Republicans see all of this as more — much more — than the results of mere political differences or mere political mistakes. We see this as the result of a fundamentally and absolutely wrong view of man, his nature and his destiny."

His message was clearly a clarion call for less government intervention at a time when blacks in the South, especially in Mississippi, were appealing for more intervention to give them exactly what Goldwater used as the theme of his speech — freedom.

"It is the cause of Republicanism," said Goldwater, "to remind ourselves and the world that only the strong can remain free — that only the strong can keep the peace.... Let our Republicanism, so focused and so dedicated not be made fuzzy and futile by unthinking and stupid labels."

And then, what turned out to be the signature message of the night: "Extremism in the defense of liberty is no vice ... and moderation in the pursuit of justice is no virtue."[3]

One analyst said afterwards, "My God, he's going to run as Barry Goldwater."[4]

The nomination of a man who voted against the civil rights bill and who espoused a survival-of-the-fittest philosophy provided one more reason for the Mississippi Freedom Democrats to be confident that Lyndon Johnson and the national Democratic party would embrace their cause in Atlantic City in just a few weeks.

Goldwater's running mate, Congressman Bill Miller of New York, was a stellar public figure but little known outside of his native New York. Miller, 50, a graduate of Notre Dame, was a lawyer who served in the army in World War II and later prosecuted German war criminals. He was the district attorney in Niagara County, New York, when he was first elected to Congress in 1951.

Miller added value to the Republican ticket because of his base of support in New York and because he had served as Republican national chairman for the past three years and had developed contacts throughout the country. But perhaps the thing that endeared him most to Goldwater was his sharp tongue. Goldwater said Miller's sarcasm and quick wit "could drive Johnson nuts."

Though Goldwater won the nomination by besting the best of the other Republican contenders, the GOP had a candidate that many in the party had trouble rallying behind. "The fervor, the frenzy and the excesses of the dedicated Goldwater troops appalled a huge and unknown percentage of Republicans of other moralities," according to historian T.H. White, "but there was no banner to which they could commit themselves. And so Goldwater and his Puritans were left alone to face the greatest pragmatist of all time — Lyndon B. Johnson."[5]

Indeed, Goldwater himself was in no mood to mend Republican fences. On the night he won the nomination, Rockefeller placed a call to his hotel suite to congratulate him. Goldwater didn't accept the call. "Hell, I don't want to talk to that son of a bitch," he said. He was pleased and gracious, however, when Scranton joined him on the podium after his acceptance speech and pledged his support in the coming campaign.[6]

The president watched Goldwater's speech and talked with advisers about whether he should comment about it. In one part of the speech, Goldwater vowed not to get personal during the campaign — to stick to issues without resorting to personal attacks. This came several hours after he had told the reporter in the Mark Hopkins Hotel that Johnson was "the biggest faker in the United States" and "the phoniest individual who ever came around."

"Somebody got a hold of him," LBJ told his press secretary George Reedy. "He said I was terrible yesterday morning. Last night he said I'm fine and he's not going to get personal at all in his victory statement. You see that?"

"I think he realized he made a boo-boo," said Reedy.

The president said, "You ought to say all day long we're not gonna get personal and he's probably tired and angry and got a lot of problems out there when he talks about fakers and phonies.

"Galbraith said this morning they spent a hundred years trying to build the institution of the presidency up and here's a wild madman — mad dog — that's gonna tear it down in 15 minutes and then wanting to succeed to the job ... I'd put that out." He was referring to John Kenneth Galbraith, a leading economist and historian of the time.[7]

In the eyes of many in the black community, the Republican convention was an example of everything they feared in government — including a lack of sensitivity. Even Milton Eisenhower, brother of the former president, had raised concerns in his nominating speech for Scranton. "Let us not be guilty of maudlin sympathy for the criminal ... roaming the streets with a switchblade knife," he declared. Roy Wilkins, head of the NAACP, said the next day that most Americans associate switchblade knives with Negroes.[8]

The nation's black press raised concerns not only about the Goldwater candidacy but how incidents at the convention were an ugly example of the attitude of the conservative movement. The *Cleveland Call and Post* reported that George Fleming, a delegate from New Jersey, said black delegates had been shoved, pushed, spat upon and were the targets of cursing and crude racial epithets. George Young, a black delegate from Pennsylvania, said angry white delegates got so close to him that they set his suit coat on fire with a lit cigarette. Jackie Robinson, a baseball Hall of Famer who was the first black to play in the Major Leagues, was a guest at the convention. "I now believe I know how it felt to be a Jew in Hitler's Germany," he said.

The *Chicago Defender* said the Republican Party, which 100 years earlier was the party in power when slavery was abolished, was now on the brink of falling apart. The *Atlanta Daily World* noted that the Democratic Party had its segregationist wing of people such as James Eastland, Strom Thurmond and Ross Barnett — and now, from what occurred at the Cow Palace in San Francisco, it was "useless for a Negro today to think he solves the race issue in politics by jumping from one major party to another."[9]

In some parts of San Francisco on the night of July 15, not far from the Cow Palace where Goldwater was nominated, groups of black citizens gathered and sang "We Shall Overcome." In another part of the city, a reporter in his hotel room had trouble getting to sleep because of the celebratory antics of victorious Goldwater supporters near his room. They were singing, among other songs, "Dixie."[10]

CHAPTER 6

The Journey

Jackson, the capital city of Mississippi, was one of the stellar cities of the South with business and industry and government providing jobs and food and clothing for its white citizenry and a legislature and a law enforcement machine that kept its black citizens from partaking in what the white community had.

To get to the SNCC office at 1017 Lynch Street from downtown Jackson, a traveler had to go into the black district — what northerners referred to as the ghetto — stripped bare of any structural dignity with its shacks that passed for homes, usually wood structures with peeling paint and broken windows; dirt yards adorned with trash amid little children playing; and streets with soup-bowl sized potholes. The Streamline Bar was next to the SNCC office and, not far from them, a cemetery. The poverty was easily visible, more visible than the fear that was also a part of the neighborhood.

"On any day a white man could just shoot a black man down and nothing could be done about it," said Charles McLaurin. "And there were lynchings and hangings."[1]

McLaurin, from Indianola, was one of the 68 delegates who boarded three chartered buses for Atlantic City on Wednesday, August 19. Two of the delegates were sons of slaves, one was a World War I veteran, several were World War II veterans. There were farmers, sharecroppers, beauticians, door-to-door salesmen, a barber, a druggist an undertaker, maids, cooks, preachers. Most of them were dressed in their Sunday best as they embarked on their 30-hour journey, paid for by Harry Belafonte, a famous black singer and activist who supported their cause.

There were four white people in the delegation — and this was no accident. Freedom Party leaders recognized the hypocrisy of angrily protesting an all-white delegation at the convention and then presenting an all-black one as an alternative. They wanted to make their point about the importance of black representation — but as part of an integrated delegation.

What identified these travelers more than name or race or occupation though, was their collective experiences— hundreds of them, most of them dreadful and terrifying — that had been forged into one movement, one journey, taking them to what they believed was their political promised land — Atlantic City.

McLaurin carried with him the memory of the day he was stopped by police and taken to a police station without being charged with any crime. He was taken to a secluded area of the station and continually beaten until he admitted that he was a "nigger." He was then released.[2]

Aaron Henry, a druggist from Clarksdale, was the chairman of the delegation. He had been arrested more than 30 times and his drugstore had been vandalized and torched several times since he had become a civil rights activist. On one occasion, his efforts to register black voters so incensed local police that he was shackled to the back of a garbage truck and dragged through town.[3]

Fannie Lou Hamer of Ruleville, vice chairman, was an uneducated sharecropper but was a fearless and relentless civil rights leader. Her life was threatened many times and she was the victim of frequent false arrests. On one of those times, she was in a jail cell and was severely beaten by another black prisoner, a man who was ordered by police to beat her while officers watched. She was known for her tenacity, her perseverance and for her singing — raising her arms, raising her voice in stirring renditions of "This Little Light of Mine" and "We Shall Overcome."

Hartman Turnbow was a farmer from Mileston who had the reputation of being a fiery orator. There were many reasons why Turnbow boarded the bus that day, including the day in April of 1963 when he tried to register to vote and was blocked from entering the registrar's office. Not long after that, his house was firebombed. As his house burned, he grabbed his rifle to drive the assailants off his property. Police arrested him and charged him with arson — setting fire to his own home.

E.W. Steptoe of McComb, the first city visited by Bob Moses, never left his house without his gun. He was a neighbor of Herbert Lee, an activist who was murdered by E.H. Hurst, a state legislator, in 1961. Hurst and Lee had been neighbors for years and had gotten along well until Lee became active in civil rights. Then their relationship turned, and one night, during an argument, Hurst shot Lee. He was arrested but later acquitted by an all-white jury.

Steptoe had seen violence and injustice all his life and knew the solution. He was convinced voting was the key to succeeding.

Dr. Adam D. "Dan" Beittel, president of Tougaloo College in Jackson, was one of four white citizens to board the bus. Tougaloo was primarily a black school, and Beittel encouraged students to be advocates of social justice and to stand up for their rights. As a result, he often found himself putting up bail money for his students after they were arrested.

Tougaloo was a private college, administered by a board in New York. Because it was not a state institution, it was free from state control. With Dr. Beittel's blessing, Tougaloo students participated in protests for racial equality and led boycotts of restaurants and lunch counters that did not serve blacks, including the Woolworth sit-in that nearly created a riot.

The school developed a reputation in the white community as a haven for troublemakers. Housing on campus became the target of drive-by shootings. By the end of the year, the board of directors in New York reportedly fired Beittel after Senator Eastland spread the word that Beittel had Communist ties and that the school would lose its accreditation if Beittel remained as president.[4]

Boarding the bus with Beittel were the Rev. Ed King, Tougaloo chaplain, and Lois Chaffee, an instructor, both of whom were white. King was an activist who suffered many injuries while taking part in demonstrations and who was a strong advocate of the Freedom Schools in Mississippi. He believed educating the children was as important as educating the adults in order to build a strong foundation because the children served as a conduit to reach the adults. The parents would, in effect, be part of the PTAs of the schools.[5]

Chaffee subscribed to the same moral philosophy as Beittel and King and encouraged students to be active participants in social justice. Chaffee sat with students during the 1963 sit-in at the Woolworth lunch counter in Jackson, experiencing the humiliation of having catsup and mustard and salt and pepper smeared on her body.[6]

Winson Hudson, like many women on the bus, put determination above fear as she fought for equal rights for black people. The Ku Klux Klan firebombed her house as a warning for her to stop her activities. In defiance, Hudson wore a bright red dress so she'd be easy to spot when she went to register to vote.[7]

Unita Blackwell and Hudson could have sat side by side as their bus rolled out of Jackson, sharing stories of trying to register to vote. When Blackwell went to register, the white registrar threw a copy of the Mississippi state constitution at her and told her to interpret it. That was the literacy test she had to pass if she wanted to register.

Literacy tests, a requirement for blacks but not for whites, often contained questions impossible for anyone to answer, such as "How many bubbles are there in a bar of soap?" and "How many people are on the government payroll?"[8]

Nicholas Katzenbach, an assistant attorney general at the time, said, "You had black Ph.Ds who couldn't pass a literacy test and you had whites who could barely write their name who had no problem being registered to vote." He said the Justice Department was aware of the problem but because of the laws at that time, its only recourse was to sue on behalf of the individual who was denied the right to register to vote. "This meant essentially that you had to bring a separate lawsuit for each person who was discriminated against, and there were thousands. It would take years ... and simply was not a solution to the problem."[9]

Blackwell picked cotton for three dollars a day in the fields until she was fired because of her civil rights activities. She was jailed more than 70 times as she sought a decent life. She boarded the bus for Atlantic City "because we didn't have shoes for our children and decent houses to stay in or just the everyday life that we wanted."

Bernice Johnson Reagon, a member of the Freedom Singers gospel group, was one of the motivators on the bus who tried to keep spirits up as the miles piled up.

Victoria Gray Adams, from Palmers Crossing, just outside Hatties-burg, was another eloquent, dedicated activist whose husband, a plumber, could not get a plumber's license because of the civil rights activities of the couple. She was a door-to-door cosmetics salesperson who believed in the power of grassroots politics. She admonished skeptics, saying there are two kinds of people in social justice, "those who are in the movement and those who have the movement in them."[10]

She remembered an experience she had as a small child when she and her mother were kicked out of a bus terminal waiting room because they were black. As a child, she was frightened. As an adult, having experienced many more instances of bigotry, she was willing to fight to see changes made.[11]

"We went to Atlantic City ... still idealistic enough to believe that constitutional rights were all there to be ours as soon as we met the requirements," she said. "So we documented being denied the right to participate ... the right to representation. You know the old story: taxation without representation."[12]

Annie Devine of Canton was elected secretary of the delegation. She had been a school teacher in Canton but later switched to selling insurance for a black-owned company in Jackson and started distributing political materials with her insurance packets. Eventually, she quit all her other work to devote all of her time to her civil rights activities.

Another passenger was C.R. Dardin, state president of the NAACP, of Meridian, where James Chaney lived and where Chaney and Mickey Schwerner and Andrew Goodman were headed when they were ambushed and killed. Dardin made his living selling class rings to students at black schools around the state. His travels provided him with good opportunities to promote civil rights causes.

Sitting nearby was Jimmy Travis, an early follower of Robert Moses, who had a scar on his neck from a bullet wound he received one night while he was riding with Moses. The bullet more than likely was intended for Moses.

In addition to Reverend King, four other ministers making the journey were the Rev. Merrill Lindsey, Aaron Henry's brother-in-law; the Rev. Clinton Collier; the Rev. R.L.T. Smith; and the Rev. W.G. Middleton.

One activist who did not make the trip was Lawrence Guyot, state chairman of the Mississippi Freedom Democrats, who was in jail — arrested in Hattiesburg on trumped-up charges to prevent him from leading the delegation to Atlantic City.

Before the buses took off, a New Jersey radio reporter snagged an interview with SNCC's Stokely Carmichael, who was not a passenger but among the many black well-wishers on hand. Carmichael talked about the oppression of black people, the violence they endured and the lack of liberty they had, as evidenced by their being denied the right to even register to vote. The reporter noticed bullet holes in Carmichael's car and asked about them.

They were the result of an ambush by Klansmen, said Carmichael, occurring on a night when Belafonte, the singer, and Sidney Poitier, a famous black actor, had come to Greenwood, Mississippi, to lend their moral and financial support. They were not injured, but the shooting occurred as Carmichael and a passenger, Silas McGhee, were driving in the area, and McGhee was shot in the head.

The reporter asked Carmichael if he thought the bullet that struck McGhee was really intended for him. He replied, "If they were aiming for Silas — and I know that they want Silas McGhee very bad because he's one of the local youth who just won't tolerate any of their nonsense — then I wouldn't feel bad. But if they were aiming for me because it was my car, and Silas took the shot, then that's something I have to deal with."[13]

At 10 P.M., after singing "We Shall Overcome," accompanied by a banjo someone had brought, everyone got on board and the buses took off with a crowd cheering. The enthusiasm of the passengers did not obscure the potential danger they faced, particularly as the buses rambled on the dark roads of Mississippi. It was arranged for someone to call SNCC headquarters in Jackson once the buses had crossed the state line and were safely out of Mississippi. Organizers expected to get the phone call at about 3 A.M.

The travelers chatted, sang songs and munched on bologna, cheese and crackers and sipped Coca-Colas they had brought along. Some dozed off as the night wore on and did not realize it when the buses crossed over into Tennessee. SNCC headquarters got the call it was anticipating at 3:02 A.M.

They arrived in Atlantic City on August 21 with bleary eyes and rumpled clothes after the three-day trip through several southern states and up the eastern seaboard. Many of the passengers had never been out of Mississippi; some had never been out of their home towns or counties. For them, the experience was like traveling through foreign lands, seeing the mountains of West Virginia and Tennessee, the lush greenery along the countryside and the skylines of big cities— an exotic adventure, a travelogue come to life on a bumpy bus.

And, after almost 30 hours on their 1,200 mile ride, they were weary but wide-eyed at seeing Atlantic City, a surreal setting after "leaving their homes where the threat of bombings and burnings was ever present, coming to a place where sun-burned vacationers lolled on the beach. The air smelled of popcorn and seaweed; pretty girls wearing LBJ boaters pranced down the boardwalk," wrote journalist Lynne Olson.[14]

Far from the dusty ghettos of Mississippi, Atlantic City was a carnival, a playground where a goal of many of its thousands of tourists on the beaches— getting a suntan — was something quite foreign to most of the visitors from Mississippi getting off the buses. The boardwalk was lined with penny arcades where tourists spent their dimes and quarters playing ski-ball and pinball machines, trying to attain high enough scores to win a pennant or an ashtray or a doll. They had come to the place where, in less than a week, the Beatles would be appearing, and in just a month, the annual Miss America pageant would be held (and won by Vonda Van Dyke, Miss Arizona). Atlantic City represented many things to many people but all the Freedom Democrats wanted was to have their fare share of America available to them.

A few miles away from the swank and swagger of the boardwalk, the tired but anxious delegation checked into the Gem Motel, a rundown, segregated place where the rates were cheap and the management allowed its new patrons to sleep four and five to a room. They could afford better housing, thanks to Belafonte, but would have been denied access— just like in Mississippi.

Their plan was to drop off the few pieces of baggage they brought with them, straighten the rumpled clothes on their backs, and hit the streets, mingling and telling their mission to anyone who would listen in the vicinity of the convention hall. Then, back to the motel they would go for a good night's sleep as best they could manage it, because many of them had to be ready to testify before the Credentials Committee the next day.

While members of the Johnson administration in Washington were putting together a strategy to prevent a floor fight at the convention, advocates of the Mississippi Freedom Democrats were putting together their own plan to present their case to the full convention and to a national television audience.

Joe Rauh, the liberal lawyer, loyal Democrat and a member of the Credentials Committee, would present the Freedom delegates' case to the committee, the first step in the process. He explained to the delegates what had to happen, describing it simply as "11 and 8." They had to win approval of 11 members of the 122-member committee who would agree to file a minority report to the convention challenging the seating of the regular Mississippi delegation. Once the matter got to the full convention, approval from eight states or territories was all that was required to force a roll call vote on the Mississippi question.

The Freedom contingent, aided by Bob Moses, John Lewis, Martin Luther King and other advocates, went about their business with a single thought — "11 and 8" — and they repeated it to one another as both a pep talk and a reminder. On Friday afternoon, with less than 24 hours before the Credentials Committee was to meet, the lobbying began in earnest.[15]

The Freedom Party lobbyists went over worksheets that Moses and others had prepared for them. They contained the names of each Credentials Committee member along with a notation such as "strong supporter" or "possible contact." Henry spent the rest of the day meeting with 20 delegations. Unita Blackwell met with delegates from Wisconsin and Minnesota. Hartman Turnbow, the man who "spoke with dancing hands," and his wife, "Sweets," lobbied the Oregon delegation. Sweets Turnbow was a charming lady who never went anywhere without her purse in one hand and a small paper bag in the other. It contained her pistol.[16]

Other Freedom lobbyists spread out and went to various venues — anywhere they could talk to delegates and pass out fliers describing the deaths of Herbert Lee and of James Chaney, Andrew Goodman and Mickey Schwerner, all at the hands of a Mississippi government that sanctioned lawlessness and police brutality against blacks. At the end of the day, a day that had started with the completion of their 30-hour bus ride, the activists trudged back to the Gem Motel, and piled together in their meager rooms to try to get at least a little sleep.

LBJ and his advisers knew that if the delegate issue got to the floor of the convention, there were more than enough northern liberal states that would side with the Mississippi Freedom delegation to prompt the roll call and would almost certainly result in delegations from Mississippi, Louisiana, Alabama, Georgia and other segregationist states walking out and, worse, supporting Barry Goldwater in the November election.

One of President Johnson's tools was the telephone. He had phones installed in the White House so they would be convenient, no matter where he might be (LBJ Library).

So while Rauh and others mapped out their strategy that would begin with the Credentials Committee, the Johnson forces worked on a compromise to be presented to the Mississippi Freedom Democrats that hopefully would satisfy them and at the same time not alienate segregationists who were part of the traditional "Solid South" voting bloc of the national Democratic Party.

Both sides had been strategizing for weeks. LBJ and Rauh had respect for one another and had known each other for a long time, but they didn't always see eye to eye. And this was clearly a case where two lifelong Democrats, one from the eastern establishment, one from the hard-boiled south, were at huge odds with one another.

Rauh had been active in Democratic Party politics since the 1940s when he and Congressman Lyndon Johnson were both FDR New Dealers. In 1941, when Roosevelt signed an executive order prohibiting defense industry bosses from discriminating in their hiring, Rauh wrote the final draft that Roosevelt signed. In the 1950s, Rauh became the chief lawyer for the United Auto Workers, headed by Reuther. Johnson would use that relationship to his advantage in seeking a compromise with the Mississippi Freedom Democrats.

In 1957, when Johnson was majority leader of the Senate, Rauh sharply criticized him for allowing the civil rights bill to be watered down to help satisfy his segregationist friends. At the 1960 Democratic National Convention, Rauh made it clear he didn't support the choice of LBJ as John F. Kennedy's running mate.

Yet, despite the animosity that often surfaced between the two men, Johnson summoned Rauh to the White House shortly after the Kennedy assassination to seek his help in passing the 1964 civil rights bill. It was typical Johnson. He had built a career on knowing his friends and his enemies—and being able to treat people as either one or the other, depending on the circumstances—keeping them at arm's length or embracing them.

Now, just a few months after Johnson and Rauh worked together on the civil rights bill, the two men were tangling again. Johnson used Reuther as his intermediary and, as Rauh described it later, the president's message was clear. There would be no shenanigans at the convention.[17]

CHAPTER 7

Political Espionage

Cartha "Deke" DeLoach had spent half his life in the FBI, beginning in 1942 as a clerk and working his way up to assistant to the director, or "deputy," as J. Edgar Hoover referred to him. At age 44, he was one of the youngest of Hoover's inner circle but had been around long enough to be a friend and confidante of many other influential people, including Lyndon Baines Johnson.

President Johnson instructs FBI Deputy Director Cartha "Deke" DeLoach (left) on the surveillance he wants on the Freedom Democrats during a meeting in the Oval Office in August of 1964 (LBJ Library).

When the president's daughter, Lynda Byrd, was dating Charles Robb, whom she eventually married, Johnson asked DeLoach to do an internal investigation of Robb to determine if there were any skeletons in his closet. DeLoach complied and found nothing unusual that would present a problem to Lynda Byrd in marrying Robb — or to the president politically.[1]

DeLoach was well aware of how presidents used the FBI for their own personal and political purposes. He told the story of how President Franklin D. Roosevelt had the FBI investigate his wife, Eleanor, when he suspected she was seeing another man. An agent posed as a milkman and knocked on the door of the place she was staying. Eleanor, dressed in a housecoat, opened the door and conversed with the "milkman" who spotted a man standing behind her and reported his findings to the president.

On another occasion, FDR had the FBI investigate an undersecretary of state who was believed to be in a homosexual relationship. Agents conducted surveillance on the man even though he was not suspected of any crime or involved with any known criminals.[2]

So it was nothing out of the ordinary for DeLoach when he received a phone call from Walter Jenkins, one of LBJ's top aides, on August 1, 1964. Jenkins had been a top administrative assistant for Johnson since 1939, when LBJ was a congressman, and it was not unusual for Jenkins to do the president's calling for him.

Jenkins told DeLoach that the president was concerned about his personal safety in Atlantic City where the convention would be held in three weeks. He wanted the FBI to have a team in place to advise him of any potential threats. Jenkins told him, "We want to make sure the president is safe — and that there aren't any disruptions at the convention." It wasn't unusual for Johnson to ask for favors from the FBI and his good friend "Edgar," as he referred to J. Edgar Hoover, but this one was a little different. The Secret Service was in charge of protecting the president. It was not a duty of the FBI to make sure there weren't any disruptions at a political convention.

What the president sought was espionage on civilians in the United States for political purposes, similar but much more far-reaching than his requests for the FBI to investigate his political nemesis, Robert F. Kennedy. In announcing two weeks earlier that no Cabinet member would be considered as a vice presidential candidate, LBJ had eliminated Attorney General Kennedy as a possibility. Johnson feared retribution from Kennedy that might come in the form of a groundswell of support for him at the convention.

The plan Jenkins laid out for DeLoach on August 1 was mind-boggling. He wanted the FBI to do thorough investigations on the Mississippi Freedom Democratic Party, on each of its 68 delegates to the convention

President Johnson orchestrated the spying on Mississippi Freedom Democrats and tapping the phones and bugging the rooms of civil rights leaders but warned his aides to keep his name out of it. "I'm Joe Glotz," he told them (LBJ Library).

and on groups sympathetic to their cause, such as the Student Nonviolent Coordinating Committee and John Lewis; the Southern Christian Leadership Conference and Martin Luther King; and the Congress of Racial Equality and James Farmer. Johnson wanted to know everything the Freedom Democrats planned to do before they did it. There not only would be no surprises, there would be White House counteractions to thwart the efforts of the Freedom Democrats.

Johnson would be fully involved in the covert operations in Atlantic City but wanted his name to stay out of it. "I'm Joe Glotz," he told advisers on more than one occasion. As for his August 1 request, DeLoach seemed astonished at the magnitude of it. He took it to Hoover who said, "Lyndon is way out of line," but nonetheless instructed DeLoach to follow through on it and to put a plan in place.[3]

Johnson was putting the pieces together from the White House. He chose Senator Humphrey to be responsible for working with the Mississippi Freedom Democrats and other black leaders to make sure there was no fight over delegates on the convention floor. Johnson had not yet named his choice for a running mate, but Humphrey was high on the list, and he knew it. Settling the delegate mess was, in Humphrey's mind and Johnson's as well, a test he had to pass if he wanted to be vice president.

Johnson also called an old ally, Walter Reuther in Detroit, president of the United Auto Workers union, a staunch LBJ supporter, a financial contributor to black civil rights organizations and someone who had some influence with Joe Rauh — because Rauh was the UAW's attorney and his most lucrative client. Rauh was also a good friend of Humphrey's.

Reflecting on it years later, Rauh said, "President Johnson was a man who believed every man has his price. He had two things on me.... I loved Humphrey and wanted him to be vice president ... [and] I was general counsel of the UAW.... My biggest account, the UAW, my best political friend, Hubert. And he had them both."[4]

To make sure there were no surprises. Hoover assigned 27 agents who, under direction of DeLoach, tapped telephones, bugged hotel rooms, infiltrated civil rights organizations to learn their plans and, later on, impersonated television reporters (using credentials NBC willingly provided to them) to talk to MFDP members and others in Atlantic City who thought they were on television.

At the White House, Johnson monitored the activities of the MFDP closely but there were other pressing developments at home and abroad. There was the discovery of the bodies of the three civil rights workers and the flare-up at the Gulf of Tonkin resulting in Congress giving the president unprecedented war powers, and there was the matter of keeping a wary eye on Robert Kennedy. Johnson toyed with the idea of creating a position of chief executive officer of the Cabinet and asked Secretary of Defense Robert McNamara to consider taking the position. McNamara said it was a job better suited to the vice president and the idea never went any further.

On Sunday, August 9, Johnson called Reuther to apply a little pressure. He said, "If you and Hubert Humphrey have got any leadership, you'd get Joe Rauh off that damn television. The only thing that can really screw us up good is to seat that group of challengers from Mississippi.... He [Rauh] said he's going to take it to the convention floor. Now there's not a damn vote that we get by seating these folks."

Johnson said he had been in frequent contact with Mississippi governor Paul Johnson, imploring him not to impede the investigation of the murders of Schwerner, Goodman and Chaney and that the governor seemed cooperative. "He's not a Johnson man," said the president, but he had done everything that was asked of him, so politically, Johnson seemed to imply, things were settling down on that front.

Johnson told Reuther he didn't want a convention fight that could result in the election of enough segregationists in November that the Civil Rights Act could be repealed. And, Johnson said, if the Mississippi Freedom Democrats raised havoc at the convention, it could cause a walkout of delegates from the other southern states— and that would impact Johnson's chances in the November election.

"That's all I'm worried about," said Johnson. "I've got to carry Georgia.... I've got to carry Texas. We don't want to cut off our nose to spite our face. If they give us four years, I'll guarantee the Freedom delegation somebody representing their views will be seated four years from now. But we can't do it all before breakfast."[5]

The Mississippi Freedom Democrats, fresh from their convention and preparing for their trip to Atlantic City, were unaware their every move was being watched. They were eager to tell their story to what they thought would be a receptive audience. They surely would have been disappointed had they heard Johnson's pronouncement that they couldn't have it all "before breakfast" because the movement itself was the result of not wanting to wait any longer to enjoy the rights they felt they deserved.

Meanwhile, Johnson was fighting political battles in Congress with two important pieces of legislation. Both the House and the Senate overwhelmingly approved the Gulf of Tonkin Resolution but there were whispers that the United States had provoked the attack in the gulf rather than being an innocent victim. LBJ's War on Poverty program also got congressional support, but not without some political carnage.

Democrats threatened to stymy the bill unless Adam Yarmolinsky was removed from the poverty task force headed by Sargent Shriver. Yarmolinsky was of Russian descent, which automatically made him suspicious in the minds of many. Worse yet, politically, he had been an advocate of integrated housing for military personnel, something that did not sit well with southern Democrats whose votes were crucial to the passage of the poverty bill. Shriver reluctantly removed Yarmolinsky, admitting that he had been "thrown to the wolves." The House passed the poverty bill 226–184.

On Saturday, August 8, Johnson held a press conference at the LBJ Ranch where he was asked whether Yarmolinsky was sacrificed for the sake of his legislation. "Your thoughts are wrong — he never left," the president answered.

Joseph Califano, a longtime Washington bureaucrat who at that time worked for the Defense Department, was troubled by Johnson's obvious untruthfulness with the press regarding Yarmolinsky and shared his concerns with Defense Secretary Robert McNamara, the man who LBJ held in such high regard that he wanted him to be the executive officer of the Cabinet.

McNamara's reply to Califano is instructive in understanding the power of Lyndon Johnson in everything, from attacks in the Gulf of Tonkin, to anti-poverty legislation, to dealing with civil rights issues in the South.

Defense Secretary Robert McNamara told an underling their work was for "the greater good" and that was defined by the president and therefore everyone was expendable (Department of Defense).

Bayard Rustin organized many important events in the civil rights movement and was a trusted adviser to Martin Luther King, Jr., and other black leaders. He is shown in a planning meeting for the March on Washington in August 1963 (Library of Congress).

McNamara told Califano that if he was concerned about the president's lies, he was missing the big picture — that "power is not for the squeamish," that the greater good is defined by the president and however he defines it supercedes everything else. "None of us is important," said McNamara. "Everyone's expendable."[6]

Meanwhile, Martin Luther King, in Florida, strategized by telephone with Bayard Rustin, one of his most trusted advisers, who tried to keep his finger on the pulse of what was going on both in Washington and in Mississippi.

Rustin, 52, was a Quaker who grew up in Pennsylvania, moved to Harlem when he was 35 and had been active in civil rights most of his adult life. As a young man, he became affiliated with the Communist Party because he was disenchanted with American racism but resigned from the party in 1941 and spent the rest of his life in organizations promoting black freedom. He helped James Farmer start the Congress of Racial Equality, helped King form the Southern Christian Leadership Conference, helped young people start the Student Nonviolent Coordinating Committee and helped plan the March on Washington in 1963. He told an interviewer he had five guiding principles: nonviolence; constitutional means; democratic procedures; respect for human personality; and belief that all people are one.[7]

Rustin foresaw a dilemma for King when all the forces converged in Atlantic City because both President Johnson and the Mississippi Freedom Democrats were going to expect him to help win over the other side.

King sent a telegram to Johnson, requesting a meeting with him. Johnson was eager to head off a convention controversy but was hesitant to meet with King at the White House because of LBJ's insistence that he be kept out of the fray — his "Joe Glotz" position. White House strategists said if a secret meeting was held and the press found out about it, Johnson's involvement would not only be public but be seen as sinister. If the meeting was public, it would be insulting to the very segregationist forces Johnson was trying to appease. So, citing schedule conflicts, the White House said a meeting could not be arranged.

Nicholas Katzenbach, the assistant attorney general, said Johnson met often with civil rights leaders but was reluctant to meet with them one-on-one although that's what King always preferred. "The president had great respect for other leaders — Jim Farmer, Roy Wilkins and others so he liked to meet with them all at once. There were some times when Dr. King wanted to meet with him alone because Dr. King considered himself to be the real leader of the black movement, with some reason to feel that way." But Katzenbach said Johnson did not want to "put a blessing upon that" for fear of alienating the other civil rights leaders. So, much to King's chagrin, he didn't have private audiences with the president as much as he would have liked.[8]

The old "Johnson Treatment" was in full swing now, except it was covert — its victims were being backed into a corner figuratively, not literally — and they were unaware of it. Not only were phone lines being tapped, hotel rooms and offices being bugged and MFDP members and supporters being duped into talking to bogus reporters and sympathizers, but LBJ had also requested lists of names of all 68 delegates as well as every potential MFDP supporter on the Credentials Committee. Their backgrounds would surely reveal bargaining chips that might pressure them into siding with the administration if all else failed.

The FBI findings were transcribed and sent to the White House every night. During an informal dinner at the White House shortly before the convention, Johnson told Senator Richard Russell that it took him several hours each night to read all the FBI reports detailing the information from wiretaps. "Hoover has apparently been turned loose and is tapping everything," Russell wrote in his diary. He also knew his old friend well enough to see through LBJ's complaints about all the late-night reading he was doing. "He loved it," Russell wrote.[9]

On Friday, August 14, eight days before the Credentials Committee would meet in Atlantic City, Humphrey talked by telephone with Johnson, giving him a progress report on his efforts to stave off a convention confrontation.

"I've been working the devil out of that Joe," he told the president, referring to Joe Rauh. "And I understand that David Lawrence and Kenny met with Joe and had quite a talk with him ... on the basis of seating both of these delegations." (Lawrence was chairman of the Credentials Committee. Kenny O' Donnell, a holdover from the Kennedy administration, was a White House aide.)

Johnson laid down the law. "You can't do that at all," he said. "You can't seat both of them because if you do, then the other one walks out. There's just no justification for messing with the Freedom Party at all."

He told Humphrey if the Democratic Party gave in to "a group of Negroes who were elected to nothing" and in doing so, threw out the governor and other Mississippi elected officials, "we'll lose 15 states without even campaigning."

He urged Humphrey to tell the Negroes they have the president, they'll have the vice president, they have the law of the land and they'll have Democrats in power for the next four years. "Why in the hell do they want to hand-shovel Goldwater 15 states?"

Humphrey understood his marching orders but told the president, "We're not dealing with emotionally stable people on this."[10]

The next night, in Mississippi, COFO organized an event in Greenwood that was like a pep rally for MFDP supporters about a week before its delegation was to head for Atlantic City. The crowd of hundreds was stunned when actor Sidney Poitier and singer Harry Belafonte walked into the hall to join them. Poitier talked about the love he felt in the room, and Belafonte sang his hit song "The Banana Boat Song," and both men told how they had been supporters of the cause for many years. Then Belafonte took a satchel he had been holding and lifted it above his head. Those in the audience cheered wildly for they knew the satchel contained money — $60,000 as it turned out — although no one in the room was told the amount. It was shortly after this presentation that Silas McGhee was shot by a Klansman as he sat in Stokely Carmichael's car near the scene of the rally.

At about the time the doors were to open for the rally in Greenwood, Johnson had a phone conversation in Washington with the FBI's DeLoach, who was overseeing the massive intelligence operation on the Freedom Democrats. DeLoach advised LBJ to have a meeting with black leaders. "Squeeze 15 minutes into your schedule," he told him, and be sure to include Roy Wilkins, "their most rational statesman." The idea would be to talk about the advancements in civil rights and the progress that would be made in the next four years. Mississippi would not be a topic of conversation per se.[11]

Johnson held the meeting at the White House on August 19. Wilkins, James Forman and A. Philip Randolph attended. King did not but instead sent a telegram urging Johnson to support the MFDP cause. The telegram read in part:

> Only you are in a position to make clear the Democratic Party's position on the basic issues involved in this case. A great number of members of the Credentials Committee have made clear their wishes to follow you in helping the Mississippi Freedom Democratic Party's cause.
>
> Indeed, these delegates have also made clear their intention to wage a fight for the MFDP on the floor of the convention.... We urge you to join with these delegates in seating the only Mississippi Party chosen democratically and which is representative of the people in Mississippi.[12]

Through wiretaps on King's home-away-from-home in New York and on Bayard Rustin's phone, the FBI provided the White House with a play-by-play description of the game plan of black leaders. Their goal in meeting with the president was to pressure him into stating publicly why he preferred a segregated all-white, pro–Goldwater delegation rather than the Freedom Democrats.

Actor Sidney Poitier (left) and singer Harry Belafonte (center), shown with actor Charlton Heston at the Lincoln Memorial, were financial supporters of the Mississippi Freedom Democrats, making it possible for them to come to Atlantic City (Library of Congress).

President Johnson and the Rev. Martin Luther King both look glum during a White House discussion with black leaders in 1964. King sought one-on-one time with the president who preferred to meet with him in a group so as not to show favoritism (LBJ Library).

But Johnson came into the meeting and announced right away that he would not discuss anything related to the potential problems at the convention. Instead, he went into a lengthy monologue on his civil rights achievements and his goals for the future. After talking for nearly an hour, he excused himself to go off to his next engagement.

He had controlled the agenda, as he usually did, but there was still the matter of the King telegram. White House officials had learned, through FBI intelligence, that King planned to give the news media a copy of the telegram, in which case Johnson would surely be asked about it and would have to respond. LBJ was prepared to tell the press that the answer to the Mississippi delegate problem was best left to those in charge of the convention — but the question was never asked because King decided not to go public with the telegram.

As the MFDP delegates made their last minute preparations for their bus ride to Atlantic City, the FBI was waiting with informants in place at the Gem Motel where the delegates would be staying and at the Union Baptist Church where they would be holding their meetings while they were there.

On August 19, the day the journey began to Atlantic City, Bob Moses gave reporters a grim score sheet on the more brutal aspect of the Summer Project: 3 murders, 52 beatings and 250 arrests. That night, in Philadelphia, Mississippi, not far from where Mickey Schwerner, Andrew Goodman and James Chaney were killed, SNCC tried to open a new project office. A *New York Times* reporter witnessed what happened as Deputy Cecil Price, the same deputy who had escorted Schwerner, Goodman and Chaney to their deaths in June, served eviction notices on the volunteers and charged them with trespassing.[13]

The next morning, Johnson held a ceremony on the White House lawn to commemorate the signing of the $947 million Economic Opportunity Act, saying it was the nation's commitment to wipe out poverty. After the bill was signed, among those receiving ceremonial pens was Adam Yarmolinsky, whose job had been unceremoniously sacrificed in order to get the legislation passed.

When the festivities were finished, Johnson took a brisk walk on the White House grounds with newsmen scurrying to keep up with him. As he walked, he reached into his pocket and pulled out a slew of pre-convention public opinion polls showing him with huge leads over Goldwater — 67–32 in Wisconsin, 77–23 in Maine, 70–30 in New York.

With his popularity soaring and with the FBI in place in Atlantic City, the president was prepared to have an incident-free convention in which he would receive his party's adulation for all that he had done.[14]

CHAPTER 8

Showdown

Saturday was cool and overcast in Atlantic City. Shortly after noon, the Freedom Democrat delegates and their supporters, wearing their very rumpled Sunday best, left the motel and headed for the boardwalk and the convention hall, located, ironically, just off of Mississippi Street. They sang and gestured and laughed as they made their way past the arcades featuring posters of busty white women in swimsuits, and the hotdog stands and the souvenir kiosks where the hottest item was the "All the Way with LBJ" T-shirts.

As they reached the convention hall at about one o'clock, one hour before the Credentials Committee was to meet, their minds must have had dozens of thoughts swirling around, but one in particular over and over again: "11 and 8 ... 11 and 8 ... 11 and 8."

Many of the hundreds of delegates who arrived ahead of time in Atlantic City attended a Young Democrats luncheon where the featured speaker was Franklin D. Roosevelt, Jr. While the convention didn't officially open until Monday, early visitors could bask in the sunlight of beaches and the boardwalk, or take part in political events staged by the Democratic Party. The Roosevelt speech to the Young Democrats was one of them. On Saturday night, Senator Hubert Humphrey of Minnesota would be the featured speaker.

Wherever delegates mingled, they were likely to be approached by members and supporters of the Mississippi Freedom Democratic Party who formed a human ring around the convention center Friday night and again on Saturday. With each day that passed as the convention drew near, they became more encouraged. They were certain they had the support of at least eight states, the number needed to force a roll call vote on the floor of the convention as to whether they should be seated as the official Mississippi delegation. And if it got to a roll call, on national television, they felt confident they would win.

Joseph Rauh fought hard on behalf of the Mississippi Freedom Democrats but could not overcome the power of hardball politics (Library of Congress).

But the first hurdle was getting the support of at least 11 members of the 110-member Credentials Committee, which met Saturday afternoon. Failing that support, the issue would die, never making it to the full convention for consideration.

Joseph Rauh, the white, liberal attorney, walked into the convention hall, bow tie neatly in place, bulging briefcase in hand, prepared to present the MFDP's case. He was in a unique position for many reasons. For 20 years, he'd had an on-again, off-again relationship with Lyndon Johnson, goading him to be stronger on civil rights when Johnson was in the Senate, opposing his bid for the presidency in 1960 and being unhappy with his selection as vice president. Johnson, a man who always kept score on his political rivals, nonetheless sought Rauh's counsel when he wanted to shepherd the 1964 civil rights bill through Congress. Now they were at odds again.

On Friday night, while MFDP delegates and supporters, tired from their long bus ride, still found the energy to lobby for their cause outside the convention center, Johnson did his own lobbying behind the scenes, on the telephone from the oval office. At 8:56 P.M., he contacted Reuther in Detroit and told him of a compromise that might prevent a floor fight at the convention. The Freedom Democrats would be seated as honored guests but could not vote. The Mississippi elected delegation would have to take a loyalty oath to the Democratic Party or they would not be seated; and, beginning in 1968, the Democratic Party would never again exclude delegates because of race. A commission would be formed to oversee the reforms.

Johnson was making the most of the hand he was dealt. He had called Reuther to tell him the proposed compromise because Reuther could apply pressure to Rauh, who was the UAW's attorney and wanted to remain in that role. Also, Reuther and Rauh were huge supporters of Humphrey, whose nomination as vice president likely hinged on his success at selling the compromise to the Freedom Democrats. It was a classic Johnson power play — involving as many people as he could who had something to gain by doing things his way.

Rauh had another compromise in mind. In preparing for this day, he and his research assistants had discovered a nugget of American history they hoped could be repeated. In 1944, two rival Texas delegations sought to be seated at the convention that would nominate President Franklin Roosevelt to a fourth term. Lyndon Johnson was one of the delegates seeking to be seated. Roosevelt had nothing to lose because his renomination was never in doubt. Roosevelt said to seat both delegations. Rauh saw that as a compromise that President Johnson could surely relate to. In addition, Rauh knew the all-white delegation would walk out if the MFDP delegation was also seated or if the regular Democrats had to sign a loyalty oath. Either way, the MFDP contingent would be the lone representation from Mississippi.[1]

Chairman of the Credentials Committee was former Pennsylvania governor David L. Lawrence, who had served three terms as mayor of Pittsburgh before being elected governor in 1959. Lawrence was considered a man of great influence in the Democratic Party and someone who would exercise pinpoint control over the 110-member committee whose duties this year would be a little more pressing than the routine business of committees at previous conventions.

Lawrence, at age 75, was one of the old breed, a big-city boss who had attended every Democratic National Convention since 1912 and had great influence over who the party would nominate because of the votes he controlled in the delegate-rich state of Pennsylvania. A story that made the rounds in Washington political circles concerned a day in 1960 when Lawrence was in Washington in the Capitol building and Johnson, then the Senate majority leader, did not notice him and brushed by him in a hallway as he made his way to approach someone else. Lawrence said to someone nearby, "All right, if he's mad at me, I don't have to support him at Los Angeles." A Johnson aide overheard him, immediately recognized him and beckoned his boss. "Quicker than you could say 81 Pennsylvania votes, the senator was pumping the governor's hand," the *New York Times* reported.[2]

Lawrence supported Johnson for president in 1960, not out of adulation or loyalty but out of political pragmatism. He didn't think Kennedy, a Catholic, could win the presidency and that his candidacy could cause trouble for Democrats in Pennsylvania. After Kennedy won a couple of primaries, Lawrence became a believer and shifted his focus to Johnson as a vice-presidential candidate on a ticket headed by Kennedy.

He and Kennedy conferred in a Los Angeles hotel room during convention week of 1960, and Lawrence convinced Kennedy that Johnson would bolster the ticket. Kennedy offered the spot to LBJ who agreed to come on board. Lawrence delivered the speech nominating Johnson, who told him later, "Dave, I'll remember what you did for me to my dying day."[3]

Lawrence was among many Democratic power brokers across the country whom Johnson courted because their success meant political success for him. Among the others were Richard J. Daley, the red-faced, portly, three-term mayor of Chicago, whose power was such that Illinois delegates pretty much did what Daley told them to do; John Bailey, a Connecticut power broker for more than 20 years, who, though never having held elective office, was chairman of the Democratic National Committee and was often seen in political backrooms with cigar in mouth and glasses propped up on his forehead as he managed his operations; and California governor Edmund G. "Pat" Brown and California legislator Jesse Unruh, who had their thumbprint on the political landscape of their state.

Johnson had roles for all of them at the convention but Lawrence had the pivotal one as chairman of the Credentials Committee.

LBJ once said of him, "The South likes David Lawrence. They respect him. Every one of them. The Dick Russells, the Lyndon Johnsons— everybody that he was against. He's never been for us. I mean he was strong for Jack Kennedy against Lyndon Johnson. But he does it in such a way that you respect him, you like him."[4]

The committee was to convene at 2 P.M. As Rauh entered the convention center, Sander Vanocur, an NBC television correspondent, one of dozens of reporters on hand, approached him and said, "Joe, they've screwed you." And Rauh replied, "My God, already?" He learned that the committee was to meet in a room barely big enough to accommodate the full committee, the staff and those who were to testify. There might be room for one pool camera but certainly not enough to seat the people who had come all the way from Mississippi to watch the events unfold.

But more than that, part of Rauh's strategy was to allow the media to convey to the rest of the nation what was happening to the people of Mississippi, and he couldn't do it in a crowded room with limited media access. So before the hearing even got under way, Rauh raised his first objection — and it made its way all the way to the oval office.

"This is a helluva thing to be taking up with you," Walter Jenkins, one of LBJ's point men in Atlantic City, said in a frantic call to the White House. He explained that Rauh was "raising hell" over the size of the room. Johnson was shrewd enough to know what Rauh wanted and why he wanted it but consented to have the proceedings moved to a large ballroom. "I don't give a damn if he puts on a little show," said Johnson, "as long as he don't just wreck us."[5]

Chairman Lawrence finally convened the Credentials Committee at 2:53 P.M. Rauh was to present his case. Then the regular Mississippi Democratic Party would give a presentation. Under normal circumstances, the committee would then vote and the proceedings would move on. But these were no ordinary circumstances. Rauh gave an opening statement in which he reminded the committee of the fairness of the American political system and the time-honored method of open participation and freedom of choice. He said the MFDP delegates were right in their cause and had proven already they were willing to die for it.

Rauh had prepared a written brief for each committee member that contained a quote from the head of the regular Mississippi Democrats who said that Mississippi could seat "a dozen dead dodos" as delegates and there wasn't anything Rauh or anyone else could do about it. As Rauh paced and talked, backers of the MFDP and of the regular Mississippi Democrats sat across from one another, on either side of Rauh, listening to him and occasionally looking at one another.

"Some of the Freedom Democrats saw their plantation bosses; some saw the women for whom they had worked as maids and cooks, and others perhaps saw their fellow townsmen," said MFDP delegate Leslie McLemore.[6]

Rauh called his first witness, Aaron Henry, the Clarksdale druggist, head of the delegation and the man who had been shackled to a garbage truck and driven through town as the result of one of his 35 arrests as a civil rights advocate.

Henry passionately and methodically told committee members of Mississippi's white supremacy and the brutality that went with it and how the black people's inability to register, let alone vote, denied them the chance to participate in the very process that created state delegations at national political conventions.

Henry told the committee he and the other 67 delegates would probably be arrested when they got back home because the state attorney general had gone to court and gotten an injunction against them attending. He

Aaron Henry, surrounded by delegates and reporters, testifies before the Credentials Committee on August 22, 1964 (Library of Congress).

Fannie Lou Hamer is shown testifying before the Credentials Committee on August 22, 1964, giving a riveting account of the beatings and abuse she received as she tried to register to vote (Library of Congress).

further stated Mississippi's racism was the biggest reason the state ranked 50th in so many academic and economic categories. "The only reason we are not 51st is because we only have 50 states," he said.[7]

The next witness, the Rev. Ed King, one of the four white MFDP delegates, continued to talk about the violence heaped upon not only black people but white supporters as well. "I have been imprisoned ... I have been beaten," he said, at which point Chairman Lawrence interrupted and in a gracious manner asked the minister to focus his remarks on the political process rather than on the quality of life.

But Rauh argued that the inhuman quality of life and terror experienced by the witnesses was directly related to their inability to participate in the political process— and that's what he wanted the committee members to hear.

Following the black pharmacist and the white clergyman to the witness stand was Fannie Lou Hamer, the gospel-singing sharecropper who walked with a slight limp, the aftermath of battling polio as a child. She put her purse on the table and leaned over to have a microphone attached to her print dress.[8]

Hamer, 46, was the last of 20 children born to Jim and Ella Townsend in Montgomery County, Mississippi. When she was two, the family moved to Sunflower County where, at the age of six, she joined other members of her family in sharecropping cotton. At an early age, she wondered why Negroes had life so tough and white people had it so good. Her family wanted her to be educated but also needed her in the fields. She went to school for a few months each year until she finished sixth grade.

She grew up and married Perry "Pap" Hamer and settled in Ruleville, where she and Pap sharecropped for a family and Fannie cleaned the people's house to earn a little extra cash. In 1962, she was invited to attend a SNCC meeting at a church near her home. It was a turning point in her life. After hearing the SNCC presentation, she became convinced that one of the reasons for black oppression in the South was fear of trying to do anything about it. And the way to do something about it was to vote.

Hamer tried many times to register to vote and was rejected for various reasons, such as not being able to pass a literacy test. On one occasion, she, like so many other black people, was asked a series of questions about the Mississippi state constitution.

But, after telling the local registrar she would be back every month, she finally was allowed to register. She became a SNCC field secretary and worked tirelessly to help other blacks register, and was beaten and had her life threatened several times because of it.

When Bob Moses came to Mississippi and started to organize the movement, it was a perfect fit for Hamer. And now, this humble but stubborn activist, who learned long ago to cast fear aside to advance the movement, was about to tell her story on a national stage. She was accustomed to singing "This Little Light of Mine" and "Go Tell It on the Mountain" to church audiences and at voter registration rallies. But today was not a day for singing and her audience was a room full of strangers.

Her appearance was in stark contrast to those who preceded her. She did not have the education or the polish of Aaron Henry, the pharmacist, or Ed King, the preacher. Some of her words tumbled out of her mouth without rhythm or cadence or even grammar. But she represented just exactly what Rauh wanted the committee to see and hear — living proof of the inhuman treatment of black citizens in Mississippi. Her presentation was not eloquent, not worthy of Toastmaster clarity, but it proved to be riveting in its honesty, simplicity and depiction of the life of a poor, southern black woman who risked her life to try to vote.

Historian Theodore White described the moment as Hamer began her testimony. "As her fine, mellow voice rose, it began to chant with the grief and the sobbing that are the source of all the blues of the world. The hot, muggy room was electrified."[9] She said:

> Mr. Chairman and the Credentials Committee, my name is Fanny Lou Hamer and I live at 626 East Lafayette Street, Ruleville, Mississippi, Sunflower County, the home of Senator James O. Eastland and Senator (John) Stennis.
>
> It was the 31st of August in 1962 that 18 of us traveled 26 miles to the county courthouse in Indianola to try to register to vote to become first-class citizens. We was met in Indianola by Mississippi men, Highway Patrolmen, and they only allowed two of us in to take the literacy test at the time. After we had taken this test and started back to Ruleville, we was held up by the city police and the State Highway Patrolmen and (ordered) back to Indianola where the bus driver was charged that day with driving a bus the wrong color.
>
> After we paid the fine among us, we continued on to Ruleville and Reverend Jeff Sunny (drove) me four miles in the rural area where I had worked as a timekeeper and a share cropper for 18 years. I was met there by my children who told me that the plantation owner was angry because I had gone down to try to register.
>
> After they told me, my husband came and said the plantation owner was raising cane because I had tried to register and before he quit talking, the plantation owner came and said, "Fanny Lou — do you know — did Pap tell you what I said?" And I said, "Yes, Sir." He said, "I mean that." He said, "If you don't go down and withdraw your registration, you will have to leave ... because we are not ready for that in Mississippi."
>
> On the 10th of September, 1962, 16 bullets was fired into the home of Mr. and Mrs. Robert Tucker for me. That same night, two girls were shot in Ruleville, Mississippi. Also, Mr. Joe McDonald's house was shot in.

And on June the 9th, 1963, I had attended a voter registration workshop, was returning back to Mississippi. Ten of us was traveling by the Continental Trailways bus. When we got to Winona, Mississippi, which is in Montgomery County, four of the people got off the bus to use the washroom and two of the people to use the restaurant....

During this time, I was on the bus. But when I looked through the window and saw they had rushed out, I got off of the bus to see what had happened, and one of the ladies said, "It was a State Highway Patrolman and a Chief of Police ordered us out."

I got back on the bus and one of the persons [who] had used the washroom got back on the bus too. As soon as I was seated on the bus, I saw when they began to get the four people in the highway patrolman's car. I stepped off the bus to see what was happening and somebody screamed from the car ... "get that one there" and when I went to get in the car, when the man told me I was under arrest, he kicked me.

I was carried to the county jail and put in the booking room. They left some of the people in the booking room and began to place us in cells. I was placed in a cell with a young woman called Miss Ivesta Simpson. After I was placed in the cell, I began to hear the sound of kicks and horrible screams and I could hear somebody say, "Can you say, yes, sir, nigger? Can you say yes, sir?"

And they would say other horrible names. She would say "Yes, I can say, yes sir." "So say it." She says, "I don't know you well enough." They beat her, I don't know how long, and after a while she began to pray and asked God to have mercy on those people. And it wasn't too long before three white men came to my cell. One of these men was a state highway patrolman and he asked me where I was from and I told him Ruleville. He said, "We are going to check this."

And they left my cell and it wasn't too long before they came back. He said, "You are from Ruleville, all right" and he used a curse word and he said, "We are going to make you wish you was dead." I was carried out of that cell into another cell where they had two Negro prisoners.

The state highway patrolman ordered the first Negro to take the blackjack. The first Negro prisoner ordered me, by orders from the state highway patrolman, to lay down on a bunk bed on my face and I laid on my face.

The first Negro began to beat and I was beat by the first Negro until he was exhausted and I was holding my hands behind me at that time on my left side because I suffered from polio when I was six years old. After the first Negro had beat until he was exhausted, the state highway patrolman ordered the second Negro to take the blackjack.

The second Negro began to beat and I began to work my feet and the state highway patrolman ordered the first Negro who had beat me to sit upon my feet to keep me from working my feet. I began to scream and one white man got up and began to beat my head and told me to hush.

One white man, since my dress had worked up high, walked over and pulled my dress down and he pulled my dress back up.

All of this is on account of wanting to register, to become first-class citizens, and if the Freedom Democratic Party is not seated now, I question America. Is this America, the home of the free and the land of the brave where we have to sleep with our telephones off the hooks because our lives are threatened daily, because we want to live as decent human beings in America? Thank you.[10]

While Mrs. Hamer was testifying, President Johnson was playing host to a meeting of southern governors at the White House, but he and his aides kept track of what was happening in Atlantic City by watching the television accounts. Johnson often watched news developments on three television sets lined up side by side in his office so he could watch CBS, NBC and ABC simultaneously.

At about the point where Mrs. Hamer started describing the beating she received in a jail cell, the president became alarmed at the potential impact her testimony might have to millions of people watching on television. He immediately notified the networks that he was about to make an important announcement. All three networks interrupted their coverage of the Credentials Committee (and Mrs. Hamer's testimony). As NBC's Edwin Newman told viewers, "We will return to this scene in Atlantic City, but now we switch to the White House and NBC's Robert Goralski."

Goralski and the other White House correspondents on the air that day speculated that the president might be about to announce his choice for vice president. But Johnson, who was adept at quickly sizing up a situation and reacting to it as if it had been a long-studied, calculated move, briefed reporters on his meeting with the governors, noting the attendance of Gov. John Connally of Texas, who exactly nine months previously, had been wounded in the attack that had thrust Johnson into the presidency. He also noted that he was narrowing his choices for vice president but had not yet made a final decision. He then retreated to the meeting with the governors without taking any reporters' questions. By the time his press conference was over, so was Mrs. Hamer's testimony before the Credentials Committee. Mission accomplished.

As his next witness, Rauh called Rita Schwerner, widow of Mickey, whose very presence was a symbol of the results of brutality not only of black people but of white people who supported their cause. As she spoke, several in the audience stood in silent tribute to her husband. Schwerner told of how she sought to talk with Mississippi governor Paul Johnson after her husband was murdered, just as she had done with President Johnson. Whereas the president had given her a few minutes of his time, the governor had unceremoniously slammed the door on her.

Outside the convention hall where she was testifying, a charred vehicle was on display, a replica of the vehicle in which Schwerner, Goodman and Chaney had driven into Neshoba County two months earlier. SNCC brought the vehicle to Atlantic City as a stark reminder of what their movement was all about.

Next up was James Farmer of CORE, followed by Roy Wilkins of the NAACP. Rauh had purposely peppered his witness list with men, women, white, black, sharecropper, professional people and national civil rights leaders.

His last witness was the Rev. Martin Luther King. He told the committee, "If you value your party, if you value your country, if you value the democratic process, then you must recognize the Freedom Party delegation, for it is in these saints in ordinary life that the true spirit of democracy finds its most profound and abiding expression."[11]

He noted that the state Democratic Party would not allow a single Negro into a state university until federal troops forced the issue and this same party was poised to snub its nose at the leader and the platform of the party.

King put the Mississippi oppression in the context of world affairs, saying, "For all the disenfranchised millions of this earth, whether they be in Mississippi or Alabama, behind the Iron Curtain, floundering in the mire of South Africa apartheid or freedom-seeking persons in Cuba who have now gone three years without an election — recognition of the Freedom Party would say to them that somewhere in the world there is a nation that cares about justice."

As King, suffering from a recently sprained ankle, hobbled out of the hearing room at about 6:15 P.M., undercover agents quickly radioed FBI agents who were in rooms 1901, 1902 and 1923 at the Claridge Hotel, King's suites, where they were busy wiretapping his phones. The agents got out just before some of King's aides returned to the hotel. Other agents placed hidden microphones in rented storefront offices of SNCC and CORE. Agents also established a command center in the room directly below King's suite with electronic monitoring equipment.[12]

Meanwhile, State Senator E.K. Collins, a lawyer from Laurel, took up the cause at the Credentials Committee for seating the all-white Mississippi delegation, claiming the Mississippi Freedom Democrats and, for that matter, all blacks, were free to be part of the Mississippi Democratic Party. He urged the committee not to seat a bunch of renegade challengers, some of whom he said had Communist ties.

"We submit, not by way of threat but as a matter of cold facts, even though we suspect our opposition to accuse us of threats, that there can be no surer way of forever killing the Democratic Party in the state of

Mississippi than to seat this rump group who represent practically no one," said Collins.

It was Collins, who, two years earlier, fought against James Meredith in his quest to be the first black person to enroll at the University of Mississippi. Collins exclaimed the crusade to desegregate the university must be resisted "regardless of the cost in money, regardless of the cost in prestige and regardless of the cost in human life."[13]

In his rebuttal, Rauh challenged every claim made by the regular Democrats but in particular their assertion of having a process open to everyone. He paced the floor and gestured as he talked, like a lawyer presenting his case to the jury. In this situation, Rauh had the unusual distinction of being one of the "jurors" since he was a delegate from the District of Columbia and a member of the Credentials Committee. When it came time to count votes, he was assured of at least his own vote being one of the 11 he needed to get this issue out of committee and on to the convention floor.

"I've got a stack of affidavits this high of people who were kept out of precinct meetings," he said. "Of course, Fannie Lou Hamer had the courage to go there. She had the nerve to lay her life on the line and you heard her here, the beating she took in that prison because she went to a voting school and she had the nerve to go to a precinct meeting."

He asked committee members if they thought Mrs. Hamer made up her story — or if Aaron Henry or Rev. King had made up their stories. Did everyone concoct tales to tell the committee?

Rauh told the committee it was wrong to consider the white Mississippi Democrats as the "legal" delegation because there were no statutes that dictated their existence. The Democratic Party was like a club or private organization that could admit anyone that met the criteria for membership. The Mississippi Freedom Democratic Party had not only tried to fulfill its responsibilities as part of the national Democratic Party, but it was pledged to support the national ticket, which the white delegation was not willing to do.

Afterward, Henry was optimistic. "We supported the national party and other state delegations seemed sympathetic to the plight of the southern Negroes. We saw no reason why we would not have the entire delegation seated. The future looked brighter than we had ever expected," he said.[14]

Chairman Lawrence adjourned the hearing at 7:10 P.M. to be continued the next day, Sunday, August 23.

The Freedom Party delegation and supporters returned to their cramped quarters at the Gem Hotel, happy that they had told their story to the nation, and then became incensed when they learned Johnson had pre-empted the testimony of Mrs. Hamer with his impromptu press conference. They talked among themselves about a plot to defeat them and how widespread it might be. But someone watching television hollered and the group gathered around a nearby TV set as Mrs. Hamer's testimony was rebroadcast in prime time.

As they watched, they shouted and hugged one another. Mrs. Hamer, humbled by the attention she received and yet obviously enjoying it, wiped away a few tears and said, "I felt just like I was telling it from the mountain. That's why I like that song, 'Go Tell It on the Mountain.' I feel like I'm talking to the world."[15]

Though no decisions had been reached, the MFDP contingent felt it had achieved a moral victory in front of the Credentials Committee, for their cause was mighty and it was presented well. The public would surely be on their side.

Walter Mondale, then the attorney general of Minnesota and a member of the Credentials Committee, said, "The impact of the Freedom Democrats' case, especially Hamer's testimony, was awesome. In fact, the emotions Hamer stirred completely changed the politics of the convention. Many of us already knew the Freedom Democrats had justice on their side. Hamer's speech ... put new pressure on us to do something about Mississippi immediately."[16]

Mondale said many Democrats had no sympathy for the Mississippi regular delegation. "They were an embarrassment to the party," he said, and there was general support to do something about it before the 1968 convention. But those in the civil rights movement had waited a long time, and they had come to Atlantic City because they wanted change now. "Because of Hamer, President Johnson was facing a different convention," he said.[17]

The national media was paying attention, too, for a number of reasons. For one, there was little mystery or intrigue at the convention to captivate the nation since President Johnson's nomination was a for gone conclusion. The one unanswered political question was who LBJ would pick as his running mate — but that was a sidelight and nothing more than a guessing game that Johnson controlled.

So with the television networks' commitment to gavel-to-gavel convention coverage, reporters were looking for a good story and they found one in the Mississippi challenge. It was a David-versus-Goliath–type of story and the racial overtones made the story even more compelling. Also, the press had heard rumblings that a compromise was in the works and of the possible floor fight over the seating of the Mississippi delegation.

Aaron Henry cited yet another reason for the press interest. "Most of the news people had never before seen 64 [sic] Mississippi Negroes in a group," he said, "and [they] were keenly interested in us and what we were trying to accomplish. They appeared to be very sympathetic."[18]

Meanwhile, the lobbying of state delegations continued. Some of the students from the North who had come to Mississippi for Freedom Summer were now in Atlantic City. They continued to help the cause by introducing MFDP supporters to members of their state delegations. Years later, Henry recalled the intense lobbying and said it seemed like most of the people they talked to supported the cause.

Henry said many of the rank-and-file delegates they talked to felt no blind loyalty to the party and seemed to have a sense of knowing right from wrong and wanting to do the right thing. "However, the leaders of the delegations, who usually sat quietly and listened to us, were generally with the party line, right or wrong, and they were important figures. This is what we didn't understand at that point — it isn't how many people you have with you, it's WHO you have with you."[19]

Those not actively involved in lobbying were supporting the cause in other ways. Since noon, a quiet demonstration had been taking place on the boardwalk. MFDP supporters gathered around large charcoal drawings of Chaney, Schwerner and Goodman, hoping to draw the attention of convention delegates and passers-by. By midafternoon the group of demonstrators had swelled to a crowd, still quiet and peaceful, that included blacks and whites from all over the country. The vigil continued for the duration of the convention.

But the political forces in Atlantic City were mighty and their cause was simple — to remain mighty. Lyndon Johnson knew about the MFDP celebration that occurred when their delegates and supporters at the Gem Hotel watched Mrs. Hamer on the television screen. FBI operatives, some posing as NBC reporters— with credentials supplied to them by NBC — were keeping the president informed of most everything taking place. Supporters not at the Gem were being monitored in their hotel rooms.

For instance, the president learned, through FBI wiretaps, that Bayard Rustin had called King and told him it was a nice touch when the television cameras showed him hobbling out of the hearing on crutches, and that his affliction gave him an excuse to get out of town before Lyndon Johnson arrived. And the president was kept informed about the whereabouts of Robert Kennedy and his operatives, for LBJ could not shake the fear he had of an attempted takeover of his convention.

He had convinced himself, if not others, that Kennedy and Martin Luther King had connived to use Johnson's inability to solve the delegate dispute as a springboard for an 11th hour movement to draft Kennedy as the nominee for president or vice president. Kennedy was young, ambitious, had a name that resonated with the American people and never had a pleasant relationship with the president. LBJ's political instincts made him aware and suspicious of his attorney general.

While Johnson fretted about this and shared his concerns with Walter Jenkins and others, Kennedy was busy with other political aspirations. Seemingly far removed from any sinister plot to take over the convention, Kennedy was about to formally announce his candidacy for the U.S. Senate seat in New York that had become vacant because of the death of Senator Kenneth Keating.

So while a Kennedy takeover was something LBJ imagined, the Mississippi problem was real. And as Johnson prepared for what he hoped would be his triumphal and perhaps majestic trip to Atlantic City to accept the nomination of his party, he was mindful of what his old friend, Texas governor John Connally, advised him concerning the Mississippi Freedom Democratic Party: "If you seat those black buggers, the whole south will walk out."[20]

He wasn't about to let that happen.

CHAPTER 9

Compromises and Consternation

On Sunday, August 23, Americans were "putting a tiger in their tanks" and heading off for family vacations at Lake Geneva, Wisconsin, or Cedar Point, Ohio, or the World's Fair in New York where Willie Mays dolls, made in Japan, were selling for two dollars. Some were seeing the Beatles, who were drawing huge crowds on their nationwide tour and who had left Seattle and were set to appear at the Hollywood Bowl, where patrons had to come up with seven dollars to get the best seats in the house.

Television, which, since the Kennedy assassination, had become an important medium for Americans to get their news, was also a source of entertainment and vicarious thrills through the broadcast of entertainment programs and sporting events. Red Skelton was making audiences laugh every Tuesday night, as Jackie Gleason was on Saturday night, while Alfred Hitchcock was scaring them with his mysteries on Sunday.

Baseball was the national pastime and on this day, the Baltimore Orioles split a doubleheader with the Chicago White Sox to remain 1½ games ahead of Chicago and five games ahead of the New York Yankees in the American League.

The exhibition football season was under way, with the Oakland Raiders defeating the Buffalo Bills in a pre-season American Football League game. In auto racing, where drivers were now topping 100 miles an hour, Parnelli Jones won the Tony Bettenhausen 200 in Milwaukee.

None of that much mattered to those embedded in the civil rights movement who were clashing with political forces in Atlantic City.

Newspaper readers in Mississippi were getting a far different account of what was occurring at the convention than readers in other parts of the country. Many of the largest newspapers in Mississippi were run by power brokers in their respective communities who stood for the common good and against any forces that might upset the common good. With segregation being a century-old accepted practice, the newspapers' reaction to the MFDP was predictable.

On Saturday, August 22, the *Jackson Clarion Ledger* reported on the MFDP presence in Atlantic City under the headline "Freedom Group Linked to Communist Fronts." An editorial said "Reds" were attempting to form "a third-party coalition of labor, Negroes and farmers" to create the image of a political party rather than a "foreign-controlled conspiracy."[1]

The *Jackson Daily News* had a story headlined "Commies Tied to Freedom Demo Group" and quoted State Senator E.K. Collins who said the MFDP "had the support of known Communists."[2]

A follow-up story in the *Daily News* went further, calling the civil rights movement an "invasion of Mississippi carefully planned by the Communist conspiracy" under a headline that proclaimed "Reds Among the Rightists."[3]

The *New York Times* covered the first day of the Credentials Committee hearings with photos of the competing delegations in the hearing room and a story describing the testimony with a headline reading "Mississippi Factions Clash Before Convention Panel." The story provided quotes from the testimony of Fannie Lou Hamer, Martin Luther King and of Senator Collins, chief spokesman for the regular Democrats.

The following day, the *Times* presented a profile on Hamer, the poor, uneducated sharecropper who was suddenly in the national limelight. In describing her testimony, the story said, "Her tone ranged from outrage to resignation to hope." Neither the *Clarion Ledger* nor the *Daily News* quoted from Mrs. Hamer's testimony.[4]

On Sunday, the Credentials Committee reconvened. Joe Rauh exuded a quiet confidence because by his count, he had 17 votes in favor of a minority report, a good cushion over the 11 he needed to bring it to the floor. He also felt certain he had ten states in line to approve a roll call vote on the seating of the MFDP delegation.

Someone leaked the LBJ compromise — that the MFDP contingent be seated as "honored guests" rather than as delegates and to give them seats in the balcony. MFDP chairman Aaron Henry was livid. To him, it wasn't much different than being told to sit in the back of the bus or in the balcony in movie theaters. "We can sit in the balcony ... in Mississippi," he said. "We won't settle for that in Atlantic City."[5]

That morning, the MFDP caucused, one of a flurry of whirlwind meetings being held in hotel suites around the convention center as Humphrey and other Johnson supporters worked to find a compromise and MFDP members and supporters talked about what they would and wouldn't accept.

Other guests arriving early for the convention could attend many functions. The Young Democrats sponsored a breakfast at the Hotel Jefferson, not far from the convention center. An invitation-only brunch for national committeewomen and newly elected committeewomen, with National Chairman John Bailey's wife as hostess, took place at the fashionable Smithville Inn in the nearby city of Absecon. New Jersey senator Harrison Williams held a reception for the New Jersey delegation at the Zaberers Restaurant. A special edition of the television news program *Meet the Press* was broadcast from the convention hall TV studio. And Young Citizens for Johnson held an orientation session in the Atlantic City High School Auditorium where Senator Birch Bayh of Indiana and New Jersey governor Richard Hughes were among the speakers.

All of that was far afield from the hotel suite where the MFDP caucused. In attendance were, among others, Martin Luther King; Bob Moses and his wife, Donna; Aaron Henry; Fannie Lou Hamer; Ed King; Verna Canson, a Credentials Committee member from California; Marjorie King, a Credentials Committee member from Washington state; and Congressmen Bob Kastenmeier of Wisconsin and Charles Diggs of Michigan, both Credential Committee members.

Earlier that morning, Hamer had breakfast with Canson, the California delegate, as part of a systematic MFDP lobbying effort to keep supporters in the fold, to try to woo opponents and to identify undecideds and work on them. The MFDP had developed lists of names of delegates with handwritten notes next to them, indicating whether they were "strong," "maybe" or "sold out."

Mrs. Canson, a civil rights activist for years, was a strong MFDP supporter who was on good terms with Edwin "Pat" Brown, the state's governor. Her husband, who was president of the Sacramento NAACP, was expected to be appointed to a federal judgeship soon.[6]

During their caucus, the group discussed a proposal by Congressman Al Ullman of Oregon that the MFDP be given two delegate seats. Congresswoman Edith Green, also of Oregon, proposed that anyone willing to take a loyalty oath to the Democratic Party be seated. This raised the possibility, at least theoretically, of both delegations being seated. It was similar to the Roosevelt plan from 1944 that Rauh had researched. But it was unlikely to occur because the regular Mississippi delegation and delegations from four or five other southern states would probably walk out if the MFDP delegation was seated.

Walter Jenkins called Johnson at the White House to talk about the Ullman proposal to seat two Freedom Party delegates in place of two regular delegates. "We have no right to take their delegates," said Johnson.

Jenkins said the proposal would lose when put to a vote. "But they have sufficient people for a minority report and a floor fight if they take it there. That's right up to the moment," he told the president.

Johnson was concerned about a vote being taken. "I thought he [Lawrence] was going to procrastinate," he said. Jenkins said the plan was for Lawrence to recess the committee until eight o'clock that night.

Johnson said he was certain the South would walk out of the convention if two Freedom Party delegates were seated. Jenkins agreed. "Two would be as bad as 52," he said. Jenkins said there was a possibility that a delegate from West Virginia would offer a motion to seat the regular delegation without a compromise.[7]

Unknown to the Johnson forces, Rauh was also disappointed in the Ullman proposal. Oregon senator Wayne Morse had told Rauh that Oregon was solidly behind them. The Ullman proposal showed that the Oregon support was not solid. But it was particularly distressing to Rauh because it showed that people he was counting on were already reducing the stakes before the fight had even begun.

There was also concern at the White House about the Edith Green proposal because of a possible southern walkout. Green, a former teacher and head of the Oregon Education Association, was the second woman from Oregon elected to Congress when she took her seat in 1955. She was a delegate to national conventions in 1956, 1960 and 1964.

Many of the MFDP supporters at the caucus thought Green's proposal was the best compromise offered so far but were still firm in their belief that no compromise should be necessary and that their position would prevail, especially if they could get it to a roll call vote on the convention floor.

Fannie Lou Hamer at first strenuously objected to the Green Compromise because she couldn't conceive of being seated equally with segregationists who had treated blacks so brutally for so many years. But as discussions continued, she softened her stand and her tone, realizing it was a way of getting her delegation seated, albeit a most discomforting way.

High-ranking Democrats loyal to President Johnson saw no value in the Green Compromise. It earned the congresswoman the label of "bitch" by Democratic National Chairman John Bailey who talked about her in a telephone conversation with President Johnson. The president agreed with his assessment.[8]

When the Credentials Committee reconvened Sunday afternoon, Henry and Ed King attended the session as representatives of the MFDP with no voice in the proceedings but merely serving as observers. Rauh continued to try to convince the committee that the issue was not whether the MFDP was a "legal" delegation because there were no laws involved.

Congresswoman Edith Green of Oregon proposed that both Mississippi delegations be seated at the convention. John Bailey, Democratic national chairman, characterized her as "a bitch" and President Johnson agreed (Library of Congress).

Years later, in reflecting on the proceedings, Henry said he thought the mindset of some committee members was that it must be illegal because it had never been done before.

As the meeting progressed, Chairman Lawrence realized discussion of the Ullman and Green proposals meant trouble for President Johnson and if they were put forward, a convention floor fight would be inevitable. He was also aware of the president's edict to procrastinate. So he stalled by forming a subcommittee to discuss the issue and come up with a recommendation to the full committee on how to handle it.

He appointed Walter Mondale of Minnesota to head the subcommittee. The recommendation had to come in time for the full committee to vote on it prior to Monday night's formal opening of the convention with its 5,600 delegates and alternates in attendance. The appointment of Mondale was a strategic move and had Johnson's approval.

Mondale, 36, was a Hubert Humphrey protégé dating back to 1948 when, at age 20, he worked on Humphrey's first Senate campaign. The son of a Methodist minister, Mondale graduated from the University of Minnesota in 1951, served two years in the army, then came back to his home state and graduated from the University of Minnesota law school in 1956. In 1960, he was appointed to fill a vacancy as attorney general and was elected to that position later that year. In 1962, he was re-elected.

As a delegate to the 1964 convention, he was appointed to the Credentials Committee. At the time of the appointment, it was treated as nothing more than routine business—filling out the scorecard for one of the standing committees. But now, as head of the subcommittee, his role was pivotal and politically significant. Johnson had his man, Humphrey, in charge of working out a settlement, and Humphrey's man, Mondale, was now in charge of seeing it through without it getting to the floor of the convention.

Other subcommittee members were Congressman Charles Diggs, a black man from Michigan; Price Daniel, former senator and governor from Texas—an obvious choice of Johnson; Sherwin Markman, a liberal political activist from Iowa, another Johnson crony; and Irving Kaler, a Jewish businessman from Georgia.

Diggs had been a supporter of the Mississippi freedom movement and had firsthand experience of the violence that came with it. On April 11, 1963, he was a guest in the home of Aaron Henry when the house was firebombed by white extremists. But Diggs was a veteran politician who knew the way Washington politics operated. He cautioned Henry and others that they wouldn't get everything they wanted in Atlantic City because that's not how the system worked. They were probably going to have to accept some type of compromise.

Price Daniel of Texas was one of the Johnson supporters on the Credentials Committee subcommittee seeking a compromise on the Mississippi delegation controversy (Texas State Library and Archives Commission).

Joe Rauh was telling anyone in Atlantic City who would listen that the best solution was to seat both delegations. Some Democrats thought neither group should be seated. Still others said to seat members from either group who agreed to sign a loyalty oath.

During the Credentials Committee session on Sunday, tension mounted as the afternoon wore on and no solution was in sight. At one point, one of the committee members stood up and called the Mississippi regulars Nazis. A regular Mississippi delegate responded by shouting that the Freedom Democrats were Cuban sympathizers. It was at this point that Lawrence realized the dispute was going to spill over onto the convention floor unless he took some action to stall it. That is when he formed the subcommittee headed by Mondale.

"So there I was, a young politician, 36 years old, barely acquainted with Mississippi and untested in national politics, but now in charge of keeping the convention from blowing apart," said Mondale. He believed in civil rights and the cause of the Freedom Democrats, but he also believed delegates to a national convention had to be part of a legal process and not a busload of well-meaning citizens who had no legal standing. Mondale also wanted Humphrey to be vice president and for Johnson and Humphrey to defeat Goldwater in the November election. "I was also very conscious of the possible implications of all of this on my own career," he said.[9]

Time was short — the full convention was to convene in about 24 hours — so two meetings were hastily arranged, one with Humphrey meeting with MFDP supporters, the other with Mondale convening a meeting of his subcommittee in his hotel room.

Humphrey met with Dr. King, Henry, the Rev. Ed King, Bob Moses, Roy Wilkins and Rauh. It was a cordial atmosphere but it was also the first time the black leaders came face to face with the hardball politics of their situation. Humphrey in a pleasant manner reminded them of his commitment to civil rights dating back to 1948 and that he wanted segregation within the Democratic Party to stop. However, there was the problem of the MFDP not being a "legal" delegation. Therefore, the best solution to the problem was to compromise and come away with everyone being a winner. He then proposed that the MFDP delegation be seated as "honored guests" at this convention and steps would be taken to make sure they had fair representation at future conventions.

Henry's reaction was, "One hell of a lot of good that was going to do. We knew that Humphrey was acting as a spokesman for President Johnson and we had every reason to believe that if he didn't settle this entreaty squabble, he wouldn't be offered the vice presidency." And the president feared that seating any of the MFDP delegation would probably cause a

Walter Mondale, the attorney general of Minnesota, had a good chance of becoming the state's next senator if he could shepherd the compromise through his subcommittee (Library of Congress).

southern walkout and, worse, loss of most of the South in the election, including his home state of Texas, which would cause him tremendous embarrassment.

"Had we been more politically sophisticated, perhaps we could have seen that, on a national level, the party comes before issues, no matter how important they may be," said Henry. But he said the MFDP contingent felt insulted and many said they would go home rather than settle for any compromise.

Following the meeting with Humphrey, Martin Luther King called a press conference in which he said if the Credentials Committee approved the White House compromise, Negroes "might go fishing" on election day. Henry was dismayed at the statement. He had pledged to support the Democratic ticket and intended to honor his pledge. It wasn't the first or last time there would be disagreement within the ranks of leaders of the movement.[10]

Late Sunday night, Mondale convened a meeting of his subcommittee in which members batted ideas back and forth into the wee hours of the morning. At one point, Daniel, tired and frustrated, looked at Mondale and said, "Can you give me one goddamn good reason why we have to stay here?" Mondale replied, "Yeah — Lyndon wants you to stay here." And Daniel said, "OK" and he stayed.[11]

During the hearing on Saturday, Markman had questioned the MFDP leaders who testified and got them to acknowledge that the Mississippi problem, while very real and hitting home with them, was really a problem that had national impact and should be dealt with that way. Now, in the hotel room Sunday night, Markman recalled that and suggested a new compromise, that the convention create some new positions — delegates at-large — and give those seats to representatives of the MFDP. The others in the room listened but did not embrace the idea.[12]

On Sunday night, black delegates from all over the country held a caucus at the Deauville Motel. The general feeling was that they must support President Johnson, the man who gave them the civil rights bill and the anti-poverty legislation. MFDP delegate Annie Devine, who was in attendance, burst into tears as she spoke. "We have been treated like beasts in Mississippi," she said. "They shot us down like animals. We risk our lives in coming here.... These politicians sit in positions and forget the people who put them there."[13]

At an MFDP meeting earlier Sunday, a man struck up a conversation with Bob Moses. He said he was a friend of Chairman Lawrence and had an idea. He asked Moses to give him a list of MFDP supporters on the Credentials Committee. The man said he would show the list to Lawrence to use as leverage to show the strength of the MFDP cause and how

President Johnson talks with Mississippi senator James Eastland in the White House in August 1964. When three civil rights workers disappeared, Eastland, a segregationist, dismissed it as a hoax (LBJ Library).

important it was to make sure their freedoms were confirmed. Moses was skeptical but others thought it was a good idea, so he provided the names.

The man turned out to be an ally of Johnson. The list never made it into the hands of Lawrence. Instead, the espionage team put together by the White House went to work. Canson, the black MFDP supporter from California, was reminded that her husband was up for a federal judgeship that he might not get, depending on how she voted.

Victorine Adams, the first black woman elected to the Baltimore City Council and a leader in black voter registration drives in Maryland for 20 years, was harassed by officials from Washington and Annapolis who threatened lack of federal support for causes she championed.

A man who had a federal job in the Panama Canal Zone was told he would lose it if he did not support the president on the MFDP issue.[14]

Johnson, of course, did not take part in the full-court press against the MFDP in Atlantic City. But he used his influence from the White House to try to defuse another concern he had — a possible walkout of southern, segregationist delegates if things didn't go their way. On Sunday night, when blacks were caucusing at the motel in Atlantic City, the president got on the phone in Washington. He called Senator James Eastland of Mississippi to talk about his concerns of a southern walkout. Finding Eastland unsympathetic, Johnson told him he might eliminate his "goddamn subsidies and cut out your $6 billion cotton program." Eastland, a wealthy cotton-plantation owner, benefited from a federal price support

Senator Hubert Humphrey had the task of working out a compromise with the Mississippi Freedom Democrats at the risk of President Johnson naming someone else as his candidate for vice-president (Library of Congress).

program in which the government paid farmers to withhold part of their land from production as a means of balancing supply and demand.[15]

Time became a critical factor for all parties. Lawrence couldn't put off a vote for too much longer. The convention was to begin Monday night. Humphrey had less than 24 hours to work out a plan agreeable to the MFDP delegates and hand it to Mondale's subcommittee, which would guide it to passage through the full Credentials Committee. And it had to meet the approval of someone who wasn't even in Atlantic City — Lyndon Baines Johnson.

At midnight Sunday, supporters of the MFDP re-enforced their picket line outside the convention hall, promising to stay there until the MFDP delegates were seated. That meant they would be there as the more than 5,000 convention delegates from across the nation began arriving at the convention site on Monday.

The predictable series of events that would occur the next four days in the convention hall — the speeches, the pageantry, the glad-handing and back-slapping were a stark contrast to the drama unfolding in Atlantic City hotel rooms and at the White House as the power brokers played hardball and invoked political realism on the hopes of the idealistic newcomers from Mississippi.

CHAPTER 10

Into the Lion's Den

Hubert Humphrey was up early Monday morning preparing for a series of closed door meetings and contemplating his political future. His task was daunting and unenviable. He was under orders from the president to fix this dispute and not to screw up. He was a hero to many in the black community, dating back to his courageous speech in 1948 calling for a civil rights plank in the Democratic platform. Yet now, he was being asked to find a way to pacify blacks whose civil rights were violated every day in Mississippi. And to do so could possibly cause a walkout of several segregationist states from the convention, perhaps triggering a tidal wave of support for Barry Goldwater.

His first meeting was at the Pageant Motel, dubbed by some as the convention White House. Congressmen Kastenmeier and Diggs were there as was Congresswoman Green, who were all on the Credentials Committee. Joe Rauh was there with Allard Lowenstein who was now an MFDP legal counsel. Martin Luther King, Aaron Henry, Ed King and Fannie Lou Hamer were also present.

Kastenmeier, 40, of Wisconsin, was white, a World War II veteran and was a small town justice of the peace when he was elected to Congress in 1959. Diggs, 41, was a licensed mortician in Michigan who had served in the Michigan state senate from 1951 to 1954 and was elected to Congress in 1955. He was a civil rights activist who once spoke to a crowd of 10,000 in Mississippi at a political rally. He drew great respect in the state when he attended the murder trial of the killers of Emmett Till, the 14-year-old boy who was slain by white supremists after he allegedly whistled at a white woman while vacationing with his family in Mississippi. Diggs was a friend of Aaron Henry and remembered well the night he was a guest in Henry's home when it was firebombed.[1]

Humphrey outlined the three-point settlement proposal: (1) each Mississippi regular delegate would have to pledge support to the Democratic candidate and the party platform; (2) segregationists would be disqualified as delegates to any future convention; and (3) the MFDP delegation would be welcome this year as "honored guests."

The proposal allowed for no MFDP representation as delegates, which is what they came to Atlantic City to achieve. Rauh and others asked if it would be possible to seat MFDP delegates in place of the Mississippi regular delegates who were sure to walk out instead of signing a loyalty pledge.

Humphrey tried to frame the problems they had to work out and the potential consequences. The crux of the problem was that, even though it was through no fault of their own, the MFDP delegates had not been elected through a normal, sanctioned process. In an emotional appeal, he mentioned his chance to become vice president was riding on the outcome of these meetings. He may have intended it as a way of showing the MFDP supporters that they stood the chance of losing a champion of their cause, but Mrs. Hamer thought he was putting his personal ambitions ahead of everything else.

"Well Mr. Humphrey," she said, "do you mean to tell me your position is more important to you than 400,000 black people's lives?" Ed King recalled later that she told Humphrey he was afraid to do what was right. The rebuke stunned Humphrey.

Bob Moses said her outburst was a result of her never having had the education or professional experience to know how to act businesslike and to try to build a relationship that would be productive. Instead, he said, Mrs. Hamer was unpredictable and uncompromising. She was not invited to future meetings.[2]

After the flare up, Rauh, Lowenstein and others brought forth a series of suggestions to try to bring the meeting back on focus, suggesting other possibilities including the Green proposal. Humphrey became upset that Congresswoman Green was even in the discussions since her plan was an obvious attempt to thwart the White House scenario of how things were supposed to go.[3]

While the meeting was getting under way at the Pageant Motel, President Johnson called Reuther in Detroit. "It's going to be a mighty hard four days," he said. "My guess is this morning you'll have a bunch of walkouts. If they see a legally elected delegation that's there and not seated, it'll have the effect of just depriving them of representation. Alabama's done gone and they tell me Louisiana and Arkansas are going with them. And I'm afraid it's going to spread to eight or ten."

Reuther told Johnson that Rau had talked to King and Wilkins at about 2 A.M. and that he had talked with Humphrey at about 3 A.M. He and Johnson talked about how Rau needed something to show for their efforts. Johnson thought allowing them on the floor of the convention with the promise that changes would be made in 1968 should be seen as signs of progress.

Reuther thought the naming of a subcommittee was an excellent move. He suggested that a partial report from the Credentials Committee be given at the convention and that delegates be told some problems were still being worked out by a subcommittee. The Mississippi problem might get lost in the shuffle in the other business of the convention, he thought, and a floor fight would be avoided.

Johnson seemed frustrated.

> I doubt if you're going to be able to keep intelligent people there. Put yourself in their place. If you were a legally elected delegate from Michigan, I doubt if you'd stay there for four days waiting. My judgment is you'd gather together your sympathizers and you'd apply the pressure. I believe that's what they'll do.
>
> I believe our greatest danger here is— if we don't seat Mississippi, we've already lost Alabama — my guess is we'll lose Georgia and states we oughten be losing. They [MFDP] talk about a seat in the back of the bus. I don't see why if you give 'em a seat on the floor and they sit there just like the Texas delegation does ... I don't see why it wouldn't be a pretty good victory for 'em.

Reuther agreed. "It would be a tremendous victory," he said, and then talked again about a stalling strategy to avoid a floor fight, saying, "We've gotta get over the hurdle."

Johnson said he hoped the convention did not give in to the Freedom Party. "I can go along with anything the Democratic Party can," he said. "I think they're diggin' their grave [if the convention gives in to the MFDP]. We're going to hurt ourselves not only in the south but other parts of the country if we refuse to seat a legally elected delegation. I think it's going to hurt us right in New York City. Abe Fortas and Clark Clifford and every boy that's studied this thing thinks it's outrageous."[4]

Shortly after the phone call to Reuther, LBJ received another telegram from Martin Luther King, urging him to allow the seating of the Mississippi Freedom Democrats. "In the last few days, the charged atmosphere of the convention has left the impression that only you are in a position to make clear the Democratic Party's position," King said in the telegram. "Members of the Credentials Committee have made clear their wishes to follow you."[5]

Johnson called his old friend Senator Richard Russell of Georgia for advice on how to respond to King. Russell, who was not attending the convention, said King was an arrogant man. "I don't see how you can do business with a man — white, black, green or yellow — that just comes out and intimidates [saying] if you don't do this we're going to take it out of your hide." The senator suggested that Johnson not give the telegram the dignity of a response and to handle any response in a press conference for everyone to hear rather than dealing specifically with King,

Johnson then shifted the conversation to the potential upheaval at the convention. "The question is: What should you do when they're getting ready to take charge of the convention? If you say they can't, and they run over you, which they will, then what do you do?" he asked Russell.

"You don't do a thing," said Russell. "You say you're sorry, you think they're ill advised and you let it go. If they do run over you, and I don't think they will, I don't think it would be disastrous if they did. It isn't going to hurt you any in the country if you get run over. It will hurt your pride like hell, I know."

But Johnson feared the American people would have another view. "I would think they'd say 'hell, the niggers have more power than the Democratic Party or the president, and the niggers are taking over and the hell with the Democratic Party.'"

Then Johnson shifted his thoughts to yet another fear, the paranoia he had regarding Robert Kennedy. "It would be best if I could stay out of that convention if I can," he said. "He [King] is trying to get me in it. I think it's Bobby's trap. Martin Luther King and his group want to put me in a position of saying I've turned on the Negro. I think that's Bobby's strategy, Dick."

Russell said, "Do you think Bobby would like to see Goldwater president?"

"No," said Johnson, "but I think he'd like to see me in all the trouble he can.... I think that's what we have to watch very carefully."[6]

The Credentials Committee spent Monday's session dealing with problems in the Alabama delegation. Lawrence, realizing no compromise had been reached on Mississippi, put off dealing with that situation for another day to give Humphrey more time to find a solution. When the convention opened Monday night, there were empty seats in the Mississippi delegation.

On Monday afternoon, Jenkins called the president and the two of them strategized. Johnson had come up with another idea. "Suppose Doug Winn got sick and resigned from the convention...," he said, referring to a member of the regular Mississippi delegation he trusted, "and we had the most respected member of the Freedom Party take his place. Of course they wouldn't do it, but that ought to satisfy them," said Johnson.

Jenkins said, "I don't think there's a chance it could be done but we could feel them out."

LBJ was on to another thought.

> Tell Governor Lawrence to say to everyone at the convention that none
> of them have talked to me, that the convention is entirely up to them. I

don't want to be involved. Martin Luther King sent me a wire. I don't even want to be replying. It's very important that everyone up there say they're not talking to me.... Be sure and say that to 'em.

Then concentrate on Harriman working on the New York one [delegation] and Williams work on the Michigan one and Luther Hodges start to work on the conservatives and have them go to television and put out a statement about what a good convention it is and how harmonious it ... and have Orville Freeman go around and say what a good farm plank it is and get some of the big talkers like Jim Patton on television.

Jenkins told the president he'd heard that Mondale's subcommittee members were getting tired and impatient. "Price Daniel and the Georgia man are getting a little rusty," he said.

"Do they understand they may have to hold it the whole convention?" asked Johnson.

"Mondale does and Lawrence does," said Jenkins.

Johnson thought a moment and said, "I'll try to get the liberals to say they're responsible for the delay — so we're not delaying it," he said.

At about 4:30 P.M., Jenkins called back and told the president about the frustrations of Humphrey after a day of talks with the Freedom Democrats and their supporters. He quoted Humphrey as telling him, "I'm a hell of a salesman. I walked into the lion's den. I argued fervently. I used all the heartstrings that I had and I made no headway. I think we can forget now any possibility of them not trying for a floor fight unless they have some votes."

Humphrey said Henry was an intelligent man and seemed to be reasonable. He suggested that perhaps some of the negotiators could come to Washington to try to get things settled. But he agreed with Jenkins who said nothing could be discussed in Washington that couldn't be discussed in Atlantic City.

Johnson was irritated. "I don't want to see them at all," he said. "If they're interested in the slightest in what concerns me, it is to go on and take the compromise that was proposed. That's what they ought to do.... If they want Goldwater, they can have Goldwater."[7]

Between phone calls from Jenkins, Johnson talked with James Reston of the *New York Times* who hoped to get a hint as to who the vice-presidential candidate was going to be. The president said he hadn't made up his mind and then asked Reston his thoughts on the convention. In a matter-of-fact way, he asked Reston if the reporter thought the Mississippi challenge was having any impact. Reston told him the buzz among Democrats was who LBJ's vice-presidential pick would be and the Mississippi situation didn't seem to be making much of an impression.

Humphrey's was the name most mentioned for the second spot on the ticket, but Johnson did nothing to stop talk among the media and in Democratic circles about the possibility of him naming Senator Eugene McCarthy, also of Minnesota, or Senator Thomas Dodd of Connecticut. Though the president had publicly ruled out any member of his cabinet as a possibility, the aura of Bobby Kennedy still hung like a cloud over any conversation about the vice presidency. Keeping the public and the press guessing while carefully calculating what he was going to do was part of the Johnson mantra, and it was in full gear as the convention began.

That evening, Johnson sat in his living quarters with friends Abe Fortas and Clark Clifford to watch the opening of the convention. How the political spectrum had changed in just four years. In 1960, the convention belonged to young John Kennedy with Johnson and Humphrey having to accept their roles as also-rans for the position both of them coveted. But Kennedy needed to carry Texas in the election and he needed Johnson. And Johnson needed to feel needed and so he agreed to run for the office that former vice president John Nance Garner once described as being as influential as a "bucket of warm spit."

But gunshots in Dallas changed everything. And as Johnson watched the television with Fortas and Clifford, he hoped to hear commentators remark about his achievements since taking office amid tragedy ten months earlier. Instead, he watched as NBC television anchors Chet Huntley and David Brinkley talked about the empty Mississippi delegation and the probable floor fight over seating one group over another.

LBJ picked up the phone and called Reuther in Detroit to vent. He told him he was "distressed beyond words" and that the Negroes are "going to set themselves back a hundred years" if they are not willing to compromise.

A sympathetic Reuther said he thought he might come to Atlantic City to get things settled before they got any worse.

Johnson said, "Hell, the northerners are more upset about this. They call me and wire me, Walter, and say ... that the Negroes are taking over the country. They're running the White House. They're running the Democratic Party. And it's not Mississippi and Alabama. [We're] catching hell from Michigan, Philadelphia, Ohio and New York. They're before that television. They don't understand that every white man in this country would be frightened if he thought the Negroes were going to take him over. But they're on television showing it."[8]

In contrast to what was happening behind the scenes, the pageantry inside the convention hall provided a hearty atmosphere of enthusiastic delegates enjoying "the land of the free and the home of the brave." At 8:30 P.M., Senator Daniel Inouye of Hawaii, America's newest state, led the 5,600 men and women present in the reciting of the Pledge of Allegiance.

As the delegates remained standing, they placed their hands over their hearts as opera singer Robert Merrill performed a stirring rendition of "The Star Spangled Banner."

Dorothy Vredenburgh Bush, secretary of the Democratic National Committee, stepped to the podium and issued the official call of the convention, a strictly procedural step but one that signaled the official business was about to begin. Governor Richard Hughes of the host state of New Jersey gave a welcoming address after which a short promotional film was shown lauding the successes of the Democratic Party in domestic affairs.

Johnson watched from his living quarters, still brooding over the Mississippi political problem and how it could singularly unravel not only the progress made through the passage of his civil rights and anti-poverty programs, but short-circuit the adulation he thought he deserved for bringing these programs to fruition.

His mood picked up as he watched Senator John Pastore of Rhode Island come forward to deliver the keynote address. Pastore, a short man with salt-and-pepper, short cropped hair just long enough to part, black moustache, and wearing rimless glasses, punctuated his words by sometimes lunging forward as if to throw the words into the arms of his appreciative audience.

He told the delegates of how he was a first generation American, born of immigrant parents, and that he had grown up to have the two greatest honors a state could bestow upon a citizen — to be its governor and its United States senator. "God bless America," he said, and the crowd roared.

Senator John Pastore of Rhode Island delivered the keynote address at the 1964 Democratic Convention (Library of Congress).

"We meet here tonight to assure the people of the world that reason, respect and responsibility still survive," said Pastore. "This is a time for plain talk. We must speak the facts of life as they are. We will not be misunderstood in Moscow or Peking or anywhere else in the world. We are a showpiece of partnership, progress and leadership."

Then, speaking of the recently-enacted Civil Rights Bill, Pastore said, "Finally, the conscience of America spoke ... the dream of President Kennedy and the fulfillment of President Johnson."[9]

As Pastore spoke, Johnson listened as he and Lady Bird dined off of portable metal trays with their dinner guests, novelist John Steinbeck and his wife, Elaine. (Fortas and Clifford had departed.) Lady Bird Johnson and Elaine Steinbeck had been classmates years ago at the University of Texas and had kept in touch. The president was an admirer of John Steinbeck and reportedly wept while watching the film of the author's renowned book "The Grapes of Wrath." He had asked Steinbeck to help him with his acceptance speech.

In Detroit, Reuther was involved in tough union negotiations. But he was moved by the anguish of his friend Lyndon Johnson. Reuther, age 57 had developed professional friendships with several presidents but felt a special kinship with Johnson whom he met with on a regular basis.

Reuther was born in West Virginia, the son of a brewery worker who was active in unionism. He said, "At my father's side we learned the philosophy of trade unionism. We got the struggles, the hopes and the aspirations of union people every day." The activism of his father made a lifelong impression on young Reuther who grew up to learn the power of unionism and political action to address social change.

As a young man, he moved to Detroit where, as a skilled tool-and-die worker, he had no trouble finding work in the auto industry. He and his brother, Victor, spent some time in Russia where they witnessed how hard laborers worked for little reward and how domineering the government was in people's lives. They returned to Detroit just as the union movement was sweeping into the auto industry. Reuther got involved and quickly learned the value of "organizing the unorganized."[10]

He was elected president of the United Auto Workers, one of the most powerful unions in the country, in 1946 and still held that position. In 1952, he was also elected president of the CIO and remained in that role until it merged with the AFL a few years later.

His empathy with the downtrodden and his belief in participation in political and social change drew him to the civil rights movement. He participated in marches in Mississippi, and in the 1963 march on Washington, D.C., and he was a big financial contributor to Martin Luther King's Southern Christian Leadership Conference.

Reuther was a friend of both President Johnson and of Martin Luther King. He was a civil rights advocate and he wanted another friend of his, Hubert Humphrey, to be the next vice president. He was an experienced negotiator who knew how to close a deal. And while he sympathized with the cause of the MFDP supporters, he had some leverage over them because of the financial support he provided them that he could easily withdraw — a tactic that smacked of the "Johnson Treatment." All of these things made him the ideal person to straighten out the mess in Atlantic City before it got out of hand.

In March of 1964, after the Mississippi Freedom Democratic Party had been formed and its leaders elected, and when plans for the Freedom Summer Project were well under way and students were being recruited, Robert Moses went to the United Auto Workers National Convention, which, ironically, was being held in Atlantic City. Moses knew that Reuther and the UAW were sympathetic to the plight of blacks in Mississippi and that he might be able to get some help if he connected with the right people.

He was able to meet with three key people — Rauh, who was the UAW's chief legal counsel; Mildred Jeffrey, director of community affairs and a political activist; and William Dodds, acting director of the union's Political Action Department. Moses explained to them what had occurred so far and the plan to challenge the seating of the regular Mississippi delegation at the Democratic National Convention. He left the meeting with the assurance that (1) Rauh would represent the MFDP at the convention and present its case to the Credentials Committee; (2) Jeffrey would use her considerable influence to get the Michigan delegation to support the MFDP challenge; and (3) Dodds would secure financial backing for the endeavor.

Dodds said, "I think it will be a pretty good test of some people who have been giving a great deal of political lip service to the subject."[11]

But the UAW position changed in July when Republicans nominated Barry Goldwater to run against Johnson. The contrast between the Republican and Democratic parties was so sharp — a president who signed the Civil Rights Act against a senator who voted against it — that the UAW wanted the ultra-liberal, pro-union, longtime civil rights advocate Hubert Humphrey on the ticket.

LBJ already had Humphrey on his "short list" for vice president. But the MFDP challenge caused potentially profound political problems. He had to find a compromise because he knew if he gave in to the MFDP — or gave the impression he was giving in — the southern states would bolt the convention and desert the party in November. He might not be able to afford to put Humphrey on the ticket to further infuriate the South.

So Johnson called Reuther, who also wanted Humphrey on the ticket, and asked that the UAW back off on its overt support of the MFDP challenge. Reuther called Rauh and asked him to do the same. But Rauh, committed to the MFDP cause, declined.

So as Senator Pastore finished his speech at the convention Monday night and President Johnson finished his dinner in Washington, Walter Reuther was packing his bags in Detroit. By midnight, he was on a flight to Atlantic City.

CHAPTER 11

A Compromise and a Lynching

President Johnson awoke Tuesday morning with a feeling of discontent that bordered on helplessness. He had used all of the tools in his political arsenal to try to resolve the Mississippi dilemma. He dangled the vice presidency over Hubert Humphrey's head. He had his hand print all over the Credentials Committee with his friend David Lawrence as chairman and Humphrey's friend Walter Mondale heading the subcommittee. He had two other allies on the five-member subcommittee — Price Daniel of Texas and Sherwin Markman of Iowa so he was virtually assured of getting a plan he approved through the subcommittee. Through his operatives, he had applied pressure to supporters of the MFDP on the Credentials Committee by threatening to stifle job promotions or to cut their jobs altogether, and suggesting to state officials that their federal subsidies might disappear. And he had Walter Reuther coming to town, who could withdraw his financial support of civil rights causes if things didn't go right and he could eliminate Joe Rauh's lucrative job as legal counsel to Reuther's UAW. In addition, the president knew just about every move the MFDP supporters were going to make before they made them because of the FBI bugs and wiretaps he had authorized.

And yet, as dawn emerged on Atlantic City and Washington, D.C., on the morning of August 25, nothing had been resolved and the possibility of turmoil on the convention floor that night was fast becoming a probability.

Johnson took a pen and paper and began scribbling out a statement he thought he would make later in the day. But he needed to talk to some people first. At 8:15 A.M., he called his old friend Senator Richard Russell, who was home in Georgia. Russell, like many other southern politicians, had decided not to attend the convention. Johnson told him he was going to Atlantic City and would tell the convention delegates Tuesday night that they should find someone else to nominate and elect. He said he had many scars to show for his efforts but was unable to unite his own party, let alone the country. He would try to hold things together until January, he said; then someone else could try to do it.

Russell was accustomed to Johnson's mood swings. He had watched him in action for nearly 20 years, smiling one moment, angry the next, patting someone on the back, then turning on them in a curse-filled tirade. Johnson, who had grown up in a home in which love was dispensed and then withdrawn just as quickly, displayed those same traits in his public life. Russell had seen and heard it all before. He told the president he was acting like a spoiled kid and to take a tranquilizer and get a couple of hours sleep.[1]

Johnson also called A.W. Moursund, a good friend from Texas, who was attending the convention. He informed him of his plan to withdraw. Moursund was also accustomed to his friend's mood swings. He advised him not to make any hasty decisions.

Next he talked with his press secretary, George Reedy, who was about to brief the press on the president's activities. "What should I tell them about this morning?" Reedy asked, unaware of the president's latest idea. Johnson and Reedy chatted about the president's schedule that day and what would be of interest to the media.

Johnson then told Reedy of his plan to go to Atlantic City and to either have a press conference or to address the convention. "I've just written out a little statement that I think I'm going to make," he said. "Here's what I'm going to say to 'em."

> Forty-four months ago, I was selected to be the Democratic vice president. On that fateful November day last year, I accepted the responsibility of the president, asking God's guidance and the help of all of our people. For nine months, I've carried on as effectively as I could.
> Our country faces grave dangers. These dangers must be faced and met by a united people under a leader they do not doubt. After 33 years in political life, most men acquire political enemies as ships accumulate barnacles. The times require leadership about which there is no doubt and a voice that men of all parties and sections and color can follow. I've learned, after trying very hard, that I am not that voice or that leader. Therefore, I suggest that representatives from all the states of this union selected for the purpose of selecting a Democratic nominee for president and vice president proceed to do their duty. And that no consideration be given to me because I am absolutely unavailable.

Reedy tried to convince Johnson that he was the right man for the times. He said if Johnson withdrew, it would throw the country into an uproar and hand the presidency to Goldwater. Johnson went into a rant about how the major newspapers and news magazines were critical of him and that he was going to make the announcement.

Johnson seemed tired and discouraged and ready to give up. He told Reedy,

> I don't want this power of the bomb. I just don't want these decisions I'm required to make. I don't want the conniving that's required. I don't want the disloyalty that's around....
>
> I'm absolutely positive that I cannot lead the north and the south and I don't want to lead the nation without my own state. I'm very convinced that the Negroes will not listen to me. They're not going to follow a white southerner and I think the stakes are too big to try to compromise.... The nation ought to have the chance to have the best available. That's who I want my children to have. I know I'm not....
>
> I know a man ought to have the hide of a rhinoceros to be in this job but I don't have the hide of a rhinoceros. I'm not seeking happiness. I'm just seeking a little comfort once in a while. I want to get away from it. I think I've earned it after 33 years.... I have a desire to unite people and the south is against me and the north is against me and the Negroes are against me and the press doesn't really have affection for me....

Johnson was particularly melancholy over a column by Henry Brandon in that morning's *Philadelphia Inquirer* that portrayed him as a "textbook caricature of a fast-dealing politician who has not aroused any excitement as a person or any emotion or enthusiasm as a human being." He read portions of the column to Reedy and then shifted his thoughts back to his announcement to withdraw as a candidate.

"If you've got any thoughts or any way you can improve this—I'm not gonna make it very long—I'm just about ready to sign off. Just let me know."[2]

His next call was to his trusted assistant Walter Jenkins. "I just don't see any reason why I should seek the right to endure anguish," he said. "People I think have mistaken judgment. They think I want power. And what I want is great solace. A little love."[3]

He also confided in Lady Bird who was to recall years later, "I do not remember hours I ever found harder." As the president went his way that morning, making telephone calls and keeping appointments, his wife tried to soothe him with a note she left for him. "Beloved, you are as brave a man as Harry Truman — or FDR — or Lincoln. You can go on to find some peace, some achievement, amidst all the pain.... To step out now would be wrong for your country and I see nothing but a lonely wasteland for your future.... Your friends would be frozen in embarrassed silence and your enemies jeering. I know it's only your choice. I love you always. Bird."[4]

Lady Bird Johnson, shown here in a White House portrait with her husband, wrote a touching note to him when he was contemplating not running for election in 1964 (LBJ Library).

Lady Bird, more than even Senator Russell, had lived through her husband's mood swings and knew which buttons to punch to console or encourage him. Johnson had often said he wanted to "out–Roosevelt Roosevelt and out–Lincoln Lincoln" and Truman was also one of her husband's heroes. Reflecting later on his wife's tender note, LBJ said she mentioned two things that really hit home with him — that withdrawing would be wrong for the country and that it would show a lack of courage on his part.

His impulse to withdraw, not out of fear but of melancholy and then just as quickly changing his mind, was nothing knew. He had done the same thing during his Senate campaign. Later, in 1968, during the height of the Vietnam War, he decided to withdraw as a candidate and didn't change his mind.

Delegates to the convention were unaware of the melancholy mood of their president in Washington or the behind-the-scenes, often heated talks in various hotel and motel rooms around Atlantic City. Instead, they were lounging on the beaches, sightseeing along the boardwalk or taking in some of the activities arranged for them by their Democratic hosts. Among them was the second in a series on "Women's Challenge in the Great Society." Today's program, hosted by Willard Wirtz, was on prosperity. Young Citizens for Johnson was hosting another campaign seminar in the Atlantic City High School Auditorium. Some delegates took in the Cumberland County Agricultural Tour while others took in a day at the races at the Atlantic City Race Track, which included lunch and a fashion show, all for $5.75. An alternative was a tour of the Renault Winery.

Walter Reuther arrived in Atlantic City at 3 A.M. and hardly had time to check into his hotel before engaging in hardball negotiations. He met with Martin Luther King, Bayard Rustin, Robert Moses and Ed King and then had breakfast with Hubert Humphrey, David Lawrence, Walter Mondale and Tom Finney, a Democratic staff assistant and Johnson ally.

After days of negotiating, the beleaguered Humphrey seemed relieved and confident when he called the president later in the day. But as Humphrey talked, it was evident there was a change in direction since Reuther arrived. In an effort to put the Mississippi problem behind them, they carved out what they determined was a final settlement, rather than a negotiated compromise with the Freedom Party. Humphrey described it in detail to the president and presented it almost as if he were giving a campaign speech.

> What we've tried to do is preserve the legal standing of the party by what we agreed to be done earlier, that the Mississippi regulars be seated if they're loyal and follow the requirements of the call of the convention. Number two, henceforth, the Democratic Party will make a

declaration in terms of an open party, that we will establish standards for full participation in the party without regard to race, creed or color and since the Freedom Party itself is not a party but a protest movement and surely can't be considered a legal entity in a political party manner, it obviously cannot be seated as a party nor should the state of Mississippi be denied any votes because of the Freedom Party.

Therefore, it has been recommended that since it is a protest movement that does represent the struggle of the Negro for his right to vote, that he wants to have a vote not only back home in the precincts but also here at the convention, that we recommend to the convention as a body that two delegates be seated in the convention not as Mississippians, not as deductible from the Mississippi vote but just two extra votes at large; for the chairman of that delegation, Mr. Henry, Dr. Henry, and for the other man, the national committeeman as they call him, Rev. Edward King, not Martin Luther King but Edward, one white and one colored, and that these men be heralded not as delegates from the state of Mississippi but as an expression of the conscience of the Democratic Party as to the importance of the right to vote, political participation by all peoples in our country; and we in this historic period when we passed a great Civil Rights Act which establishes a whole new pattern of social conduct in our country, that we take the lead here in our Democratic Party by showing that we mean business and that we are prepared to make official recognition of the all-important right to vote and active participation in political affairs.

Reuther was with Humphrey when he called the president and Reuther took the phone and continued making the pitch. "I think this will go together and we can avoid a floor fight and unite the party behind your leadership," he told the president, "and I think everyone can go home feeling good because what we will have demonstrated is the capability of harmonizing legal problems with moral obligations."

Reuther said he and Humphrey had set up a meeting that afternoon with Aaron Henry and Martin Luther King with the hope of "getting this Credentials Committee fight off the television cameras and get the positive image of the Democratic Party on the television cameras."

Humphrey got back on the line and made a telling statement about the status of the talks with the Freedom Party advocates. "Mr. President, we want to make it clear we're not meeting with Dr. Martin Luther King or anybody else to negotiate," he said. "We've taken a position now.... All we want to do is to tell them the decision we've made and that we're prepared to move on it and ask them to give this serious consideration and cooperate."

Johnson, who still had his handwritten note expressing his withdrawal as a candidate, which he had not yet made public, now seemed buoyed by the settlement terms and began talking like a candidate.

"Our party's always been one you could come to with any bellyache of injustice," he said, "whether it was a pecan-shelling plant that paid 4 cents an hour, sweatshop wages ... or discrimination to vote or the Ku Klux Klan whipping somebody, all of these injustices have been wound up [solved] and we've symbolized them. That's what the Democratic Party's for and why it was born and that's why it survives and that's why it thrives and exists. As long as the poor and the downtrodden and the bended know that they can come to us and be heard, and that's what we're doin'—we're hearing them."

The president then characteristically evaluated the political potential. He said, "If by stopping this damn foolishness, you can elect a ticket and pick up four to five seats in the Senate so we'll have 70 instead of 67 and pick up 20 or 30 in the House, then we can do something about this in the next four years."

"Ram that damn thing through," he said. "Don't tell anyone you talked to me. I'm Joe Glotz."[5]

At 3:30 that afternoon, Humphrey and Reuther met with Henry, Martin Luther King, Bayard Rustin, Robert Moses and Ed King and laid out the details of the settlement:

- The Mississippi Freedom Democratic Party would have two at-large delegates, Aaron Henry and Ed King, on the convention floor. The others would be honored guests.
- Members of the regular Mississippi delegation would have to sign a loyalty pledge to the Democratic nominee or they would not be seated.
- In the future, no delegation would be seated if it discriminated in any way regarding race, creed or national origin. The Democratic Party would establish a commission to make sure that happened.

When Rauh learned of what had been worked out, he saw it as a sign of progress for the civil rights movement but also saw it as a declaration rather than an agreement worked out by all involved.

He said once Reuther hit town, things happened quickly. "I get a call from Reuther. He said, 'This is what the convention has decided.' What he meant was, this is what he and Johnson had agreed to and want you to accept it." Rauh thought it was a good compromise—the Freedom Democrats would have some representation, they would have a guarantee of fair representation at conventions from now on, and the administration would avoid a floor fight at the convention on national television.

But he told Reuther he couldn't agree to it—not yet, at least. He had to talk to Henry, because he and Henry had agreed that neither of them would agree to anything without checking with the other. But the

Credentials Committee was about to meet. Rauh asked Reuther to get the hearing postponed so he could find Henry and confer with him.[6]

In the 3:30 meeting with black leaders, Reuther had made it clear to Martin Luther King that "your funding is on the line," just as he had told Rauh a few minutes earlier to accept the compromise or forget about representing the UAW any more.[7]

Ed King said he and Henry were willing to talk about it, but Moses was vigorous in his objections to it. And King and Moses did not want to commit to anything until the entire MFDP delegation could vote on it. Reuther and Humphrey were frustrated. They had made their final offer, one they felt was a fair settlement, and they didn't want to talk about it any further. Their plan was for it to be in place by the time the convention reconvened Tuesday night.[8]

Martin Luther King, who was an interested party not directly impacted, felt it was a decision that Henry, Ed King and Moses had to make. They questioned the fairness of having only two at-large delegates who wouldn't even be representing Mississippi or sitting in that delegation. But Humphrey argued it was an incredible piece to the puzzle, tantamount to increasing the size of Congress.

Ed King said if there could only be two delegates, he would withdraw in favor of having one of the sharecroppers take his place. Humphrey saw where King was headed and cut him off, saying Fannie Lou Hamer would not be a delegate. "The president will not allow that illiterate woman to speak from the floor of the convention," he said. When Moses again objected, Humphrey said he was certain the president just meant that Hamer's style of speaking would not help the cause.[9]

Meanwhile, Rauh went into the Credentials Committee meeting room where the hearing was about to begin. He touched base with Chairman Lawrence about postponing the hearing until he could meet with Henry. Lawrence told him to talk to Mondale who was just coming up a nearby stairway. As Mondale entered the room, Rauh touched base with him and Mondale said, "Of course, Joe, you can have a postponement."

Then, in Rauh's words, "some little punk, I think his name was Sherman [*sic*] Markman from Iowa says, 'no postponement. We're going ahead.' He was the one Johnson had put in there to watch Mondale. And so Mondale says, 'Well, Joe, that's the way the ball bounces.' I tried to get the floor for a postponement. I couldn't."[10]

The hearing began and Rauh tried to get the floor but was denied. Mondale announced the compromise proposal and extolled its finest points—the MFDP would receive some delegate recognition; the regular Democrats would have to pledge support to the party; and discrimination would be prohibited in selecting delegates for future conventions. A commission would be formed to set the anti-discrimination guidelines and to see they would be carried out.

The inclusion of at-large delegates was the idea Markman had come up with two nights ago in the sweaty motel room when Mondale convened the subcommittee for the first time. The idea of the commission reportedly came from Lawrence at the breakfast meeting with Reuther and Humphrey.

As Mondale continued to praise the compromise proposal, Rauh rose and said, "I'm not arguing whether this is good or bad. Life alone will tell that. But what I am saying is we ought to have a postponement so Aaron Henry's views can be injected in here and we can decide probably that we're all in agreement."

But the Johnson forces were in full command and Rauh's pleadings were not only not heeded, they were hardly heard over the din of shouting in the committee room. As Rauh recalled the scene years later, he said, "Have you ever been in a lynch mob? Because if you haven't, you haven't heard anything like this. A hundred people shouting 'vote, vote, vote' while I'm trying to speak."

Rauh chided committee members for their rudeness and kept repeating he had the floor and had the right to speak. But the chorus of "vote, vote, vote" continued to drown him out. "It was like a machine — and it mowed me down," he said. "I moved for a postponement, I moved for a roll call, I moved for everything but didn't get it."[11]

Lawrence called for a vote and, as near as Rauh could tell, eight delegates, including him, voted no — three short of what he needed to get it out of committee. It would not go to the convention floor; there would be no roll call vote of the states where approval of only eight states was needed for floor debate and Rauh had more states than that ready to support the MFDP cause.

Mondale's recollection of the days events starts with a Tuesday morning breakfast with Humphrey, Reuther, Lawrence and Finney. At that point, the compromise plan included the nondiscrimination rule at future conventions and the commission to implement the rule; the required signing of a loyalty oath by the regular Mississippi delegation; and the seating of all the Mississippi Freedom Democrats as honored guests. It was at that breakfast that a new provision was included — the seating of two at-large delegates "to affirm the justice of the Freedom Democrats cause." To emphasize that even further, the convention would be urged to seat Henry and Reverend King, the co-chairs of the MFDP, as the at-large delegates.

Then the meeting broke up and Humphrey and Reuther spent the next several hours with the Freedom Democrat supporters, trying to win their approval. Finney contacted the White House to get Johnson's approval and Mondale reconvened his subcommittee to get its approval. The subcommittee approved it but only by a 3–2 vote with the two southerners voting against it, because of the loyalty oath provision. Mondale's next challenge was to get the full Credentials Committee to approve it.

His version of what took place next coincides with Rauh's. He said he bumped into Rauh as they were both headed for the hearing room and Rauh asked for a postponement so he could discuss the proposal with Henry. Mondale told him he would see what he could do.

"When the committee reconvened — in closed session — I made my presentation," said Mondale. "I acknowledged that our proposal didn't go as far as either side wanted but it recognized the problem of discrimination in the party and outlined a plan of action to end it."

Rauh then asked for the recess that he says set off the "vote, vote, vote" lynch mob behavior initiated by Sherwin Markman. Mondale put it more politely. He said that "the committee was demanding action" and Lawrence called for a voice vote. The compromise was approved. All of this occurred quickly — and occurred at the same time that Humphrey was still trying to sell the plan to Henry, Ed King, Moses, Martin Luther King and the others who had been discussing it in Humphrey's hotel room.[12]

As Mondale left the committee room, he was besieged by newspaper, radio and television reporters who surrounded him. He announced that a compromise had been reached that provided the Mississippi Freedom Democrats with representation at this convention and the assurance of nondiscrimination at all future conventions.

In the Humphrey hotel suite, where the compromise package was still being discussed, one of Humphrey's aides burst into the room where they were meeting and urged everyone to come quickly to the adjoining room where a television was on. There they heard the news that a compromise had been approved by the full Credentials Committee.

Moses was furious. He turned to Humphrey and shouted, "You tricked us," for it seemed certain that Humphrey had purposely kept the MFDP supporters at bay while Johnson's compromise sailed through the committee. Somehow, the news stories reported that the vote was unanimous when in fact Rauh and seven others had voted against it. Nonetheless, the feeling in the hotel room was that Humphrey had tricked them and Rauh had sold them out. Not only had they lost their cause, they felt they had been betrayed by two people they trusted, but more important, by the government and political party they trusted.

Henry felt he was a pawn in a conspiracy cooked up by the Democratic party to railroad the compromise. He said he was contacted Tuesday along with other members of the delegation who were asked to meet with

Humphrey that afternoon at the Pageant Motel. He said he tried to reach Rauh to let him know what was going on but couldn't find him. When they arrived, they were shocked to see Reuther, a champion of their causes, in the room with Humphrey.

Henry thought it was another masterful ploy of Lyndon Johnson — using Humphrey and Reuther, two sympathizers of the movement — to push for the administration's compromise. But Henry said he was offended by Reuther's approach in speaking to him and the others, including Roy Wilkins and Martin Luther King.

He quoted Reuther as saying, "When the NAACP needed $40,000 to get buses for the Washington march, I got it for you, Roy. And Martin, when you needed $6,000 for the Montgomery boycott, I got it for you, didn't I?" Reuther was correct on both counts but it was as if he was asking Wilkins and King to repay a debt when the issue at hand was the seating of the Mississippi Freedom Party delegates — who didn't owe Reuther anything, said Henry.

Henry and the others also strongly objected to the idea of having two at-large delegates who wouldn't be representing Mississippi. After all, that's why they had made the trip to Atlantic City. And to further the insult, the white political establishment was handpicking who the delegates would be. The whole thing was unacceptable.

"If only they had said we could have two votes and left it at that. Maybe then we could have taken the two votes and divided them among all 64 delegates, giving each delegate one thirty-second of a vote and all of us would have been admitted to the convention," said Henry. But it was not to be. (Though there were actually 68 delegates, Henry, in recounting the events years later, used the 64 figure.)

The Credentials Committee had been scheduled to convene at 6 P.M. but the meeting was moved up to 4 p.m., said Henry, and was going on while Humphrey and Reuther were meeting with the black leaders at the Pageant Motel.

"So while Humphrey and Reuther were trying to persuade us to accept the compromise, that same compromise was being accepted by the Credentials Committee without us there to express our objections. Rauh was telling the committee he could not accept the compromise without talking to me, as chair of the delegation," said Henry.

He said Humphrey knew what was going on. He knew where Henry was and he knew where Rauh was, though neither Rauh nor Henry knew where the other was.[13]

In Washington, President Johnson was informed that the compromise was accepted. His mood was jubilant. He no longer talked of any intentions of withdrawing his name from consideration as a candidate.

When word spread about the compromise, there were mixed emotions among the MFDP supporters. No one felt more torn than Rauh. The proposal was nowhere near what the MFDP wanted; yet it was a step in the right direction. Small as it was, the two at-large seats meant representation, something they had been fighting for. The administration had selected both a black man and a white man as the at-large delegates as a symbol of unity. But the very fact that the administration had chosen who would represent them was an affront to all of those who had come to Atlantic City seeking freedom from people making decisions for them.

SNCC activist Stokely Carmichael said, "The delegates of the FDP did not feel it was a compromise but rather a decision that was handed down to them. If it was a compromise, then the FDP would have had a chance to say something. They were not consulted. The Democratic Party said: Here — take this; it's all we will give you."[14]

Michael Miller, a field secretary for SNCC, agreed that it was a decision made for them rather than a compromise made with them. He said it was the government telling an oppressed people how their constitutional rights were going to be distributed.[15]

Moses, shaken, hurt and angry, called a caucus meeting of MFDP supporters at the Union Baptist Temple. They had the right to accept or reject the compromise even though the Credentials Committee had ramrodded it through. He discovered that rather than uniting the movement followers in a feeling of betrayal, the compromise had just the opposite effect. They were clearly divided. Some said accept it as a small victory but a victory nonetheless. Others were defiant, saying they were told what they were getting and it was nowhere near what they sought.

Fannie Lou Hamer, whose testimony captivated the nation but whose outbursts caused her to be excluded from negotiations, was outraged at the compromise. "We didn't come all the way here for no two votes," she said.

Roy Wilkins, longtime executive director of the NAACP, was more pragmatic but just as blunt. He told Mrs. Hamer and the others to accept the compromise. "You people have put your point across. You don't know anything, you're ignorant, you don't know anything about politics. I've been in the business over 20 years. You people have put your point across. Now why don't you pack up and go home?"[16]

Moses fumed. He talked about the difference between the morality of politics and the politics of morality. SNCC's John Lewis was also against accepting the compromise. He said he was proud of how the Mississippians had taken a stand and did not go along with backtracking since they had come so far.

Henry urged the group to listen to Wilkins and other black leaders

Roy Wilkins, head of the NAACP, confers with President Johnson in the Oval Office in 1964. Wilkins was a pragmatist who understood the nuances of politics. After the Credentials Committee had acted, he told the Freedom Democrats they had made their point and should pack up their things and go home (LBJ Library).

who were experienced in national civil rights battles and had expertise to share with the others. But Mrs. Hamer said none of them had spent more than two weeks in Mississippi — so what kind of experience was that? Henry and Ed King wanted the compromise approved. When Henry said he was tempted to go before the TV cameras to tell the public the MFDP approved the plan, Hamer threatened to cut his throat, though she said later she had never carried a weapon in her life and of course didn't mean it literally.

Another disturbing aspect of the afternoon's activities occurred when Henry, after learning of the Credentials Committee vote, tried to find 11 members who would be willing to continue to fight for a minority report at the convention. His old friend and ally Congressman Diggs was nowhere to be found. For Henry, it was yet another lesson in hardball politics. "Perhaps this shows that the very best kind of people can become so much a part of the machine that they can only think in terms of the party's welfare," he said. "Then it becomes impossible for them to support anything which might cause difficulty within the party."[17]

Martin Luther King told those assembled that Humphrey had promised big changes in Mississippi if the compromise was accepted. Bayard Rustin said if the proposal was rejected, it would be a slap in the face to the very people who were in the best position to help them in the long run. He reminded them they were in the world of politics now — and politics was the art of compromise.

Andrew Young, later to become mayor of Atlanta, told them political power at a convention was worthless unless it helped elect a president — and that's where the focus should remain.

MFDP delegate Unita Blackwell was not impressed with the pleadings of Wilkins, Dr. King and Rustin. "They had a certain clique they'd talk to," she said. "The big niggers talk to the big niggers; the little folks, they couldn't talk to nobody but themselves."[18]

When all the discussion and haggling was over, the MFDP voted to reject the compromise, a symbolic gesture that had no bearing on what took place at the convention.

Lewis said one of the saddest ramifications of the day's activities was the impact on the relationship many in the movement had with Rauh, who had worked so hard on their behalf. Rauh was caught in Lyndon Johnson's cross hairs. He had done all he could to support and promote the MFDP's cause and was up against the forces of domestic spying; reprisals against those who would vote against the president's plan; withdrawal of funding for future civil rights movements; placement of Johnson allies in key positions on the Credentials Committee; and the threat of losing his biggest client in the private sector.

In addition to all of that, there was the perception that Rauh, as a member of the Credentials Committee, had voted in favor of the compromise, which in fact he hadn't, but was the victim of news reports that the vote was unanimous.

Lewis said, "When the smoke finally cleared, Joe Rauh would be seen as a villain, a traitor, a backstabber. And that was a shame. He was a good man who worked incredibly hard to bring this moment about. It's ironic that the situation he worked so hard to create wound up skewering his reputation, at least in the black community."[19]

Meanwhile, President Johnson got word that southern delegations would walk out if the full convention approved the compromise, and he began to angrily work the phones to keep things in order. He had expected the regular Mississippi delegation to bolt, and probably Alabama too, but the walkout fever was spreading. The president called his friend and political ally Georgia governor Carl Sanders.

He told Sanders,

> What's happening here is we're doing four or five things. Number one, we're coming in there and seating the state of Mississippi. Every damn

one of them. Now they oughtn't to be, Carl. They oughtn't.... You and I just can't survive our political modern life with these God damn fellows down there [Mississippi whites] that are eating them for breakfast every morning. They've got to quit that. And they've got to let them vote. And they've got to let them shave. And they've got to let them eat, and things like that. And they won't do it....

I'd come up there myself [to Atlantic City], walk naked and take it [the oath] if it would ease Bull Connor's pressure any. [Connor, the Birmingham, Alabama, police commissioner who gained notoriety by ordering high-powered fire hoses turned on black demonstrators a year ago, was head of the Alabama delegation at the national convention.][20]

Governor Carl Sanders of Georgia was a segregationist to whom President Johnson made an appeal to try to prevent the southern states from walking out of the convention (Library of Congress).

When the convention reconvened Tuesday night, delegates took care of some routine business. They heard a report from the Committee on Permanent Organization given by Norman Stahl, a national committeeman from Oregon and a report on the nomination of national committeemen and committeewomen. They heard an address by the permanent chairman, Speaker of the House John McCormack of Massachusetts, and an address by Senator Birch Bayh of Indiana in which he praised the Democratic platform and lit into the one approved a month ago by the Republicans.

Sandwiched in the middle of all of this, David Lawrence presented the report from the Credentials Committee that included the Mississippi compromise. It was approved by a voice vote — "in the opinion of the chair, the ayes have it" — and that was that. It was over in three minutes.

There were only three "ayes" from the Mississippi delegation because all of the other regular delegates left rather than stay and sign a loyalty oath. One of the three who stayed, Doug Wynn of Greenville, was married to the daughter of a Texan who was Lyndon Johnson's attorney.

Outside, Rauh and Aaron Henry led a march down Pacific Avenue from the hotel to the convention hall where the vigil around the arena had turned into a protest demonstration. As the group marched, they were joined by others who were not part of the movement but who had become sympathizers with the cause. Together, they began to sing, "We Shall Overcome."

Author Sally Belfrage, who was there, said the voices seemed to lose all restraint as they grew louder and louder. "The hands hold each other tighter. Mrs. Hamer is smiling, flinging out the words, and crying at once. 'Black and white together,' she leads the next verse and a sort of joy begins to grow in every face. 'We are not afraid' — and for just that second, no one is afraid."[21]

The MFDP contingency had been given tickets to get into the convention hall as "honored guests," but many of them, buoyed by the show of support they received on the street, decided to go in and get onto the convention floor and try to sit in the seats now empty because of the exodus of the regular Mississippi delegation.

Fannie Lou Hamer, Annie Devine and Ed King were offered seats by members of the Michigan and North Dakota delegations. White House aide Marvin Watson, one of Johnson's watchdogs at the convention, ordered security to remove the intruders from the Mississippi section, but Walter Jenkins, LBJ's top aide, said to leave them alone, fearing a live broadcast of them being dragged out would be far worse for the administration than the floor fight they worked so hard to avert.

Historian Theodore H. White, reflecting on the night's activities, said the Freedom Democrats had won a significant victory and not only didn't realize it but spoiled it by their actions. White, a Caucasian, said the Negroes "invaded" the convention floor, in effect repudiating their triumph.

He wrote about how they locked arms and scoffed at a Democratic Party that had tried to balance morality and law to accommodate them. In so doing, "they defied law. It was as if the illegality of Mississippi had authorized them to commit a counter-illegality on a national body.... The Freedom Party had stained the honor that so much courage and suffering had won it."[22]

Tom Wicker, reporting the events for the *New York Times*, opened his story by reporting that the Mississippi delegation had walked out of the convention. He quoted Mississippi governor Paul Johnson as saying state Democrats were now "absolutely free to take such action as we feel to be in the best interest of our state, of our nation and of our people."

It was precisely the kind of coverage President Johnson did not want to have at his convention and had pulled so many strings from the supposed sanctity of the White House to try to avoid.

Wicker's story included the oath the regular Mississippi delegates refused to sign: "We the undersigned members of the Mississippi delegation to the 1964 Democratic National Convention hereby each formally assure the convention of our intention to support the convention's nominees in the forthcoming general election."

Wicker quoted Jack Pittman, a regular Mississippi delegate, who read a statement explaining why most of the Mississippi delegation left the floor. He said the oath they were asked to take was a "blind oath" and he referred to the Mississippi Freedom Democrats as "an outside pressure group which represents no one but itself."

In summation, Pittman said, "The Mississippi Democratic delegation did not leave the National Democratic Party. It left us."[23]

When the convention proceedings ended at about midnight Tuesday, Johnson summoned George Reedy, his press secretary to the White House. LBJ's on-again, off-again thoughts of withdrawing his candidacy were on again. He was glum about the walkouts and the feeling of betrayal by those in the civil rights movement; Johnson felt it was he who had been betrayed. "By God, I'm going to go up there and quit," he told Reedy. "Fuck 'em all."[24]

CHAPTER 12

Power, Protest and Politics

Leaders of the movement spent a restless night and awoke Wednesday morning ready to gather and decide their next move. The MFDP had rejected the compromise Tuesday night, but that decision had no impact on an unsuspecting convention so there was still time for further discussion and perhaps a change of heart.

Joe Rauh contacted Humphrey, who was emotionally drained from the intensity of the negotiations and his anxiety over his chances of becoming the vice-presidential nominee. He told Humphrey, "I'm sure it wasn't you, Hubert," and then blasted "the dumb bastards on your side who chose our two people [the at-large delegates] instead of letting them choose their own people."[1]

At a meeting of delegates and their supporters at the Union Baptist Temple, Aaron Henry convinced the delegates they should hear from proponents of both sides one more time. A meeting was arranged for that afternoon.

Among those speaking were Jack Pratt, Arthur Thomas and Bob Spike, all officers of the National Council of Churches; Bayard Rustin, the immensely well-respected black leader and adviser who had organized the March on Washington the previous year; and Senator Wayne Morse of Oregon, a white maverick politician who took part in the "sit-in" the night before in the empty seats of the Mississippi delegation.

Joe Rauh and Bob Moses were there as well as James Farmer of CORE, James Forman and John Lewis of SNCC and Rev. Martin Luther King of the Southern Christian Leadership Conference. Lewis called it "an emergency summit conference of sorts."[2]

The National Council of Churches had been a financial contributor to the civil rights movement and all three of their spokesmen urged acceptance of the compromise. So did Senator Morse. Rauh was in a tough position. He wasn't happy with the compromise but saw it as a step forward.

Though he had voted against it as a member of the Credentials Committee, he had lost the trust of many of those he was defending because they mistakenly thought he had "sold out" and voted in favor of it.

Forman remembers looking around the room and marveling at the manipulation of the federal government. "There we were, all of us amazed — dumbfounded — at the array of power that the administration had dished up, thinking that these distinguished gentlemen could deliver," he said.

Rustin, as was his way, looked at the matter philosophically. "There is a difference between protest and politics," he said. "You must be willing to compromise, to win victories and go home and come back and win some more. That is politics. If you don't, then you are still protesting."[3]

Many in the room felt betrayed by Rustin's remarks and began shouting derisive comments while he was speaking. Henry urged the listeners to stay orderly and respectful and that everyone would get their chance to speak.

King chose not to lecture the delegates or make a recommendation. But he told the delegates that Humphrey had promised him he could get the Civil Rights Commission to hold a hearing in Mississippi, something that had never happened before. Humphrey also promised that segregation would leave the Democratic Party, that seats at the next convention would be open to people of all races and creeds, and that he would arrange for them to have their audience with President Johnson. But King also well understood the difference between national politics and state turmoil. He said as a Negro leader, he would hope they would accept the compromise, but if he was a Mississippi Negro, he would reject it.

Forman was not impressed. He felt that blacks would get all of those things regardless of whether they approved the compromise and urged the delegates to turn it down. He asked the delegates what they would tell their friends back home in Mississippi if they came all this way and settled for so little. Victoria Gray, Annie Devine and Fannie Lou Hamer all said the people back home expected more and deserved more. Hamer said once again, "We didn't come all this way for no two seats."[4]

Lewis was also passionate in his opposition to the compromise. Looking back on it years later, he said, "The idea that Johnson was dictating everything, from the number of delegates to who those delegates would be, was outrageous.... Too many people had worked too hard, too long, to be told that now they would be treated as honored guests and nothing more. We'd shed too much blood."[5]

After all the talk and after all the dignitaries had left the room, the MFDP delegates voted once again to reject the proposal.

At the White House, President Johnson, apparently forgetting his threats to withdraw, was preparing for the night he would be nominated at the convention. He had not publicly announced his choice for vice president. He had decided on Humphrey but wanted to keep his decision a secret, even from Humphrey, for as long as possible. Meanwhile, his speech writers were busy trying to figure out how best to deal with everything from Vietnam to civil rights in his acceptance speech. And Johnson was still grousing about the Bobby Kennedy influence on the convention. Earlier in the week, Kennedy had announced he was a candidate for the Senate from New York and LBJ had agreed to help him. Now Johnson was looking to see if Bobby would return the favor by showing support for him at the convention.

Bill Moyers called from Atlantic City, telling him suspense was mounting at the convention hall over the vice-presidential pick. Johnson mentioned that when John F. Kennedy was nominated in 1960, he made a brief appearance that night to announce his choice for running mate, then came back the following night to give his acceptance speech.

"I don't want to sit around here and let Bobby and them dominate the convention. You know he's got all these Irish Catholic girls writing for him," Johnson told Moyers. He then read a headline from the *Washington Star* newspaper. "Bobby Sweeps Atlantic City — Kennedy Magic." The "Irish Catholic girls" Johnson mentioned was an apparent reference to Mary McGrory, who had written the story for the *Star*.[6]

A half hour later Johnson was on the phone with Walter Jenkins in Atlantic City. "I sure want Bobby to nominate me," he said. "If we're going to work as a team here — why, I see in the paper that we're going to work for Bobby in New York — we want him to work with us tonight and put an end to all this hell-raising," a reference to Johnson's suspicions that Kennedy had ties to the Mississippi Freedom Democrats.

"By God, I want that done," said Johnson. "If he doesn't want to do it, all right. I'll remember that when he wants me to do something." He then told Jenkins to arrange a plane for Hubert Humphrey and to have Humphrey at the White House at 4 P.M.

Switching back to his thoughts about Kennedy, he told Jenkins, "Try to wind up that Bobby thing." But then he paused and said, "Maybe we oughtn't shove that. I don't know whether we need him seconding us or not." As it turned out, Kennedy did not speak for Johnson that night.[7]

Weeks before the convention, Humphrey had been told by White House insiders that he was on the short list for vice president, a position he admitted he coveted. He was interviewed twice by LBJ confidante James Rowe in which much of the questioning had to do with Humphrey's loyalty to the president. But Johnson enjoyed leaking names to the press (through his aides) — names such as Mayor Robert Wagner of New York; Senator

Eugene McCarthy — the other senator from Minnesota; Governor Edmund "Pat" Brown of California; and, before announcing that no Cabinet member would be considered (a polite way of eliminating Bobby Kennedy), Defense Secretary Robert McNamara's name was in the vice-presidential pool.

Humphrey said the name game was classic Johnson — keeping people in suspense, name-dropping and keeping the focus on himself for he and only he could make the final decision. One night, at a White House dinner, Johnson leaned over to Humphrey and said, "I think I'm going to drop Mike Mansfield's name into the hopper. He'll like it and it will give a lot of people something to talk about."[8]

Humphrey went to the convention confident he would be the vice-presidential nominee — as confident as anyone could be, considering the frequent mood swings of the president. But when Johnson realized the Mississippi problem could boil over on to the convention floor, he designated Humphrey as the man to stop it.

In his autobiography, Humphrey devotes about half a page to the Mississippi compromise and focuses his attention on the political challenge it created for him. His only reference to the deliberations is, "We worked out a compromise of sorts that didn't really please anyone but kept the convention from falling apart." There is a footnote mentioning that discrimination and intimidation would not be tolerated in the future. But there is no mention of Fannie Lou Hamer or Joe Rauh or Aaron Henry or Martin Luther King. Humphrey's reflection: "Johnson was testing me one more time.... Had I failed, would Johnson have chosen McCarthy or someone else? It is a question I have never been able to answer."[9]

Johnson summoned Humphrey to the White House late Wednesday afternoon to formally offer him the opportunity to be vice president. But he was still intent on keeping the press and the public guessing. So he also invited Senator Thomas Dodd of Connecticut though he had no intention of naming Dodd as his running mate. Humphrey and Dodd flew to Washington together and were met at the airport by Jack Valenti, a Johnson aide, in a Cadillac. They drove around Washington for a few minutes, instead of going straight to the White House. Humphrey said he later learned the president needed some time to tantalize the press. When they arrived at the White House, Dodd was instructed to go in, with Humphrey waiting in the car. Exhausted from the strenuous week and the bizarre trip with Dodd, Humphrey fell asleep in the car, parked a few feet from the White House entrance.

Several minutes later, he was awakened by a knock on the car window and ushered into the White House and into a room just off of the oval office. It was there that the president came in and formally offered

President Johnson liked to keep the press and the public in limbo about his selection of a running mate. He summoned Senator Thomas Dodd of Connecticut to the White House as a decoy when he had already decicied on Hubert Humphrey as his vice presidential candidate (LBJ Library).

Humphrey a spot on the ticket. The two men talked about the role of the vice president, that it was a thankless job that demanded 100 percent loyalty to the president, a job Johnson described as "a marriage with no chance for divorce."

Johnson told him to expect to be looked down upon by people associated with the president because the president had the power; the vice president was virtually meaningless to those seeking power or who were awed by it. And he said to beware of people who would try to create friction between the president and vice president. There's no reason for it, said Johnson. It's just the way it is.

At the conclusion of the conversation, Johnson took Humphrey into the Cabinet Room where Secretary of Defense Robert McNamara, Secretary of State Dean Rusk and others greeted him. The president also placed a call to Muriel, Humphrey's wife, in which he told her "we're going to nominate your boy."

Even now, all involved were told not to make any public statements. Humphrey was taken back to the Cadillac where Dodd was waiting, and the two men were driven to the airport for the return trip to Atlantic City. Humphrey empathized with Dodd, who was obviously LBJ's shill. "I'm sure the trip back was as endless for him as it was quick for me," said Humphrey.[10]

Prior to meeting with Humphrey, Johnson took a phone call from Chicago mayor Richard Daley, a staunch Johnson ally, who was concerned about a possible sit-in at the convention that night by the Mississippi Freedom Party.

"You know, we're at our peak tonight when you're nominated," said Daley. "Hell, I'd really like to see you ride up there and surprise all of them."

Johnson was hesitant. "The experts thought that right after you're finished nominating, they [TV networks] would switch to the White House office where I'm working. Then they'd let me recommend my man for vice president."

But Daley was insistent. "Tonight I think the president belongs in the convention," he said. "Sometimes these experts—all these guys who sell Campbell's Soup and Coca-Cola — they don't feel the human things."

Johnson laughed and told Daley, "I got Hubert here. I'm going to see him in about 30 minutes. I'm probably going to try to have a meeting of the mind with Hubert."

But Daley pressed on. "I would love to see you be in Atlantic City tonight. What the hell, all this thing about the vice president," he said.

Johnson laughed again and said, "Is it all right with you if I go along with Humphrey?"

"Anything you want, I'm with you 100 percent," said Daley, who then reminded LBJ that in 1960 John F. Kennedy had called the Chicago mayor and asked him about Johnson as a possible running mate. He said he told Kennedy it was the "greatest choice he could make."[11]

Johnson, who just a day earlier had scrawled out a letter withdrawing his name as a candidate, was now in full campaign mode. Moments after getting off the phone with Daley, he contacted Reedy and told him Daley wanted him to fly to Atlantic City that night.

"Dick Daley just says to hell with everything, you're crazy not to do it — and I don't like to get into an argument with Dick Daley when I need those votes in Chicago,"[12] said the president.

Johnson ended the conversation with Daley, then called another big city boss, Francis Smith, chairman of the Philadelphia Democratic Executive Committee, to inform him of his choice and asked that he keep it secret. He also told Smith he'd be going to Atlantic City in a couple of hours to tell the convention he wanted Humphrey as his running mate. In the space of a few minutes, the president had made the decision to go to Atlantic City — on short notice for his staff. The call to Muriel Humphrey was placed at 6:34 P.M. Johnson planned to arrive in Atlantic City between 9:30 and 10 P.M.

Humphrey, arriving back in Atlantic City, kept a commitment for a radio interview with WCCO in Minneapolis, being careful to keep his pledge to Johnson not to reveal what was to be the big news of the evening. In the middle of the interview, the newsman told Humphrey they were going to have to pause for a moment because a bulletin was forthcoming from CBS national news.

Chicago mayor Richard Daley, shown conferring with President Johnson at the White House in 1964, was a political power broker whose Johnson advice Johnson sought and acted on (LBJ Library).

The bulletin was the announcement that President Johnson was on his way to Atlantic City to recommend Humphrey as his vice president.

At the White House, military aides and the Secret Service scrambled to get helicopters to take the presidential entourage from the White House to Andrews Air Force Base and from Andrews to Atlantic City. The president drank Sanka from a paper cup and watched the convention from a television on Air Force One. He watched his name placed in nomination by his old friend Governor John Connally of Texas and by California Governor Edmund G. "Pat" Brown. "All right," he shouted so he could be heard over the roar of the plane's engines. "We've got this show on the road."

But the president's usual impeccable timing was a little off. After the nominating speeches had concluded, delegates stomped and jumped and hollered their approval just as Johnson's plane arrived at the Atlantic City Airport. All three television networks switched from the love fest on the convention floor to the scene at the airport and the arrival of the president.

A few minutes later, Lyndon Johnson entered the convention hall and received the adulation of the delegates, who screamed their approval as he made his way through the rush of people and to the podium. He took the gavel from the permanent chairman, John McCormack, and, smiling broadly, pounded it repeatedly to quiet the crowd. He then informed the crowd of his choice of Humphrey as his running mate. Delegates approved them both by acclamation.

CHAPTER 13

The Forces of
Human Decency

Early in 1964, when organizers were planning the Democratic National Convention, they set aside Monday, August 24, the first day of the convention, as "Kennedy Night" as a tribute to the slain president and to give proper, gracious and emotional attention to his widow, Jackie, and his brothers, Attorney General Robert Kennedy and Senator Edward Kennedy. Planners thought it would be a fitting way to begin a week in which the Democratic Party would go about its business.

The Johnson forces believed pragmatically that it would also be a way of giving the Kennedy family its just due and be done with it. The president continued to have suspicions about Bobby Kennedy's motives and his possible involvement with Martin Luther King and the Mississippi Freedom Democratic Party.

As convention time approached, President Johnson got some advice from an unlikely source — Thomas E. Dewey, former governor of New York and two-time Republican presidential candidate. Dewey paid a visit to the White House in the summer of 1964, and in the course of his conversation with LBJ, he mentioned he had seen the proposed schedule for the Democratic convention with the "Kennedy Night" on Monday.

Dewey told the president there would be an enormous emotional response from the convention at seeing Bobby at the podium, and that all the Kennedys would be there, including Rose, Bobby's mother and the matriarch of the Kennedy family. Dewey warned Johnson it was possible that convention would force Bobby on him as his running mate. Not long after Dewey's visit, Johnson made some phone calls and the Kennedy tribute was moved back to Thursday night, after the presidential and vice-presidential nominations had been secured.[1]

When Kennedy was introduced that night, delegates reacted in a boisterous demonstration of affection that lasted a full 22 minutes of standing ovation, placard waving, hooting, hollering, whistling and stomping of feet that left the attorney general with moist eyes as he looked over the crowd. He nodded his head occasionally as if in recognition of someone waving at him and offered a smile that appeared to be one of embarrassment at the extent of the tribute.

Chet Huntley, reporting on the convention for NBC television, said it was hard to determine whether the outpouring of emotion was for Kennedy; for his brother, the slain president, or as an indication of who the delegates thought should have been the vice-presidential candidate.[2]

When the hoopla subsided, Kennedy thanked Democrats for the support they had given his brother as he sought the presidential nomination in 1960, in helping him win the election and in standing by him during periods of both triumph and difficulty during his administration.

"The same energy must be given to Lyndon Johnson and Hubert Humphrey," he said, causing the delegates to erupt in applause again. The statement also provided solace to the president, who, on this his 56th birthday, had still been wondering what kind of support he would be getting from the Kennedy wing of the party.

The most poignant moment in Kennedy's talk, which was actually an introduction to a film tribute to John F. Kennedy, came when he quoted Shakespeare in assessing his brother's legacy: "When he shall die, take him and cut him into little stars and he shall make the face of heaven so fond that all the world will fall in love with night and pay no worship to the garish sun."

Humphrey used his acceptance speech for the vice-presidential nomination to point out the stark differences between the Democratic and Republican platforms and, more pointedly, between President Johnson and Barry Goldwater.

> Most Democrats and Republicans in the Senate voted for an 11½ billion dollar tax cut for American citizens and American business, but not Senator Goldwater.
> Most Democrats and Republicans in the Senate — in fact ⅘ of them — voted for the Civil Rights Act — but not Senator Goldwater.
> Most Democrats and Republicans in the Senate voted last year for an expanded medical education program — but not Senator Goldwater.

By this time, Humphrey had his audience caught up in the cadence of his speech and, as if on cue, they chanted at the appropriate moment, "Not Senator Goldwater."
And Humphrey provided the ammunition.

> Most Democrats and Republicans in the Senate voted for education legislation — but not Senator Goldwater.

The stage of the Atlantic City Convention Center is adorned with huge banners of President Johnson with smaller images of Franklin Roosevelt, John Kennedy and Harry Truman above them (Library of Congress).

> My fellow Americans, most Democrats and Republicans in the Senate voted to help the United Nations in their peace-keeping functions when it was in financial difficulty — but not Senator Goldwater.

The culmination of the evening, the culmination of the week, occurred when the 36th president of the United States, speaking on his 56th birthday, spoke not only to the more than 5,000 delegates to the convention, but to the nation as a whole and to anyone anywhere in the world allowed to hear his voice.

Johnson, lacking the Kennedy charisma or the Humphrey rhythm, spoke for 42 minutes in the slow, deliberate, lackluster tone that was in such sharp contrast to the fire in the belly he possessed but could not seem to put into words that excited people. LBJ had but one rule for the parade of speech writers he had over the years. "Give me a headline," he would tell them.[3]

"Tonight we offer ourselves— on our record and by our platform — as a party for all Americans, an all–American party for all Americans," he began. "This prosperous people, this land of reasonable men, has no place for petty partisanship or peevish prejudices. The needs of all can never be met by parties of the few. The needs of all cannot be met by a business party or a labor party, not by a war party or a peace party, not by a southern party or a northern party. Our deeds will meet our needs only if we are served by a party which serves all of the people."

Johnson touched on many aspects of governing and then zeroed in, without mentioning it specifically, on the problems that brought the Mississippi Freedom Party to Atlantic City. He said,

> Here at home one of our greatest responsibilities is to assure fair play for all of our people. Every American has the right to be treated as a person. He should be able to find a job. He should be able to educate his children. He should be able to vote in elections and he should be judged on his merits as a person....
>
> So long as I am your president, I intend to carry out what the Constitution demands — and justice requires — equal justice under the law for all Americans. We cannot and we will not allow this great purpose to be endangered by reckless acts of violence, Those who break the law, those who create disorder, whether in the north or the south, must be caught and must be brought to justice. And I believe that every man and woman in this room tonight joins me in saying that in every part of this country, the law must be respected and the violence must be stopped....
>
> And I say tonight to those who wish us well — and to those who wish us ill — the growing forces in this country are the forces of human decency and not the forces of bigotry and fear and smear.[4]

Johnson was sincere in his conviction to use the power of the federal government to end discrimination, and he felt he had proven it by passing a civil rights bill and pushing Congress to enact anti-poverty programs. But many of the people who had been within his easiest reach, the people who had in fact reached out to him, were not in the hall to hear his words. The Mississippi Freedom Party delegation was preparing to go home to decide its next move, frustrated that the government they counted on had let them down.

When the president finished speaking, the convention was essentially over and it took on a party atmosphere. Actress Carol Channing, famous at the time for starring on Broadway in "Hello, Dolly," sang "Hello, Lyndon" as the president was presented with a huge birthday cake in the shape of a map of the United States.[5]

It was after midnight by the time Johnson arrived at the home where he was to stay overnight. Tired and emotionally drained, he was irritated to discover the house had no air conditioning. Abe Fortas and Clark Clifford joined him for a drink and then departed as the president had a rubdown, ate a couple of sandwiches and some ice cream, and went to bed.

He was awakened by a phone call from Reedy, his press secretary, who was distressed to learn of a *Houston Post* story, to be published that morning, claiming Reedy resigned over a dispute with Johnson over his coming to the convention Wednesday rather than Thursday. Reedy wanted LBJ to know there was nothing to it.

Johnson told Reedy not to worry about it, that the person most responsible for him coming to the convention a day earlier than expected was Chicago's Mayor Daley, a man Johnson wanted to keep on his good side for political reasons.

"The only man that I know of who had anything legitimate to do with me coming up here was Dick Daley.... He thought we could really take charge if we'd make an appearance.... He didn't say so, but what he meant did happen — he wanted us to run the Freedom Party completely out of town There was only nine of 'em they could locate after I got in."

"It was a damn good idea," said Reedy.[6]

CHAPTER 14

Turning Points

The irony of the civil rights clamor at the Democratic Convention is not the result it achieved but how it was achieved. Angered and frustrated by being shut out of the political system by the domineering government in their own state, 68 Mississippi residents boarded buses and traveled to Atlantic City seeking redemption, only to be rebuffed by the strong-arm tactics of top leaders of the national government they thought would come to their aid.

They came to Atlantic City determined and confident, aware of their cause but unaware of the threat they posed to unravel the political strength of the national Democratic Party.

Lyndon Johnson, the white southern president who was sympathetic to their plight, nonetheless used his considerable political clout to squash their efforts. In fact, he expressed satisfaction in having "kicked most of them out of town" by the time he arrived at the convention on Wednesday night.[1]

The goal of the Mississippi Freedom Democratic Party was forthright. It sought to have its delegates seated at the convention in place of the all-white delegation that had been elected in a process they were prevented from taking part in. Historian Theodore H. White put it succinctly. "There were two absurdities face to face.... There was the all white Mississippi delegation — legal but morally absurd. And there was the Mississippi Freedom Party delegation — impeccably moral but legally absurd because it had no lawful standing."[2]

Actually, there was a third absurdity at play. Two of the most influential white politicians in advancing civil rights for black Americans, Johnson and Hubert Humphrey, wanted this civil rights dispute settled amicably — and out of public view — for more than ethical or moral reasons. They each aimed to protect and advance their individual political legacies.

Johnson wanted an unobstructed, landslide election in November that would rid him of the curse of being remembered only as the "accidental president." Rather, he wanted to be remembered and beloved in his own right instead of being seen as such a contrast in background, style and achievement to his slain predecessor, the revered John F. Kennedy.

Humphrey, one of the Senate's strongest advocates for civil rights, who had sought the presidency in 1960 and still had hopes of achieving that pinnacle, knew the vice-presidential nomination — the stepping stone he wanted so much — was dependent on how well he cleaned up this potential political land mine for President Johnson.[3]

A third politician who benefited from the outcome was young Walter Mondale, the attorney general of Minnesota, a protégé of Humphrey's, who was on the Credentials Committee, and who helped shepherd the Johnson compromise through the committee. When Humphrey was subsequently elected vice president, Mondale was appointed to fill his Senate seat. He later became vice president under President Jimmy Carter and ran for president on his own right in 1984.

Edith Green, the Credentials Committee delegate from Oregon who proposed that both delegations be seated, said afterwards, "I am absolutely persuaded that the scenario was as follows: that LBJ said to Hubert Humphrey, 'If you can prevent a floor fight over civil rights, you will be the next vice president of the United States.' And Hubert Humphrey said to the then-attorney general of Minnesota [Walter Mondale], 'If you can prevent a minority report from coming out of the Credentials Committee, you will be the next senator from Minnesota.[4]

There was division even within the Mississippi Freedom Democratic Party as to whether to accept the compromise. Aaron Henry, the druggist from Clarksdale who was head of the MFDP delegation, thought it was a step in the right direction, a foot in the door that blacks in Mississippi had not previously experienced and could open bigger doors for more blacks in the future.

Others, such as Fannie Lou Hamer, the Ruleville sharecropper, were outraged, saying her delegation hadn't come all the way from Mississippi to get just two seats. Many in the Freedom Party were insulted that Johnson's forces not only decreed they would get two seats — but named the people who would have them. To them, that was tantamount to the white man telling the black man what he could and couldn't have, which, to blacks, was business as usual. It was like being told to sit in the back of the bus or refused service at a lunch counter or denied the right to vote. It was a crushing blow to those who came to Atlantic City seeking change.

Freedom Party delegate Unita Blackwell said she understood why Henry and other black leaders thought it was best to take whatever they could get and be satisfied they had advanced their cause. But she didn't agree. "The

Democratic Party offered us two seats at large. We thought it was, for them, a compromise. But that wasn't what we wanted," said Blackwell.

She said she knew when the delegation got back to Mississippi, they probably would be thrown off their plantations and would lose whatever jobs they had because of the stand they took in Atlantic City. So it was important for them to return home with more than having gained two seats on the convention floor.[5]

Another black delegate, Victoria Gray Adams, put it this way. "You may get home and not have a house. You may get home and a member of your family may be missing — or you may not get home at all. So we weren't going to accept anything less than what we came after, which is the real thing, which is representation, which is the right to participate. And if we don't get that, then we'll go back and take our chances and regroup and come to fight another day."[6]

Robert Moses was so disgusted that not long after the convention he went to Africa to disassociate himself from white people for a while. "Up until Atlantic City," he said, "the idea had been that you were working more or less within the Democratic Party. We were working with them on voting, other things like that. With Atlantic City, a lot of movement people became disillusioned.... You turned around and found your support was puddle-deep."[7]

But Leslie McLemore, another of the 68 who came to Atlantic City with high hopes, said though the short-term goal was not achieved, there was a long-lasting impact that was more important. "We changed the rules of the national Democratic Party convention system," he said. "And that changed the body politic of this country."[8]

Lawrence Guyot, the MFDP president who couldn't take the bus trip to Atlantic City because he was in jail in Hattiesburg, Mississippi, for participating in a voter registration drive, agreed with McLemore on the long-term impact of what happened in Atlantic City. "The convention challenge in Atlantic City changed the entire party apparatus as to allowing black people in," he said.[9]

CORE's James Forman said, "Atlantic City was a powerful lesson. No longer was there any hope ... that the federal government would change the situation in the Deep South. The fine line of contradiction between the state governments and the federal government, which we had used to build a movement, was played out."[10]

Hollis Watkins, an MFDP supporter who went to Atlantic City but was not a delegate, said, "By analyzing the whole thing, we could clearly see the victories that had come about, even though we didn't get seated — including the awakening of the American public about the system and the conditions people were living under."[11]

Gray Adams, another nondelegate MFDP supporter in Atlantic City, put it succinctly: "We didn't lose. We refused to be used."[12]

Mondale said the Democratic Party recognized the problem of discrimination in the Deep South and particularly in Mississippi. But he said the challenge for the Credentials Committee was to create a fair and long-lasting solution, and the task was not easy.

"There was no question the Mississippi regular Democratic delegation was segregated," he said. "And there was no question the black competing delegation was also a single non-party group that came up to present themselves as a party.

"How to resolve the basic underlying injustice of it all, and, at the same time put into place something that would create integrated parties in the south — that was the tough part of it."

Mondale said the idea of kicking out the white delegation and seating the black delegation wouldn't have solved the underlying problem. "It didn't establish any rule of law for civil rights and if all it was going to do was be a fight of blacks against whites, one winning, one losing, there was no hope for a healthy political party."[13]

Mondale believes the compromise was the best solution. "I was on the Credentials Committee. I had no other role than being a member," he said,

> but the Mississippi Freedom Democratic Party issue was too explosive to be handled at the committee level. Everybody could see that. So I was picked as one of six or seven people on the committee to work out the compromise.
>
> What we did is still controversial today. I know that. But it has proven the test of history. We made everyone take a loyalty oath to the Democratic Party and a lot of them didn't like us for that. We seated two members of the Freedom Party as delegates. Some thought they shouldn't have been seated at all. The Freedom Party thought more of them should have been seated. But the big thing was we put into effect what I call the Civil Rights Act of the Democratic Party because it opened up the process to blacks. The party had been hypocritical. We were saying one thing in Washington but ignoring what was happening in the south. We took the steps needed to change that.[14]

Clearly, in Mondale's view, the compromise represented a turning point in Democratic politics. Others also saw it as a turning point but with a far different impact.

SNCC leader John Lewis said, "The ramifications of not seating the MFDP were immeasurable. They permeated the political climate for years to come. The same questions that were asked by all of us that August are still echoing today," he wrote in his autobiography. The questions jump off the printed page as if they were shouts:

Congressman John Lewis of Georgia, who headed the Student Nonviolent Coordinating Committee (SNCC) as a young man, says the Mississippi controversy at the convention was a turning point for many reasons.

Can the people trust their government?

Can the people trust their political leaders?

Can the people trust their president?

Do we live in a country in which the president and the government lie to the people?

Has anything really changed from the Lyndon Johnson era to today?

"That [compromise] was the turning point for the country, for the civil rights movement and certainly for SNCC. People began turning on each other. The movement started turning on itself. Fingers of blame and betrayal were pointed both left and right," said Lewis.[15]

One of the ramifications of what happened in Atlantic City was the transformation of SNCC. Lewis was replaced as president by Stokeley Carmichael who believed "the national conscience was unreliable.... Black people in Mississippi and throughout this country could not rely on their so-called allies." Carmichael coined the phrase "black power" as he tried to re-energize the movement.[16]

Historian Randall Bennett Woods wrote, "The MFDP brouhaha was a watershed in the history of the civil rights movement. It helped radicalize SNCC and CORE and in the minds of some activists, it painted King, Whitney Young, Rustin and Randolph as Uncle Toms. Civil rights activists in general became dubious about working within the Democratic Party."[17]

Former Pennsylvania governor David Lawrence, who was handpicked by President Johnson to chair the Credentials Committee, also saw the compromise as "a turning point in history" but for far different reasons than Lewis stated.

Lawrence was also appointed chairman of the commission that was to reform the delegate selection process, which would allow for inclusion of blacks and other minorities beginning in 1968. He believed the national party had committed itself to a new goal, "a breakthrough for all minorities in that the party's presidential nominating process in the South would be democratized"—and that, in his view, was a huge turning point for the Democratic Party.[18]

Joseph Rauh, the white attorney who fought so hard for the Mississippi Freedom Democrats before the Credentials Committee, also saw the experience as a turning point. He said, "I believe this was the greatest legal revolution, and I stress 'legal,' in the history of a democracy. What we did was to take a legal system which supported segregation and discrimination and turned it upside down into one that opposed it. That does not give you equality. It gives you the opportunity for equality."[19]

Humphrey, whose political fate dangled as he worked diligently to achieve the compromise that Johnson wanted, makes little mention of it in his autobiography. In the scant six paragraphs he devotes to it,

Humphrey said, in part, "We worked out a compromise of sorts that didn't really please anyone involved but kept the convention from falling apart."[20]

He chose to look at it politically and personally rather than discussing its long-term impact on the Democratic Party or the civil rights movement. "Johnson was testing me again. Was I capable of handling a difficult negotiation? Could I be relied on?... Had I failed, would Johnson have chosen McCarthy or someone else? It is a question I have never been able to answer."[21]

Aaron Henry said his hope from the beginning was that the Mississippi Freedom Democratic Party would become a viable political party, one of inclusion with blacks and whites and labor organizations and professionals all working together for noble causes such as racial equality.

"In retrospect, I think we did the best we could at the Atlantic City convention and I lost no personal respect for the people who had tried to help us," he said. "They gave us what President Johnson would allow. We did all we could do and learned a great deal about the way things work up in the world of high-level politics—heartbreak and all."[22]

With all the historical emphasis on the politics and the civil rights movement clashing at the convention, another turning point is easily but wrongfully overlooked—the impact it had on the thousands of young white people from the North who gave up comfortable lives—and in some cases gave their lives—in recognition of doing something for the greater good.

Writer Elizabeth Sutherland put it this way: "What happened [at the convention] went beyond the greatest expectations of all who had trudged the backwoods with their registration forms.... There, by the sea, across from a huge billboard of Barry Goldwater ... a band of young people from nowhere brought the machinery of a powerful political party to a halt for four days."[23]

Patti Miller, the white college student from Audubon, Iowa, reflected, 46 years later, on her journey to Mississippi:

> Time has given everyone a much broader picture of what was accomplished—and I think it was many things on many levels.
> The relationships of the native black Mississippians and Northern whites were wonderful and transforming. The chance to be involved in the plans for the Freedom Democratic Party were great. But most of all, having the Voting Rights Act passed was truly the crowning glory.
> I truly believe that without Freedom Summer, many of the changes that have been seen and experienced since would have never happened.
> And I think it's due to the fact that the attention of the entire country, and world for that matter, were drawn to the conditions in the South. And after being made aware of all the injustices, people could not continue to condone them. They realized change needed to come.
> Schools were desegregated. Lunch counters, theaters, libraries,

Patti Miller, who went to Mississippi as an Iowa college student in 1964, sees some successes that resulted from Freedom Summer (courtesy Patti Miller).

restaurants, parks— all were desegregated after that. And of course, hundreds of thousands of blacks registered to vote and many black officials were elected. The visible changes were many and were great. But as the lady I lived with that summer told me when I returned in 2004, "Many things have changed. Many things have not. It's still a white man's world,' she said."[24]

President Johnson, shown here in retirement at his Texas ranch, said all he wanted for his work on civil rights was a little thanks. He said what he got was riots (LBJ Library).

The political fallout of the Johnson compromise was palpable and predictable. Forty years later, Joshua Zeitz, writing in *American Heritage* magazine, observed: "Nobody knew it then but that 1964 Democratic National Convention would be a turning point for the Democratic Party. It was Atlantic City that sowed the seeds of the wars that tore apart the Democratic coalition four years later in Chicago and that have left it wounded ever since."[25]

For Johnson, the convention compromise was a necessary political maneuver and, he hoped, would not even be a small blip on the radar screen of his civil rights accomplishments. He ordered that he not be mentioned in the negotiations—he was "Joe Glotz"—and he never publicly acknowledged his influence on them afterwards. Looking back on his career after his presidency was over, Johnson seemed baffled and heartbroken that he was not held in higher esteem by the black community.

"How is it possible that all these people could be so ungrateful to me after I had given them so much?" he told his biographer Doris Kearns Goodwin. "Take the Negroes. I tried to make it possible for [them] to grow up in a nice house, eat a solid breakfast, attend a decent school and get a good job. I asked so little in return. Just a little thanks ... appreciation.... But look at what I got.... Riots in 175 cities. Looting. Burning. It ruined everything."[26]

Johnson never lost sight of the political implications of anything he did, for he knew without political power, he could do nothing, and that was not in his nature. So when LBJ learned of the Mississippi Freedom Democrats' plan to try to be seated at the convention, he knew if he let that happen, he would lose support of the segregationist southern states that were a core of the Democratic existence; yet if he gave in to the segregationists, he would not only lose support of the northern liberals but also of future historians—and that was always a concern of his.

Not long after he signed the Civil Rights Act, he accurately predicted the political outcome. "I think we just delivered the South to the Republicans for a long time to come," he told White House aide Bill Moyers.[27]

He was right. And the party leadership agreeing to seat two Mississippi Freedom Party delegates at the convention was two too many for the segregationists. That, on the heels of signing the Civil Rights Act led to the once "Solid South" abandoning the Democratic Party.

In five presidential elections since Johnson predicted "delivering the South to the Republicans," Democrats have been shut out in the South — getting no electoral votes from the region that was once their stronghold. In two other elections, they carried only one southern state, Lyndon Johnson's home state of Texas in 1968 and Jimmy Carter's home state of Georgia in 1980.

Here is a comparison of how Democratic presidential candidates fared in southern states before and after the 1964 elections:

1952 — Democrats won Alabama, Arkansas, Georgia, Louisiana, Mississippi, North Carolina, and South Carolina.

1956 — Democrats won Alabama, Arkansas, Georgia, Mississippi, North Carolina, and South Carolina.

1960 — Democrats won Texas, Arkansas, Louisiana, Georgia, South Carolina and North Carolina. (Alabama and Mississippi electors were divided among many candidates— which means Democrats failed to win them.)

1964 — Democrats won Texas. Republicans swept the rest of the South.

1968 — Democrats won Texas. (Alabama governor George Wallace had the most electoral votes in Louisiana, Arkansas, Mississippi, Alabama and Georgia. Hubert Humphrey, the Democratic candidate, finished third behind Richard Nixon and George Wallace, respectively, in Tennessee, North Carolina and South Carolina.)

1972 — Democrats won no southern states.

1976 — Democrats (Carter) won Alabama, Arkansas, Georgia, Louisiana, Mississippi, North Carolina, South Carolina, and Texas.

1980 — Democrats won Georgia.

1984 — Democrats won no southern states.

1988 — Democrats won no southern states.

1992 — Democrats (Clinton) won Arkansas, Louisiana, Georgia, Tennessee, and Florida.

1996 — Democrats (Clinton) won Arkansas, Louisiana, Florida, and Tennessee.

2000 — Democrats won no southern states.

2004 — Democrats won no southern states.

2008 — Democrats won Florida, North Carolina, and Virginia.

As has been noted, many who participated in the events of August 1964 — Walter Mondale, John Lewis, Joseph Rau, David Lawrence —consider them turning points in the history of the civil rights movement and of the Democratic Party and the politics of the country.

Yet, ever mindful of his legacy and how he wanted to be remembered, Johnson made no mention of the Atlantic City compromise in his autobiography.

Once again, he became Joe Glotz.

CHAPTER 15

Political Espionage Documented

As an outgrowth of the Watergate scandals of 1972–1974 that led to the resignation of President Richard Nixon, the United States Senate established a committee to look into intelligence operations of the federal government.

Given the cumbersome name of Senate Select Committee to Study Governmental Operations With Respect to Intelligence Activities, it was headed by Democratic Senator Frank Church of Idaho. Church, 40, a former army intelligence officer, was elected to the Senate in 1957 and was considered one of the Senate's leading experts on intelligence.

Republican Senator John Tower of Texas was vice chairman of what came to be known as the Church Committee, a more user-friendly and headline-friendly term than its formal title. Other Democratic members were Senators Philip Hart of Michigan, Walter Mondale of Minnesota, Walter Huddleston of Kentucky, Robert Morgan of North Carolina and Gary Hart of Colorado.

Republicans on the committee, besides Tower, were senators Howard Baker of Tennessee, Barry Goldwater of Arizona, Charles McMathias of Maryland and Richard Schweiker of Pennsylvania.

The committee met for several months taking testimony from dozens of witnesses regarding all types of U.S. intelligence operations. It eventually published a series of 14 reports examining abuses of power and possible illegal activity within the intelligence community, focusing on both the Central Intelligence Agency and the Federal Bureau of Investigation. One of the reports dealt exclusively with the 1964 Democratic National Convention.[1]

That report says:

A Senate committee looking into abuses of power concluded that President Johnson and his aides acted far from properly in authorizing spying on U.S. citizens for political purposes at the Democratic National Convention (LBJ Library).

On August 22, 1964, at the request of the White House, the FBI sent a special squad to the Democratic National Convention at Atlantic City, New Jersey. The squad was assigned to assist the Secret Service in protecting President Lyndon Johnson and to ensure that the convention itself would not be marred by civil disruption.[2]

But it went beyond these functions to report political intelligence to the White House, Approximately 30 special agents, headed by Assistant Director Cartha DeLoach were able to keep the White House fully apprised of all major developments during the convention's course by means of informant coverage, by use of various confidential techniques, by infiltration of key groups through use of undercover agents and through use of agents using inappropriate cover as reporters. Among these confidential techniques were: a wiretap on the hotel room occupied by Dr. Martin Luther King Jr. and microphone surveillance of a storefront serving as the headquarters for the Student Nonviolent Coordinating Committee and other civil rights organizations.

Neither of the electronic surveillance devices in Atlantic City were specifically authorized by the attorney general. At that time, Justice Department procedures did not require the written approval of the attorney general for bugs such as the one directed against SNCC in Atlantic City. Bureau officials apparently believed that the wiretap on King was justified as an extension of Robert Kennedy's October 10, 1964, approval for surveillance on King at his then-current address in Atlanta, Georgia, or at any future address to which he might move. The only recorded reason for instituting the wiretap on Dr. King in Atlantic City, however, was set forth in an internal memorandum shortly before the convention:

Martin Luther King Jr., head of the Southern Christian Leadership Conference, an organization set up to promote integration, which we are investigating to determine the extent of Communist Party (CP) influence on King and the Southern Christian Leadership Conference, plans to attend and may indulge in a hunger fast as a means of protest."

Walter Jenkins, an administrative assistant to President Johnson, who was the recipient of information developed by the Bureau, stated that he was unaware that any of the intelligence was obtained by wiretapping or bugging. DeLoach, moreover, has testified that he was uncertain whether he even informed Jenkins of these sources.

Walter Jenkins and presumably President Johnson received a significant volume of information from the electronic surveillance at Atlantic City, much of it purely political and only tangentially related to possible civil disturbances. The most important single issue for President Johnson at the Atlantic City convention was the seating challenge of the Mississippi Freedom Democratic Party to the regular Mississippi delegation. From the electronic surveillance of King and SNCC, the White House was able to obtain the most intimate details of the plans of individuals supporting the MFDP's challenge, unrelated to the possibility of violent demonstrations.

Jenkins received a steady stream of reports on political strategy in the struggle to seat the MFDP delegation and other political plans and discussions by civil rights groups under surveillance. Moreover, the 1975 Inspection Report stated that several congressmen, senators and governors of states were overheard on the King tap.

According to both Cartha DeLoach and Walter Jenkins, the Bureau's coverage in Atlantic City was not designed to serve political ends. DeLoach testified:

"I was sent there to provide information which could reflect on the orderly progress of the convention and the danger to distinguished individuals, and particularly the danger to the president of the United States as exemplified by the many, many references (to possible civil disturbances) in the memoranda furnished Mr. Jenkins."

Jenkins has stated that the mandate of the FBI's special unit did not encompass the gathering of political intelligence and speculated that the dissemination of any such intelligence was due to the inability of Bureau agents to distinguish dissident activities which represented a genuine potential for violence. Jenkins did not believe the White House ever used the incidental political intelligence that was received. However, a document located at the Lyndon B. Johnson Presidential Library suggests that at least one political use was made of Mr. DeLoach's reports.[3]

Thus, although it may have been implemented to prevent violence at the convention site, the Bureau's coverage in Atlantic City—which included two electronic surveillances—undeniably provided useful political intelligence to the president as well.

The overall conclusion of the Church Report refers to many incidents over many years involving many presidents and intelligence agencies. But its final conclusion resonates with memories of the 1964 Democratic Convention: "Domestic intelligence activity has threatened and undermined the Constitutional rights of Americans to free speech, association and privacy. It has done so primarily because the Constitutional system for checking abuse of power has not been applied."

EPILOGUE

Three passionate factions collided at the 1964 Democratic Convention in Atlantic City — the all-white segregationist delegation from Mississippi; the upstart Freedom Democratic Party intent on unseating the segregationists; and President Lyndon Johnson, who wanted no trouble at the convention, and unleashed the overt and covert powers of the federal government to get his way.

The convention lasted a week. Its ramifications have influenced politics for generations since then. Those involved in the tumult of Atlantic City carried on with their lives and careers, some more successfully than others, but with no less passion than what motivated them at that convention nearly 50 years ago.

President Johnson easily won re-election in 1964 in a landslide victory over Senator Barry Goldwater. He received 61 percent of the popular vote, a 22 percent margin that is still a record for a presidential election. But just as he had predicted, his civil rights policies caused him to lose the Deep South states of Louisiana, Alabama, Mississippi, Georgia and South Carolina — the first time a Democrat had lost those states since Reconstruction.

In the next four years, racial unrest continued to plague the nation and the war in Vietnam escalated and became increasingly unpopular. As the 1968 election year began, Johnson was seeing opposition even within his own party. Senator Eugene McCarthy of Minnesota, an avowed opponent of the Vietnam War, challenged the president in the New Hampshire primary. Though he did not win, he bruised the president's tough political skin and fragile ego. A few days after the primary, Senator Robert Kennedy of New York, Johnson's old nemesis, announced his candidacy for president.

In addition to the war and the racial unrest, there were signs that the American economy was faltering. Johnson had fears of a stock market crash similar to the devastating one of 1929. The president told people privately that he felt like "a stampede was coming at him from all directions."

On March 31, 1968, at the end of a televised speech to the nation in which he outlined the latest developments in Vietnam, Johnson told the country something they clearly did not expect to hear from this political warrior. He said, "I shall not seek and I will not accept the nomination of my party for another term as your president."

He had threatened to quit during the difficult times prior to the 1964 convention but changed his mind. This time, there was no change of heart.[1]

In January of 1969, after Republican Richard Nixon took office as president, Johnson retired to his home in Texas. In 1971, his memoir, *The Vantage Point*, was published. That same year, the Lyndon Baines Johnson Library and Museum opened in Austin, Texas.

On January 22, 1973, Johnson suffered a massive heart attack and died at his ranch.

Johnson's death came less than a month after the death of former president Harry Truman and two days after the inauguration of Richard Nixon for a second term in office. Truman and Johnson had been the nation's only two living ex-presidents.

Senator Hubert Humphrey, the man handpicked by Johnson to work out a compromise with the Mississippi Freedom Democrats in Atlantic City, was Johnson's choice for vice president and served in that capacity during Johnson's first full term in office. When Johnson announced he would not seek a second term, Humphrey had the opportunity to stake his claim to the nation's highest office.

He was nominated at a volatile convention in Chicago in which anti-war protesters took to the streets and were subdued, sometimes violently, by Chicago police. Humphrey waged a valiant campaign but many observers thought his role as a loyal vice president prevented him from speaking out against the war policies of the president. In a turbulent year which saw a president withdraw from running and two national icons, Kennedy and Martin Luther King Jr., assassinated, Humphrey lost the election to Richard Nixon by less than 1 percent of the popular vote.

He returned to Minnesota and taught at Macalester College and the University of Minnesota and became chairman of the board of consultants for Encyclopedia Britannica. But politics was his lifeblood and in 1970 he ran for the United States Senate when McCarthy chose not to seek re-election. Humphrey defeated Republican Clark MacGregor and was re-elected in 1976.

Humphrey sought the Democratic presidential nomination in 1972 and won some early primaries but eventually lost the nomination to

Senator George McGovern of South Dakota, a staunch anti-war candidate. In 1976, he considered another run but decided against it. He then ran for the post of Senate Majority Leader but was defeated by Senator Robert Byrd of West Virginia.

Humphrey became gravely ill with bladder cancer and died at his home in Waverly, Minnesota, on January 13, 1978.

Walter Mondale, the attorney general of Minnesota, was one of the key players on the Credentials Committee in the dispute over seating the Mississippi Freedom Party delegation. On December 30, 1964, Mondale was appointed to succeed Humphrey in the United States Senate after Humphrey was elected vice president. He filled out Humphrey's unexpired term and then was elected to a full term in 1966 and was re-elected in 1972.

The succession of political events involving Johnson, Humphrey and Mondale was thought by many, including Oregon Congresswoman Edith Green, as being a direct byproduct of the compromise Johnson wanted at the convention. He picked Humphrey as the point man to resolve the problem. Humphrey tabbed his political protégé, Mondale, to give him some help on the Credentials Committee. In the end, Johnson was re-elected, Humphrey got the vice presidency and Mondale got the Senate seat.[2]

In 1976, Jimmy Carter won the Democratic presidential nomination and picked Mondale as his running mate. They won the November election and Mondale served as vice president until 1980 when Carter was defeated for re-election by Ronald Reagan. In 1984, Democrats nominated Mondale for the presidency and he selected New York congresswoman Geraldine Ferraro as his running mate, making her the first female to run on a national ticket. They were defeated as Reagan and vice president George Bush easily won re-election.

Mondale returned to Minnesota and practiced law. He was a popular public speaker. In 1993, President Bill Clinton appointed him as ambassador to Japan, a position he held for four years. In 2002, when Senator Paul Wellstone was killed in a plane crash while campaigning for re-election, Mondale ran in his place but was defeated by Republican Norm Coleman. He retired from active politics and returned to his law practice in Minneapolis.

Mondale always acknowledged the weaknesses in the compromise reached at the 1964 Democratic convention but contends it was like a Civil Rights Bill for the Democratic party. He also believes that had it not been for the Vietnam War, Johnson and Humphrey, who helped launch his national political career, would be remembered as the greatest civil rights president and vice president in American history.[3]

Robert Moses became disillusioned with the American political process and with the divisions within the civil rights leadership after the Democratic convention. In December of 1964, in an effort to withdraw from the limelight, he began going by his middle name, Parris, and he took a leave of absence from the Student Non-Violent Coordinating Committee (SNCC) which he believed had become more radical under the leadership of Stokely Carmichael.

Moses also turned his attention to the anti-war movement and in 1966, after receiving his draft notice, he fled to Canada rather than fight in a war he did not believe in. He spent two years there and then moved to Africa where he taught mathematics in Tanzania for eight years.

In 1976, when President Carter instituted an amnesty program for draft dodgers, Moses and his second wife returned to the United States. In 1982, using funds from a MacArthur Foundation grant, Moses established what came to be called The Algebra Project, a math and science program for inner city and minority school children. His goal was to broaden the educational level of needy children so that someday they would have the same opportunities to go to college and get a job as children from better backgrounds.

In 1992, a little more than 40 years after he had started his civil rights work in Mississippi, Moses returned to Mississippi and started the Delta Algebra Project with the same objectives. He said the same principles that motivated him in the Mississippi struggles of almost a half-century earlier were still in force — educate the children and get the parents actively involved.

In 2011, Moses was appointed as a distinguished visiting fellow in the Center for African American Studies at Princeton University.[4]

Dr. Martin Luther King Jr. continued his work as head of the Southern Christian Leadership Conference. In 1964, at the age of 35, he became the youngest person ever to be awarded the Nobel Peace Prize. In 1965, he organized a march from Selma, Alabama, to the state capitol in Birmingham to protest racial inequality. It was stopped before marchers ever left Selma because of mob and police violence which drew national attention. Later, King organized another demonstration in Selma. But instead of marching, supporters took part in a prayer vigil led by King.

In 1966, King, who by now had also become a critic of the Vietnam War, moved his focus north to demonstrate how racial inequality was not confined to the south. In Chicago, he started what came to be known as the Chicago Freedom Movement in quest of fair housing, fair wages, equal education opportunities and better living conditions for minorities. His efforts there were also met with violence. When he left Chicago, his organizational structure was left with the Rev. Jesse Jackson, a young black activist who later would become a national advocate. Jackson twice sought the Democratic presidential nomination.

Dr. King continued to zero in on economic equality for minorities. On March 29, 1968, he and his entourage traveled to Memphis to support black public works employees who were on strike for better wages and better working conditions. On April 4, 1968, while standing on the balcony of the Lorraine Motel in Memphis, King was shot and killed. James Earl Ray was subsequently arrested and convicted of the assassination.

In 1983, President Ronald Reagan signed a bill establishing a federal holiday in honor of King to be observed on or near January 15, the anniversary of his birth. As evidence of the controversial figure that he was in life, it was not until 2000 that all 50 states recognized the holiday.

In 2011, a memorial sculpture of King was unveiled in Washington, D.C.

John Lewis is one of many who took part in the civil rights movement in the 1960s who were elected to public office. He was one of hundreds of blacks beaten during the aborted march from Selma to Montgomery, Alabama, in 1965 that was organized by Dr. Martin Luther King. In 1966, he resigned from the Student Nonviolent Coordinating Committee because of differences of opinion on the direction SNCC was taking under the direction of its new leader, Stokely Carmichael, whose emphasis was on "Black Power" and a decidedly more militant philosophy.

Lewis made his home in Atlanta and became executive director of the Southern Regional Council's Education Project and then became associate director of ACTION, a federal government agency advocating volunteer service.

In 1981, Lewis made his first bid for public office and was elected to the Atlanta City Council. Five years later, he ran for Congress, defeating an old friend in the civil rights movement, Julian Bond, in a hotly-contested primary election and then won the general election. He has been in Congress ever since and has held leadership positions in the House Democratic caucus.[5]

Fannie Lou Hamer, the sharecropper from Ruleville, Mississippi, who delivered riveting testimony of racial injustice before the Credentials Committee at the 1964 convention, continued to be an activist for the rest of her life. She ran unsuccessfully for Congress in 1964 and 1965 and for the Mississippi State Senate in 1971.

But she served as a delegate from Mississippi to the Democratic National Conventions in both 1968 and 1972, and was a Democratic National Committeewoman from Mississippi from 1968 to 1971. She continued to speak out about inequality and one of the lines from her speeches has been widely quoted in referring to Hamer and her causes. She said, "I'm sick and tired of being sick and tired."

She worked on Head Start programs and Farm Cooperative programs in Mississippi and also worked on Martin Luther King's Poor People's Campaign. Hamer died of breast cancer on March 14, 1977.

Aaron Henry, the Clarksville, Mississippi, druggist who led the Freedom Democrats at the Democratic convention and testified before the Credentials Committee, was active in civil rights for 30 years after the convention.

Henry, who headed the Mississippi NAACP for 33 years, was elected to the board of directors of the national organization in 1965. In 1976, he achieved a personal and a symbolic victory when he was elected as Mississippi delegate to the Democratic National Convention and served as the delegation's co-chair, just 12 years after the Freedom Democrat delegation had to settle for an unsatisfying compromise at the 1964 national convention.[6]

In 1982, Henry was elected to the Mississippi House of Representatives and served there until 1996. He also served on the Rural America board from 1976 to 1989 and was its chairman from 1983 to 1989.

In his later years, Henry suffered a series of strokes and died of congestive heart failure on May 19, 1997.

Joseph Rauh, the liberal lawyer who represented the Mississippi Freedom Democrats at the 1964 convention and was wrongly accused by some of selling out to Lyndon Johnson because of the compromise, continued his legal work on behalf of liberal and labor causes, often donating his time.

One of his clients was Joseph Yablonski, who had worked his way up in the mining industry and decided to challenge Tony Boyle as head of the United Mine Workers union. When Yablonski and his family were murdered in 1970, Rauh was convinced that Boyle and his supporters were behind it. Rauh pushed for a federal investigation into the killings. In 1974, in a celebrated case at the time, Boyle was convicted of first degree murder.

As Rauh grew older, he devoted less time to his law practice and more time to giving speeches on topics that aroused his passion such as civil rights and continued to support liberal organizations such as Americans for Democratic Action, which he helped found 50 years earlier and the NAACP.

Rauh died in Washington on September 3, 1992. On November 30, 1993, President Bill Clinton awarded him posthumously the Presidential Medal of Freedom.[7]

David Lawrence, former Pittsburgh mayor and Pennsylvania governor who, as chairman of the Credentials Committee, controlled activities until a Johnson compromise could be worked out, served in many capacities for the Democratic party. He was chairman of the President's Committee on Equal Opportunities in Housing under both presidents Kennedy and Johnson.

On November 4, 1966, while campaigning in Pittsburgh for gubernatorial candidate Milton Shapp, Lawrence collapsed and was rushed to a hospital. He died 17 days later, on November 21, without ever regaining consciousness. Lawrence was 77.[8]

Walter Reuther, the labor leader and shrewd negotiator who Johnson summoned to broker the compromise with the Freedom Democrats, continued his efforts toward social justice on the national scale and for better living and working conditions for the working man.

One of his dreams was to build an education center that would be used as a training ground for future labor leaders. The center was built near Black Lake in northern Michigan. As it was nearing completion, on May 9, 1970, Reuther and his wife May boarded a private plane so they could fly to the center to get a look at the new facility. The plane crashed en route, killing all aboard. Reuther was 62. The education center was later named in honor of Walter and May Reuther.[9]

Edith Green, the congresswoman from Oregon who proposed a compromise plan that earned her the label of "bitch" by Democratic National Chairman John Bailey, continued her work in Congress and had a highly successful and highly acclaimed legislative career.

As chair of the subcommittee on higher education, Green helped pass the Higher Education Act of 1965 which, together with earlier legislation she championed, was one of the first acts of providing federal aid to undergraduate college students. Then, in 1972, working with Congresswoman Patsy Mink, a Hawaii Democrat, and Democratic Senator Birch Bayh of Indiana, she helped pass landmark legislation prohibiting discrimination against women in federally-funded education programs. It was Title IX of the 1972 Education Act, known today as simply Title IX, the provision that opened the door for women to more fully participate in athletics and gave them fuller access to academic programs that had been dominated by men.

Green supported President Johnson in his War on Poverty and civil rights legislation but did not support the escalation of the war in Vietnam. She was one of seven House members who voted against additional funding for the war effort.

She retired from Congress in 1974 and returned to Oregon where she taught government at Warner Pacific College and was on the state Board of Education. Ever the independent thinker, in 1976 Green served as the national chairwoman for Democrats for Ford. President Ford, seeking election to a full term as president, had been a longtime colleague and friend when he and Green both served in Congress. In 1981, another Republican president, Ronald Reagan, appointed her to the President's Commission on White House Fellowships.

Mrs. Green died of cancer on April 21, 1987. She was 77.[10]

Adam Yarmolinsky, who helped develop the War on Poverty program but lost his job because he was not liked by southern congressmen whose votes were crucial to the program's passage, was not out of work long.

He had gained favor in both the Kennedy and Johnson administrations for his work in developing programs for the Defense Department and was "on loan" from that department to help Sargent Shriver with the anti-poverty program. Yarmolinsky returned to the Defense Department and remained there until 1966 when he accepted a position at the Harvard Law School and the Harvard Institute of Politics.[11]

In 1977, he returned to Washington and became a lawyer with the U.S. Arms Control and Disarmament Agency. He also taught law at the University of Maryland.

Yarmolinsky died of leukemia in Georgetown Hospital on January 7, 2000, at age 77.

Senator Barry Goldwater of Arizona, the Republican who voted against the Civil Rights Bill and was Johnson's opponent in the 1964 presidential election, carried only six states and received just 36 percent of the popular vote. But with his nomination, the conservative wing of the Republican gained some strength. Hollywood actor Ronald Reagan gave Goldwater's nominating speech and it helped propel him into fulltime politics, winning two terms as California governor and two terms as president.

Goldwater returned to the Senate in 1969 and served there until 1985. He was known for his fearlessness and his candor. In 1974, during the height of the Watergate crisis, it was Goldwater whom fellow Republicans turned to when they needed someone to convince President Nixon he had lost congressional support. Goldwater went to the White House but did not advise Nixon to resign because he thought that would be inappropriate. Instead, he informed the president that there were not sufficient votes to stop his impeachment. The next day, Nixon resigned.[12]

After retiring from the Senate, Goldwater returned to Arizona where he continued to speak out on issues for which he had a passion. Often, he was criticized for abandoning conservative principles that he had been so instrumental in establishing. In 1994, he supported a woman's right to an abortion. When conservatives challenged him, Goldwater responded, tongue sharp as ever. He said, "They think I've turned liberal because I believe a woman has a right to an abortion. That's a decision that's up to the pregnant woman, not up to the pope or some do-gooders on the religious right."[13]

Goldwater suffered a stroke in 1996 that damaged part of the brain and in 1997 went into the beginning stages of Alzheimer's disease. He died on May 29, 1998, at his home in a suburb of Phoenix. He was 89.

Cartha "Deke" DeLoach, the FBI official and confidante of President Johnson who oversaw the FBI's clandestine operations in Atlantic City, had the title of assistant director. He was considered to be a possible successor to J. Edgar Hoover if Johnson had been re-elected in 1968 and if Hoover had retired in Johnson's second term.

DeLoach retired from the FBI in July 1970. He moved to New York and became vice president of corporate affairs for Pepsico Corp. He retired from that position in 1985 and moved to Hilton Head, South Carolina. In full retirement, he has given speeches and written extensively about his career.[14]

Walter Jenkins, Johnson's trusted aide from his days in Congress, was an LBJ operative on the floor of the convention in 1964. Less than two months later, he was arrested by Washington, D.C., police in a YMCA restroom. He and another man in the restroom were charged with disorderly conduct. Publicity about the arrest forced him to resign. Johnson said, "I couldn't have been more shocked about Walter Jenkins than if I'd heard Lady Bird had tried to kill the pope."

Though the arrest came a month before the presidential election, it had little effect on the campaign. Historian Theodore White wrote, "Perhaps the most amazing of all events of the campaign of 1964 is that the nation faced the fact fully — and shrugged its shoulders."[15]

Jenkins returned to Texas and worked as a certified public accountant and management consultant. He also operated a construction company for a short time. He died in 1985 after suffering a stroke. He was 67.

Patti Miller, the Drake University music major who went to Mississippi to take part in Freedom Summer, returned to Drake and became active in trying to change the university's housing policies which allowed racial discrimination in off-campus housing. After she graduated, Miller worked in Chicago for two years with Dr. Martin Luther King and the Southern Christian Leadership Conference to try to improve conditions in the city's slum neighborhoods. She also organized civil rights marches in the Chicago suburbs.[16]

At the time of Dr. King's death, she was teaching music in Chicago's largest all-black inner city high school.

Today, Miller has developed a web site, *www.keepinghistoryalive.com*, in which she relives her civil rights experiences. She also lectures extensively about her experiences and is working on both a book and a documentary about the civil rights movement as a way of educating today's generation about the struggles of the past.[17]

Roy Wilkins, the head of the National Association for the Advancement of Colored People (NAACP) who told the Mississippi Freedom Democrats that they had made their point at the 1964 convention and should go home, believed in achieving goals through the legislative process. He did not believe militancy would bring desired results and strongly opposed the "Black Power" movement that developed after the convention.

Wilkins, who headed the NAACP from 1955 to 1977, testified before many congressional committees and conferred frequently with presidents Kennedy, Johnson, Nixon, Ford and Carter. In 1967, President Johnson presented him with the Presidential Medal of Freedom, the highest honor the government can confer on a civilian.

Wilkens died on September 8, 1981. His autobiography, *Standing Fast: The Autobiography of Roy Wilkins*, was published posthumously the following year. In 1992, the Roy Wilkins Center for Human Relations and Human Justice was established at the University of Minnesota. It is part of the Hubert Humphrey Institute of Public Affairs, linking two men of different races who championed civil rights in their lifetimes.[18]

Senator Frank Church, the Idaho Democrat, whose committee pointed out abuses of power by the Johnson administration at the 1964 Democratic convention, was considered one of the Senate's experts on intelligence. He was an early supporter of the Vietnam War but later became an outspoken critic of it.

In 1976, Church sought the Democratic presidential nomination and won primary elections in Nebraska, Oregon, Montana and his home state, Idaho. When Jimmy Carter was assured of the nomination, he contemplated Church as a running mate but chose Senator Walter Mondale of Minnesota instead. Church lost his bid for re-election to the Senate in 1980 and began practicing international law for a Washington law firm.

He died of pancreatic cancer on April 7, 1984, at his home in Bethesda, Maryland. He was 59.[19]

Many of the people who boarded the bus in Jackson, Mississippi, on that sweltering day in August 1964 and headed, with their bologna sandwiches and their principles, to Atlantic City never made the national limelight in the same way Fannie Lou Hamer and Aaron Henry did, but they still carved out their own niches in the civil rights movement for many years after the convention.

Lawrence Guyot graduated from Tougaloo College in Jackson, Mississippi, when he was elected chairman of the Mississippi Freedom Democratic Party. He was unable to accompany his delegation on the bus to Atlantic City because he had been arrested in Mississippi for assisting black people as they tried to register to vote.

Guyot has remained active in civil rights issues and in educating future generations about the lessons of the past. He earned a law degree from Rutgers University in 1971. He currently works for the Department of Health and Human Services in Washington, D.C., and conducts leadership training seminars.[20]

Victoria Gray Adams, along with Fannie Lou Hamer and Annie Devine, is credited with being a co-founder of the Mississippi Freedom Democratic Party. She continued her work in civil rights long after the convention and was the first woman to run for the U.S. Senate from Mississippi, though she did not win.

In 1968, she, Hamer and Devine were recognized by Congress for their civil rights work and, as honored guests, were seated on the floor of the House. Adams moved to Thailand with her second husband and worked for several years in projects to help African American servicemen.

She died of cancer on August 12, 2006, at her son's home in Baltimore, Maryland. She was 79.[21]

Annie Devine, the third woman in the trio of civil rights trail blazers, continued to work toward open, nonviolent voter registration for blacks in Mississippi. The efforts of the three women, and the publicity that resulted from their struggles, are credited with helping build momentum toward the passage of the Voting Rights Act in 1965. For many years after that, she was active in the Head Start program, another Johnson era program to help the under privileged.[22]

Dr. Adam Beittel, one of four white people on the bus to Atlantic City, became president of Tougaloo College, an all-black school in Jackson, Mississippi, in 1960 and began exchange programs to bring white students to Tougaloo and black students to primarily white schools. He was a friend of Medgar Evers, the black civil rights activist who was assassinated in the driveway of his home.

Tougaloo students became active in the civil rights movement and Beittel supported them, even bailing them out of jail from time to time. In a famous sit-in at a lunch counter in a Jackson restaurant, Beittel joined protesting students.

His advocacy of civil rights angered white segregationists in Mississippi, including Senator James Eastland, chairman of the Senate Judiciary Committee. Eastland began hearings to determine whether Beittel had Communist ties. Finding none, Eastland then pressured the school's board of trustees to remove Beittel for being "inefficient"— an accusation so subjective, it would be hard to disprove in court. Eastland threatened that the school's accreditation would be stripped if Beittel was not removed. He was fired in the fall of 1964 after returning from the convention.

He continued his career in education at several other institutions until his retirement. He died July 26, 1988, at the age of 89.[23]

The Rev. Ed King, who came to Tougaloo College in 1963 as a young chaplain, was another of the white passengers on the bus to Atlantic City and testified before the Credentials Committee. He did not get caught up in the politics that led to Dr. Beittel's dismissal and remained at Tougaloo until 1968.

He has been a frequent advocate and speaker on civil rights issues and was an adjunct professor of sociology and religion at Millsaps College, Jackson, Mississippi, from 1974 to 2004. He has also been an associate professor with tenure at the University of Mississippi Medical Center since 1974.

King, an ordained United Methodist minister, has received honors from many organizations for his work in race relations, including the Catholic Council of Civil Liberties and the Mississippi Religious Leadership Conference for 40 years of work in communications between races and religious groups.[24]

Winson Hudson, the black woman who taunted segregationists by wearing a red dress when she went to register to vote — so she would be easy to spot — continued her civil rights activism long after the 1964 convention.

In 1965, she testified before the U.S. Commission on Civil Rights. In 1976, 12 years after she was denied a seat as a Mississippi Freedom Democrat delegate, she was elected as a delegate to the Democratic National Convention in Florida. In 1978, she was one of a select group of blacks who was invited to have lunch with President Jimmy Carter to talk about racial issues.

In 1994, she testified before President Bill Clinton's Health Reform Task Force Commission. In 2002, Mrs. Hudson published her autobiography, *Mississippi Harmony: Memories of a Freedom Fighter*.

She died in Carthage, Mississippi, on May 1, 2004. She was 87.[25]

Unita Blackwell remains a champion of civil rights and help for the underprivileged today just as much as she was nearly 50 years ago. In 1967, she co-founded Mississippi Action Community Education, an organization that helped teach small town communities the importance of incorporating as cities. In the early 1970s, she worked for the National Council of Negro Women which became associated with the U.S. Department of Housing and Urban Development in developing and implementing programs for low-income housing. In this capacity, she traveled throughout the country, educating people in low-income areas about the opportunities available to them.

In 1976, she was elected mayor of Mayersville, her home town, a community of 500 people, thus becoming the first black woman mayor in Mississippi. Mayersville had no paved streets, no water system, no police department, and no money to handle its many challenges. Blackwell used her experience from a decade earlier with Mississippi Action Community Education to work toward incorporating, Mayersville. When it was incorporated, the city became eligible for much needed federal and state grants to pave the streets, put in a water system and improve law enforcement.

In 1990, she was elected president of the National Conference of Black Mayors. She remains the mayor of Mayersville today, making her one of the longest serving mayors in Mississippi.[26]

Dr. Leslie McLemore also became a public official and a noted educator in Mississippi. He served on the faculty of Jackson State University for 40 years, founded and headed its political science department and was also dean of its graduate school. In 2010, a year after his retirement, he served as interim president of the university.

McLemore also served for 10 years on the Jackson City Council, a remarkable feat for someone who, years earlier, had trouble even registering to vote in that city. He served for a short time as interim mayor.

"Since the movement was the defining moment of my life, it changed my outlook on the world and my role in it," he said. "In Mississippi we tried for so many years to work it out as two separate bodies, two separate entities. It didn't work. I believe in the spirit of the civil rights movement, people of color working together."[27]

Charles McLaurin became a great friend of Fannie Lou Hamer as they both worked tirelessly to register black voters. Upon returning to Mississippi after the convention, McLaurin continued his efforts on civil rights. Today he is still a frequent speaker at various events, recounting his days in the civil rights movement. He spent more than 10 years working in the public works department for the city of Indianola, retiring as assistant director. He is an active volunteer with the Fannie Lou Hamer National Institute on Citizenship and Democracy at Jackson State University.[28]

Four segregationist politicians went on with their political careers, long after the 1964 convention, some more successfully than others.

Senators James Eastland and John Stennis were two of the longest-serving tandem of senators from one state in U.S. history. Eastland, who thought it was a hoax when three slain civil rights workers were reportedly missing and later forced the ouster of the president of Tougaloo College, served in the Senate until 1978. He resigned three days before his term was up so Governor Cliff Finch could appoint his successor, Thad Cochran — giving Cochran seniority over other incoming senators.

Eastland was president pro tempore of the Senate, a largely ceremonial title but twice became second in line to the presidency — in 1973 when Vice President Spiro Agnew resigned and in 1974 when Vice President Gerald Ford became president, leaving the vice presidency temporarily unfilled. Eastland was chairman of the powerful Senate Judiciary Committee for 22 years.

In retirement, he returned to Mississippi where he died February 19, 1986, at the age of 81.

Stennis, described by the *New York Times* as "the last of the Southern barons" in the Senate, had served the second longest tenure in the Senate, 41 years and one month, when he retired on January 3, 1989. Only Carl Hayden of Arizona had served longer.[29]

His seniority awarded him chairmanships on many Senate committees and his age and experience made him a mentor to many young senators. Like Eastland, he too served as president pro tempore of the Senate. A staunch segregationist during the civil rights movement, Stennis tried to change with the times and was a more moderate voice by the time he retired. He died on April 24, 1995, at the age of 93.[30]

A.K. Collins, the Mississippi state senator who equated the civil rights movement with Communism and who testified for the segregationist delegation before the Credentials Committee at the 1964 Democratic convention, remained in the state senate until 1971 when he was defeated in a re-election bid.

Governor Paul Johnson Jr., who had to balance the political juggernaut of a segregationist constituency and a growing civil rights movement, is the man who, as lieutenant governor, said in 1963, "The NAACP stands for Niggers, Apes, Alligators, Coons and Possums."[31]

As governor, in his inaugural speech, he said, "Hate or prejudice or ignorance will not lead Mississippi while I sit in the governor's chair." He worked to enforce the Voting Rights Act of 1965.

Johnson did not seek re-election and dropped out of politics after leaving office in 1968. He incurred a series of health setbacks and died October 18, 1985, at the age of 69.

Chapter Notes

Notations citing "LBJ tapes" refer to tape recordings of President Johnson's telephone conversations that are available through the Lyndon Baines Johnson Library and Museum in Austin, Texas. Many of them can also be accessed at www.lbjlibrary.org.

Preface

1. Taylor Branch, *Pillar of Fire* (New York: Simon & Schuster, 1998), pp. 444–445.

Introduction

1. Cartha DeLoach, *Hoover's FBI: The Inside Story by Hoover's Trusted Lieutenant* (New York: Regnery, 1995), p. 1.

Chapter 1. The Movement

1. Interview with civil rights activist Victoria Gray Adams for *Eyes on the Prize* documentary series for Public Broadcasting System, conducted November 9, 1985, 2. Ivanhoe Donaldson, interview, *Eyes on the Prize*, conducted October 4, 1979.

3. A summary of civil rights murders can be found in the archives of the Southern Poverty Law Center at www.splcenter.or/civilrights-memorial/civil-rights-martyrs.

4. Ibid.

5. Text of Humphrey's speech is accessible through many sources. Both transcript and recording of the speech are available at http://www.americanrhetoric.com/speeches/hubert humphey1948dnc.html.

6. Henry Wallace, who served as Franklin Roosevelt's secretary of agriculture and as his vice president during Roosevelt's third term, also broke from party ranks, and ran for president in 1948 on the Progressive Party ticket. Wallace's run was prompted by his disagreement with Roosevelt/Truman policies and was not connected with the civil rights issue.

7. Historian Theodore White has pointed out an irony in this case. The court ruling in effect stopped the child from having to be bused across town to go to school. In years to come, enforcement of desegregation led to court-ordered busing of school children to achieve integration in school systems.

8. Congressional Record, 84th Congress, second session, v. 102, pt. 4, March 12, 1956, Washington, DC: Government Printing Office.

9. Senator A. Willis Robertson of Virginia, who signed the manifesto, had a son, Marion "Pat" Robertson, who became a famous television evangelist and sought the Republican presidential nomination in 1988.

10. Nick Kotz, *Judgment Days: Lyndon Baines Johnson, Martin Luther King Jr. and the Laws That Changed America* (New York: Houghton Mifflin, 2005), 45. Kefauver, Gore and Kennedy all contended for the 1956 vice-presidential nomination, won by Kefauver. But the national exposure helped set the stage for Kennedy's successful 1960 presidential run. Gore's son, Albert Gore Jr., was a senator from Tennessee, vice president from 1993 to 2001 and an unsuccessful candidate for president in 2000.

11. Kotz, *Judgment Days*, 50.

12. John Lewis and Michael D'Orso, *Walking with the Wind: A Memoir of the Movement* (New York: Harcourt Brace, 1998), 91–93.

13. Kotz, *Judgment Days*, 51–52.

14. Lewis and D'Orso, *Walking with the Wind*, 156–157.

15. "Letter from Birmingham Jail," quoted in Kotz, *Judgment Days*, 57–58.

16. Kay Mills, *This Little Light of Mine: The Life of Fannie Lou Hamer* (Lexington: University Press of Kentucky, 1997), p. 56.

17. Audio and text versions of the Kennedy speech can be found on the website americanrhetoric.com.

18. Anne Moody, *Coming of Age in Mississippi* (New York: Delta, 2004), 252.

19. *A Sense of History: The Best Writing from the Pages of American Heritage* (New York: American Heritage Press, 1985), 792.

20. Kotz, *Judgment Days*, 22, 32, 63.

Chapter 2. Robert Moses

1. Lewis and D'Orso, *Walking with the Wind*, 182.

2. Mills, *This Little Light of Mine*, 32.

3. Robert Moses, interview, *Eyes on the Prize*, conducted May 19, 1986.

4. Ibid.

5. Amzie Moore, interview, *Eyes on the Prize*, conducted 1979, exact date unknown.

6. Kotz, *Judgment Days*, 161.

7. Lewis and D'Orso, *Walking with the Wind*, 182.

8. Theodore H. White, *America in Search of Itself* (New York: Harper & Row, 1982), 105.

9. Joshua Zeitz, "Democratic Debacle," *American Heritage*, June/July 2004.

10. Robert Moses' testimony before the United States Senate Judiciary Committee, September 4, 2007.

11. Eric Burns, *And Gently He Shall Lead Them: Robert Parris Moses and Civil Rights in Mississippi* (New York: NYU Press, 1995), 2.

12. Joseph Rauh, interview, *Eyes on the Prize*, conducted October 31, 1985.

13. Ibid.

14. While it was significant for the civil rights movement in Mississippi for the various organizations to form a coalition, there was a practical reason behind it as well. Aaron Henry, president of the state NAACP, had been trying to meet with Governor Ross Barnett to discuss grievances. Barnett was not sympathetic to the NAACP's cause and declined to meet. COFO was formed to provide a little more political clout. When COFO sought a meeting with the governor, he consented — and wound up meeting with the same people he would have if he had agreed to meet with the NAACP. Henry discusses the COFO meeting with the governor in his autobiography, *Aaron Henry: The Fire Ever Burning.*

15. Aaron Henry and Constance Curry, *Aaron Henry: The Fire Ever Burning* (Jackson: University Press of Mississippi, 2000), 161.

16. Mills, *This Little Light of Mine*, 80–81, 106.

17. Ibid., 105.

18. Mississippi Freedom Party position paper, 1964; Section II, Organizational Structure, paragraph 1.

19. Use of the term "Nigra" in quoting Johnson is appropriate because that is how he often pronounced the word "Negro." He meant no disrespect but his use of the term made his speechwriters cringe.

20. Michael R. Beschloss, *Taking Charge: The Johnson White House Tapes, 1963–1964* (New York: Simon & Schuster, 1997), 312–313. In an effort to make sure his actions were accurately noted by future historians, Johnson made sure most of his telephone conversations were taped, no matter where he happened to be. Many of the recordings are available to hear on various Internet websites and at the LBJ Library in Austin, Texas. A collection of them is found in Beschloss's book.

21. David Levering Lewis, review of *Freedom Summer* by Bruce Watson, *SFGate*, June 27, 2010, http://www.sfgate.com/cgi-bin/article.cgi?f=/c/a/2010/06/27/RVL41E0CS8.DTL.

22. Lewis and D'Orso, *Walking with the Wind*, p. 256.

23. Craig Gilbert, "Doar Stood Tall for Civil Rights in South," *Milwaukee Journal Sentinel*, August 9, 2009.

24. Tracy Sugarman, *We Had Sneakers, They Had Guns* (Syracuse, NY: Syracuse University Press, 2009), 9.

25. Lewis and D'Orso, *Walking with the Wind*, 248.

26. Mississippi Freedom Party position paper, 1964; Appendix C, The Convention Challenge, paragraph 1.

27. Online Archives of California, California Digital Library, 2007.

Chapter 3. Lyndon Johnson

1. Doris Kearns Goodwin, *Lyndon Johnson and the American Dream* (New York: St. Martin's Press, 1991), 20–26.

2. Kotz, *Judgment Days*, 26.

3. Ibid., 12.

4. Goodwin, *Lyndon Johnson*, 84–85.

5. Kotz, *Judgment Days*, 89.

6. Goodwin, *Lyndon Johnson*, 93. Goodwin suggests that one of the reasons Johnson chose not to allege vote fraud is the possibility that an investigation would have revealed stolen votes on his side as well.

7. *The Texas Observer*, June 10, 1960, as quoted in Theodore H. White, *The Making of the President, 1964* (New York: Atheneum, 1965), 253.

8. Goodwin, *Lyndon Johnson*, 74–75.

9. Ibid., 120.

10. Marshall Frady, "The Big Guy," *New York Review of Books*, November 7, 2002.

11. Rowland Evans and Robert Novak, *Lyndon B. Johnson: The Exercise of Power* (New York: Signet, 1968), 74.

12. Katherine Graham was the publisher of the *Washington Post*; Meg Greenfield was a columnist. Together they were two of the most influential women in Washington journalism. Bradlee's recollections are recounted in Robert Dallek's comprehensive biography *Lyndon B. Johnson: Portrait of a President* (New York: Oxford University Press USA, 2005), 87.

13. Goodwin, *Lyndon Johnson*, 125.

14. Many sources make reference to Johnson and "jumbo." One of them is Marshall Frady, "The Big Guy," *New York Books*, November 7, 2002.

15. Goodwin. *Lyndon Johnson*, 242.

16. LBJ tapes.

17. White, *Making of the President, 1964*, 56.

18. Arthur M. Schlesinger Jr., *Robert F. Kennedy and His Times* (New York: Balentine Books, 1978), 674.

19. Ibid., 742.

20. Hubert Humphrey, *The Education of a Public Man: My Life and Politics* (Minneapolis: University of Minnesota Press, 1991), 181, 216–218.

21. White, *Making of the President, 1964*, 33–34.

Chapter 4. A Nation Awakened

1. Bruce Watson, "The Summer of Our Discontent," *American Heritage*, Summer 2010, 44–45.
2. Ibid.
3. Schlesinger, *Robert Kennedy*, 314.
4. Burke Marshall, interview, *Eyes on the Prize*, conducted November 4, 1985.
5. LBJ tapes.
6. Ibid.
7. Ibid.
8. Ibid.
9. Ibid.
10. Lewis and D'Orso, *Walking with the Wind*, 245.
11. Watson, "Summer of Our Discontent," p. 49.
12. Information on the Gulf of Tonkin incident was taken from a report written by Edward J. Marolda, senior historian, Naval Historical Center, Washington, DC. The report is entitled, "Tonkin Gulf Crisis, August 1964" and was published July 13, 2005.
13. Information gleaned from the Lyndon Johnson diary, August 4, 1964, available for view at the LBJ Library or on the LBJ Library web site, www.lbjlibrary.org. Johnson didn't actually keep the diary. His secretaries did, rotating the duty. They were not privy to the specifics of all of his telephone calls, his visits with individuals, nor to the meetings he held, but they did make a record of every phone call, visit, or meeting and wrote a note about the subject matter as best they knew. The practice started on November 22, 1963, the day Johnson assumed office after the Kennedy assassination, and continued throughout his presidency.
14. Joshua Zeitz, "1964: The Year the Sixties Began," *American Heritage*, Special Issue, October 2006, p. 45.
15. Marolda, "Tonkin Gulf Crisis, August 1964," Naval Historical Center, Washington, DC.
16. Mills, *This Little Light of Mine*, 109.
17. Lynne Olson, *Freedom's Daughters: The Unsung Heroines of the Civil Rights Movement from 1830 to 1970* (New York: Scribner, 2002), 307.
18. The delegates: Lawrence Guyot, Peggy J. Conner, Victoria Gray, Edwin King, Aaron Henry, Fannie Lou Hamer, Annie Devine, Helen Anderson, A.D. Beittel, Elizabeth Blackwell, Marie Blalock, Sylvester Bowens, J.W. Brown, Charles Bryant, James Carr, Lois Chaffee, Clint Collier, Willie Ervin, J.C. Fairley, Dewey Green, Winson Hudson, Johnny Jackson, N.L. Kirkland, Mary Lane, Merrill W. Lindsay, Eddie Mack, Lulu Matthews, Yvonne MacGowan, Charles McLaurin, Leslie R. McLemore, Robert Miles, Otis Millsaps, Hazel Palmer, R.S. Porter, William D. Scott, Henry Sias, Slate Stallworth, E.W. Steptoe, Robert Lee Stinson, Joseph Stone, Eddie Thomas, Jimmie Travis, Hartman Turnbow, Abraham Washington, Clifton R. Whitley, Robert W. Williams, J. Walter Wright, C.R. Darden, Ruby Evans, Oscar Giles, Charlie Graves, Pinkie Hall, George Harper, Macy Hardaway, Andrew Hawkins, William Jackson, Alta Lloyd, J.F. McRae, W.G. Middleton, Joe Newton, M.A. Phelps, Beverly Polk, Henry Reaves, Harold Roby, Emma Sanders, Cora Smith, R.L.T. Smith, Elmira Tyson and L.H. Waborn.

Chapter 5. The Republican Revolution

1. Rick Perlstein, "1964 Republican Convention: Revolution from the Right, " *Smithsonian*, August 2008.
2. White, *Making of the President, 1964*, 216–217.
3. Goldwater's acceptance speech is available in many venues, including www.americanrhetoric.com.
4. White, *Making of the President, 1964*, 217.
5. Ibid., 220.
6. Taylor Branch, *Pillar of Fire: America in the King Years, 1963–65* (New York: Simon & Schuster, 1998), 402.

7. Beschloss, *Taking Charge*, 456–457.
8. Branch, *Pillar of Fire*, 401.
9. Ibid., 404
10. White, *Making of the President, 1964*, 220.

Chapter 6. The Journey

1. Debbie Elliott, "When Students Ignited a Change in Racial Politics," NPR, April 14, 2010, http://www.npr.org/templates/story/story.php?storyId=125908995.
2. Sugarman, *We Had Sneakers*, 5.
3. "Aaron E. Henry," *Baltimore Sun*, May 20,1997.
4. Marcel Dufresne, "Exposing the Secrets of Mississippi Racism," *American Journalism Review*, October 1991, http://www.ajr.org/Article.asp?id=1311.
5. Moody, *Coming of Age*, 206.
6. Ibid.
7. Douglas Martin, "Winson Hudson, Tireless Civil Rights Leader, Dies," *New York Times*, May 9, 2004.
8. Examples of literacy test questions were contained in a television interview between correspondent Mike Wallace and Senator James Eastland of Mississippi that was broadcast on July 28, 1957.
9. Nicholas Katzenbach, interview, *Eyes on the Prize*, conducted December 10, 1985.
10. "Victoria Gray Adams, Civil Rights Leader, Is Dead at 79," *New York Times*, August 19, 2006.
11. Mills, *This Little Light of Mine*, 110.
12. Yvonne Lamb, "Victoria Gray Adams, Civil Rights Advocate," *Washington Post*, September 9, 2006.
13. Kotz, *Judgment Days*, 455.
14. Olson, *Freedom's Daughters*, 317.
15. Bruce Watson, *Freedom Summer: The Savage Season That Made Mississippi Burn and Made America a Democracy* (New York: Penguin, 2010), 152–153.
16. Ibid.

Chapter 7. Political Espionage

1. Brian Lamb interview with DeLoach, broadcast on C-SPAN, August 20, 1995.
2. Ibid.
3. Kotz, *Judgment Days*, 199–200. Johnson used the "Glotz" reference often in asking to be kept in the background and advised others to do the same. In a telephone conversation with Walter Reuther on September 5, 1964, he asked Reuther to call several newspapers in Michigan to complain about Barry Goldwater and suggested he identify himself as Oscar Glotz. Later that same day, he asked a friend, Bernard Boutin, to make some calls chiding Goldwater and to identify himself as John Glotz. Both calls are among the recordings in the LBJ Library.
4. Joseph Rauh, interview, *Eyes on the Prize*, conducted October 31, 1985.
5. Beschloss, *Taking Charge*, 510–511.
6. Branch, *Pillar of Fire*, 444–445. Yarmolinsky worked for both the Kennedy and Johnson administrations in various capacities. He remained a liberal, intellectual icon whose views were solicited and appreciated long after the episode that led to his departure from the antipoverty program. His boss at the time, Sargent Shriver, told him, "You've been thrown to the wolves."
7. *New York Times*, August 25, 1987.
8. Nicholas Katzenbach, interview, *Eyes on the Prize*, conducted December 10, 1985.
9. Kotz, *Judgment Days*, 200.
10. Beschloss, *Taking Charge*, 516–517.

11. Ibid., 518.
12. Kotz, *Judgment Days*, 209.
13. *New York Times*, August 20, 1964.
14. Branch, *Pillar of Fire*, 454–455.

Chapter 8. Showdown

1. Mills, *This Little Light of Mine*, 117.
2. Mark Stricherz, *Why the Democrats Are Blue: Secular Liberalism and the Decline of the People's Party* (New York: Encounter, 2007), 33–34.
3. Ibid., 65.
4. Mark Stricherz, "King David's Legacy," *America: The National Catholic Weekly*, September 22, 2008.
5. Branch, *Pillar of Fire*, 457–458.
6. Mills, *This Little Light of Mine*, 117.
7. Ibid., 118.
8. Branch, *Pillar of Fire*, 458.
9. White, *Making of the President, 1964*, 278.
10. There are numerous sources for Mrs. Hamer's testimony, including www.americanrhetoric.com, which contains both written transcription and film of her delivering her testimony.
11. Kotz, *Judgment Days*, 205.
12. Branch, *Pillar of Fire*, 460–461.
13. Jere Nash, Andy Taggert and John Grisham, *Mississippi Politics: The Struggle for Power, 1976–2006* (Jackson: University Press of Mississippi, 2006), 20.
14. Henry and Curry, *Aaron Henry*, 183.
15. Larry Still, a reporter for *Jet* magazine, a periodical aimed at black audiences, reported on the hotel scene for the magazine. Parts of his story are recounted in Taylor Branch's book, *Pillar of Fire*, 461.
16. Excerpts from speech given by Walter Mondale in Minneapolis on February 11, 2000.
17. Ibid.
18. Henry and Curry, *Aaron Henry*, 183.
19. Ibid., 184.
20. Kotz, *Judgment Days*, 191.

Chapter 9. Compromises and Consternation

1. *Jackson Clarion Ledger*, August 22, 1964.
2. *Jackson Daily News*, August 22, 1964.
3. *Jackson Daily News*, August 25, 1964.
4. *New York Times*, August 23–24, 1964.
5. Mills, *This Little Light of Mine*, 124.
6. Chana Kai Lee, *For Freedom's Sake: The Life of Fannie Lou Hamer* (Champaign: University of Illinois Press, 2000), 87.
7. LBJ tapes.
8. Ibid.
9. Mondale speech, Minneapolis, February 11, 2000.
10. Henry and Curry, *Aaron Henry*, 189.
11. Mondale speech, Minneapolis, February 11, 2000.
12. William Marvin Watson and Sherwin Markman, *Chief of Staff: Lyndon Johnson and His Presidency* (New York: Thomas Dunne Books, 2004), 66.
13. Mills, *This Little Light of Mine*, 124.
14. Kotz, *Judgment Days*, 217. Also information from John Dittmer, *Local People: The Struggle for Civil Rights in Mississippi* (Urbana: University of Illinois Press, 1994), 288–290.
15. Kotz, *Judgment Days*, 209.

Chapter 10. Into the Lion's Den

1. Diggs was the first chairman of the Congressional Black Caucus but his political career ended 10 years later when he was convicted on 11 counts of mail fraud. He served 14 months of a three-year sentence.
2. Mills, *This Little Light of Mine*, 125.
3. Branch, *Pillar of Fire*, 465.
4. LBJ tapes.
5. Branch, *Pillar of Fire*, 463.
6. LBJ tapes.
7. Ibid.
8. Ibid.
9. Pastore's stem-winding speech led some to believe he might be an 11th-hour pick for vice president, which wasn't to be. His speech can be viewed in its entirety at http://abcnews.go.com/video/playerIndex?id=9315932.
10. Information gleaned from research at the Walter Reuther Library, Wayne State University, Detroit.
11. Kevin Boyle, *The UAW and the Heyday of American Liberalism, 1945–1968* (Ithaca, NY: Cornell University Press, 1998), 93.

Chapter 11. A Compromise and a Lynching

1. Kotz, *Judgment Days*, 212–213.
2. LBJ tapes.
3. Ibid.
4. Lady Bird Johnson, *A White House Diary* (Austin: University of Texas Press, 1970), 192.
5. LBJ tapes.
6. Joseph Rauh, interview, *Eyes on the Prize*, conducted October 31, 1985.
7. Branch, *Pillar of Fire*, 469.
8. Dittmer, *Local People*, 297.
9. Branch, *Pillar of Fire*, 469–470.
10. Joseph Rauh, interview, *Eyes on the Prize*, conducted October 31, 1985.
11. Ibid.
12. Mondale speech, Minneapolis, February 11, 2000.
13. Henry and Curry, *Aaron Henry*, 188–192.
14. Mills, *This Little Light of Mine*, 126.
15. Excerpts from critique written by the SNCC leader of the Mondale speech of February 1, 2000.
16. Mills, *This Little Light of Mine*, 128.
17. Henry and Curry, *Aaron Henry*, 194.
18. Mills, *This Little Light of Mine*, 129.
19. Lewis and D'Orso, *Walking with the Wind*, 290.
20. LBJ tapes.
21. Sally Belfrage, *Freedom Summer* (New York: Viking Press, 1965), 245–246.
22. White, *Making of the President, 1964*, 280.
23. *New York Times*, August 26,1964.
24. Branch, *Pillar of Fire*, 472–473.

Chapter 12. Power, Protest and Politics

1. Branch, *Pillar of Fire*, 473.
2. Lewis and D'Orso, *Walking with the Wind*, 289.
3. Dittmer, *Local People*, 300.

    4. Ibid., 132.
    5. Lewis and D'Orso, *Walking with the Wind*, 289.
    6. LBJ tapes.
    7. Ibid.
    8. Hubert Humphrey, *The Education of a Public Man: My Life and Politics* (Minneapolis: University of Minnesota Press, 1991), 221.
    9. Ibid., 222.
    10. Ibid., 226.
    11. LBJ tapes.
    12. Michael R. Beschloss, *Taking Charge* (Simon & Schuster, 1997), p. 539.

Chapter 13. The Forces of Human Decency

    1. It was unusual for a staunch Republican like Dewey, a two-time presidential candidate, to give advice to a Democratic president and might have been an indication of Dewey's disdain for Goldwater, at that time the likely Republican candidate, or for the Kennedys.
    2. Beschloss, *Taking Charge*, 536.
    3. Robert Schlesinger, in his book *White House Ghosts*, devotes a chapter to Johnson's relationship with his speechwriters.
    4. Lyndon Johnson acceptance speech, widely quoted.
    5. Channing was a respected Broadway actress and singer known more for her talent than for her sex appeal. Her appearance at the convention, though, brought back memories of a birthday celebration a few years back when Marilyn Monroe, a Hollywood actress whose fame was based largely on her sex appeal, used her sultry voice to sing "Happy Birthday" to President Kennedy.
    6. LBJ tapes.

Chapter 14. Turning Points

    1. LBJ tapes.
    2. White, *Making of the President, 1964*, 279.
    3. Johnson's dangling of the vice presidency in front of Humphrey is cited in many sources, some of which have already been referenced.
    4. Edith Green Oral History, National Archives.
    5. Unita Blackwell, interview, *Eyes on the Prize*, conducted May 7, 1986.
    6. Victoria Gray Adams, interview, *Eyes on the Prize*, conducted November 9, 1985.
    7. Zeitz, "Democratic Debacle."
    8. Lou Dubose, "The Black Vote in a Red State," *Washington Spectator*, November 15, 2008.
    9. Lawrence Guyot, interview, *Eyes on the Prize*, conducted May 15, 1979.
    10. James Forman, *The Making of Black Revolutionaries* (New York: Macmillan, 1972), 395–396.
    11. Vern Smith. "Showdown," *Crisis*, July-August 2004.
    12. Ibid.
    13. Walter Mondale, interview, *Eyes on the Prize*, conducted May 5, 1986.
    14. Interview with author, March 11, 2009.
    15. Lewis and D'Orso, *Walking with the Wind*, 292.
    16. Zeitz, "Democratic Debacle."
    17. Randall Bennett Woods, *LBJ: Architect of American Ambition* (New York: Simon & Schuster, 2006), 533.
    18. Stricherz, *Why the Democrats Are Blue*, 72. Lawrence's commission did make changes in the process that took effect in 1968 as promised, but they were overshadowed by the anti-war demonstrations that led to the so-called "police riot" outside the convention center in Chicago.

19. Joseph Rauh, interview, *Eyes on the Prize*, conducted October 31, 1985.

20. Humphrey, *Education of a Public Man*, 222–223.

21. Ibid.

22. Henry and Curry, *Aaron Henry*, 198.

23. Elizabeth Sutherland, "Letters from Mississippi" as quoted in Guy and Candie Carawan. *Sing for Freedom: The Story of the Civil Rights Movement Through Its Songs* (Montgomery, AL: NewSouth Books, 2007), 182.

24. Interview with the author, February 23, 2011.

25. Zeitz, "Democratic Debacle."

26. Goodwin, *Lyndon Johnson*, 340.

27. Kotz, *Judgment Days*, 154. There are several versions of what Johnson said, perhaps because he said it often. Another version has him telling aide Joseph Califano, "I think we've delivered the South to the Republican Party for your lifetime and mine." Zeitz, "Democratic Debacle."

Chapter 15. Political Espionage Documented

1. More than a decade after the 1964 Democratic convention, two of the senators involved in investigating domestic intelligence were Walter Mondale, LBJ's subcommittee chairman for the Credentials Committee at the convention, and Barry Goldwater, Johnson's opponent in the 1964 presidential election.

2. As the report states, the FBI work started in Atlantic City on August 22, 1964 — but it had been discussed and planned in Washington for several weeks prior to the convention.

3. Jenkins was shading the truth when he said it was not the FBI's mandate to gather political intelligence. While not a written mandate, it was clearly the ulterior motive from the outset.

Epilogue

1. A stirring account of Johnson's decision to withdraw as a candidate for re-election is found in Doris Kearns Goodwin's biography, *Lyndon Johnson and the American Dream*, pp. 343–349.

2. Edith Green Oral History, National Archives.

3. Interview with author, March 11, 2009.

4. www.planetprinceton.com.

5. Lewis and D'Orso, *Walking with the Wind: A Memoir of the Movement*, p. 294.

6. Henry and Curry, *The Fire Ever Burning*, pp. 199–233.

7. "Joseph Rauh, Ground-breaking Civil Rights Attorney Dies," *New York Times*, September 5, 1992.

8. "Ex-Governor David Lawrence Dies, *Pittsburgh Post Gazette*, November 22, 1966.

9. www.reuther100.wayne.edu, as well as many other sources.

10. www.oregonencyclopedia.org, as well as many other sources.

11. Goodwin, *Lyndon Johnson and the American Dream*, p. 320

12. "Barry Goldwater, GOP Hero Dies, *Washington Post*, May 30, 1998.

13. Ibid.

14. Athan G. Theoharis. *The FBI: A Comprehensive Reference Guide.* (Westport, CT.: The Greenwood Group, 2000), p. 322.

15. White, *The Making of the President 1964*, p. 308.

16. As part of the research for this book, the author interviewed Miller about her civil rights experiences. Miller and the author had never met. As they discussed her organizing of marches in the Chicago suburbs nearly 40 years ago, they discovered their paths might have crossed in Aurora, Illinois, when the author, as a young newspaper reporter, covered a demonstration and march for fair housing that Miller had organized.

17. www.keepinghistoryalive.com.
18. www.naacp.org.
19. "Former Sen. Frank Church of Idaho Dies," *New York Times*, April 8, 1984.
20. www.thehistorymakers.com.
21. "Civil Rights Activist Victoria Gray Adams Dies," *New York Times*, August 13, 2006.
22. *Eyes on the Prize* interview for Public Broadcasting Network, May 5, 1986.
23. *American Journalism Review*, October 1991.
24. *Millsaps College Alumni Awards Program*, Spring 2011.
25. "Winson Hudson, Civil Rights Hero, Dies, *New York Times*, May 1, 2004.
26. www.blackpast.org.
27. Tracy Sugarman, *We Had Sneakers, They Had Guns*, pp. 197–198.
28. www.malcolmxinstitute.com.
29. Since Stennis left, two other senators passed him in longevity, Strom Thurmond of South Carolina and Robert Byrd of Virginia.
30. "Former Senator John Stennis Dies," *New York Times*, April 24, 1995.
31. "If You Try and Don't Succeed," *Time*, August 16, 1963.

Bibliography

Books

Abbott, Dorothy. *Mississippi Writer: Drama*. Jackson: University Press of Mississippi, 1991.

Barwell, Marion. *A Place Called Mississippi*. Jackson: University of Mississippi Press, 1997.

Belfrage, Sally. *Freedom Summer*. New York: Viking Press, 1965.

Beschloss, Michael. *Taking Charge: The Johnson White House Tapes, 1963–1964*. New York: Simon & Schuster, 1997.

Boyle, Kevin. *The UAW and the Heyday of American Liberalism, 1945–1964*. Ithaca, NY: Cornell University Press, 1998.

Branch, Taylor. *Pillar of Fire: America in the King Years, 1963–65*. New York: Simon & Schuster, 1998.

Burns, Eric. *And Gently He Shall Lead Them: Robert Parris Moses and Civil Rights in Mississippi*. New York: NYU Press, 1995.

Carawan, Guy, and Candie Carawan. *Sing for Freedom: The Story of the Civil Rights Movement Through Its Songs*. Montgomery, AL: NewSouth Books, 2007.

Caro, Robert. *The Years of Lyndon Johnson: Master of the Senate*. New York: Knopf, 2002.

Dallek, Robert. *Lyndon B. Johnson: Portrait of a President*. New York: Oxford University Press USA, 2005.

Dittmer, John. *Local People: The Struggle for Civil Rights in Mississippi*. Urbana: University of Illinois Press, 1994.

Evans, Rowland, and Robert Novak. *Lyndon B. Johnson: The Exercise of Power*. New York: Signet, 1968.

Forman, James. *The Making of Black Revolutionaries*. New York: Macmillan, 1972.

Goodwin, Doris Kearns. *Lyndon Johnson and the American Dream*. New York: St. Martin's, 1991.

Henry, Aaron, and Constance Curry. *Aaron Henry: The Fire Ever Burning*. Jackson: University Press of Mississippi, 2000.

Humphrey, Hubert. *The Education of a Public Man: My Life and Politics*. Minneapolis: University of Minnesota Press, 1991.

Johnson, Lady Bird. *A White House Diary*. Austin: University of Texas Press, 1970.

Johnson, Robert David. *All the Way with LBJ*. New York: Cambridge University Press, 2009.

Klopfer, Susan, Fred Klopfer, and Barry Klopfer. *Where Rebels Roost: Mississippi Civil Rights Revisited*. lulu.com.

Kotz, Nicholas. *Judgment Days*. New York: Houghton Mifflin, 2005.

Lee, Chana Kai. *For Freedom's Sake: The Life of Fannie Lou Hamer*. Champaign: University of Illinois Press, 2000.

Lewis, John, and Michael D'Orso. *Walking with the Wind*. New York: Simon & Schuster, 1998.

Marsh, Charles. *God's Long Summer: Stories of Faith and Civil Rights*. Princeton, NJ: Princeton University Press, 2008.

Matusow, Allen J. *The Unraveling of America: A History of Liberalism in the 1960s*. Athens: University of Georgia Press, 2009.

McAdam, Doug. *Freedom Summer*. New York: Oxford University Press, 1988.

Mills, Kay. *This Little Light of Mine: The Life of Fannie Lou Hamer*. Lexington: University Press of Kentucky, 2007.

Mills, Nicolaus. *Like a Holy Crusade — Mississippi 1964 — The Turning of the Civil Rights Movement in America*. Lanham, MD: Ivan R. Dee, 1993.

Moody, Anne. *Coming of Age in Mississippi*. New York: Delta, 2004.

Nash, Jere, Andy Taggert, and John Grisham. *Mississippi Politics: The Struggle for Power, 1976–2006*. Jackson: University Press of Mississippi, 2006.

Olson, Lynne. *Freedom's Daughters: The Unsung Heroines of the Civil Rights Movement from 1830 to 1970*. New York: Scribner, 2002.

Rothman, Hal K. *LBJ's Texas White House*. College Station: Texas A&M University Press, 2001.

Schlesinger, Arthur H. *Robert Kennedy and His Times*. New York: Ballantine Books, 1978.

Schlesinger, Robert. *White House Ghosts: Presidents and Their Speechwriters*. New York: Simon & Schuster, 2008.

A Sense of History: The Best Writing from the Pages of American Heritage. New York: American Heritage Press, 1985.

Silver, James W. *Mississippi: The Closed Society*. New York: Harcourt, Brace & World, 1964.

Solberg, Carl. *Humphrey: A Biography*. St. Paul: Borealis Books, 1984.

Stricherz, Mark. *Why the Democrats Are Blue: Secular Liberalism and the Decline of the People's Party*. New York: Encounter Books, 2007.

Sugarman, Tracy. *We Had Sneakers, They Had Guns*. Syracuse, NY: Syracuse University Press, 2009.

Thompson, Julius. *The Black Press in Mississippi, 1865–1985*. Gainesville: University Press of Florida, 1993.

Watson, Bruce. *Freedom Summer: The Savage Season That Made Mississippi Burn and America a Democracy*. New York: Penguin, 2010.

Watson, William Marvin, and Sherwin Markman. *Chief of Staff: Lyndon Johnson and His Presidency*. New York: Thomas Dunne Books, 2004.

Watters, Pat. *The South and the Nation*. New York: Pantheon Books, 1969.

Weber, Michael. *Don't Call Me Boss: David L. Lawrence, Pittsburgh's Renaissance Mayor*. Pittsburgh: University of Pittsburgh Press, 1988.

Weisbrot, Robert. *Freedom Bound: A History of America's Civil Rights Movement*. New York: Norton, 1990.

White, Theodore H. *America in Search of Itself: The Making of the President, 1956–1980*. New York: Harper & Row, 1982.

_____. *The Making of the President, 1964*. New York: Atheneum, 1965.

Williams, Juan. *Eyes on the Prize: America's Civil Rights Movement*. New York: Penguin, 1987.

Woods, Randall Bennett. *LBJ: Architect of American Ambition*. New York: Simon & Schuster, 2006.

Media

"Aaron E. Henry." *Baltimore Sun*, May 20, 1997.

"Aaron Henry Fought Racial Injustice." *Chicago Sun-Times*, May 20, 1997.

"Annie Devine, 88, Rights Advocate in Mississippi." *New York Times*, September 1, 2000.

Asher, Aaron. "I Reckon You're One of Them New York Doves." *American Heritage*, November/December 2006.

"Aug. 24, 1964: DNC Keynote Speaker." ABC News. 2011. http://abcnews.go.com/video/playerIndex?id=9315932.

"Bayard Rustin Is Dead at 75." *New York Times*, August 25, 1987.

Biography of Allen Lowenstein. Yale Law School. 2011. http://www.law.yale.edu/intellectuallife/lowensteinbio.htm.

Cohen, Adam. "Widow and the Wizard." *Time*, May 18,1998.

"Commies Tied to Freedom Demo Group." *Jackson Daily News*, August 22, 1964.

Dallek, Robert. "My Search for Lyndon Johnson." *American Heritage*, September 1991.

Dubose, Lou. "The Black Vote in a Red State." *Washington Spectator*, November 15, 2008.

Dufresne, Marcel. "Exposing the Secrets of Mississippi Racism." *American Journalism Review*, October 1991. http://www.ajr.org/Article.asp?id=1311.

Elliott, Debbie. "When Students Ignited a Change in Racial Politics." NPR, April 14, 2010. http://www.npr.org/templates/story/story.php?storyId=125908995.

Frady, Marshall. "The Big Guy." *New York Review of Books*, November 2002.

Fraser, C. David. "60s Voices: Reflections on Civil Rights Movement." *New York Times*, April 18, 1988.

"Freedom Group Linked to Communist Fronts." *Jackson Clarion Ledger*, August 22, 1964.

Gilbert, Craig. "Doar Stood Tall for Civil Rights in South." *Milwaukee Journal Sentinel*, August 9, 2009.

Hofstadter, Richard. "The Paranoid Style in American Politics." *Harpers*, November 1964.

Holland, Dick. "The Johnson Treatment." *Austin Chronicle*, May 3, 2002.

Humphrey, Hubert H. 1948 National Democratic Convention Address. American Rhetoric. 2001–2011. http://www.americanrhetoric.com/speeches/huberthumphey1948dnc.html.

Klopfer, Susan, Klopfer Fred, and Klopfer, Barry. *Where Rebels Roost: Mississippi Civil Rights Revisited*. lulu.com.

Lewis, David Levering. Review of *Freedom Summer* by Bruce Watson. *SFGate*, June 27, 2010. http://www.sfgate.com/cgi-bin/article.cgi?f=/c/a/2010/06/27/RVL41E0CS8.DTL.

Marolda, Edward J. "Tonkin Gulf Crisis, August 1964." Naval Historical Center, July 13, 2005.

Martin, Douglas. "Winson Hudson, Tireless Civil Rights Activist, Dies." *New York Times*, May 9, 2004.

Mayer, Jeremy D. "LBJ Fights the White Backlash." *Probe* 33, n.1 (Spring 2001).

"Mississippian Relates Struggle of Negro in Voter Registration." *New York Times*, August 24, 1964.

"Mississippi Factions Clash Before Convention Panel." *New York Times*, August 23, 1964.

Morrison, Donald. "Books: The Making of a President." *Time*. November 29, 1992.

Moses, Robert. Testimony Before the United States Senate Judiciary Committee, September 4, 2007.

Neshoba news.blogspot.com/2005/06.

Nunnelley, William A. "T. Eugene 'Bull' Connor." Alabama Department of Archives and History. Alabama Moments in American History. http://www.alabamamoments.state.al.us/sec62.html.

Perlstein, Rick. "1964 Republican Convention: Revolution from the Right." *Smithsonian*, August 2008.

"President Johnson Orders Pants from Joe Haggar." August 9, 1964. American RadioWorks. 2011. http://americanradioworks.publicradio.org/features/prestapes/lbj_haggar.html.

"Reds Among the Rightists." *Jackson Daily News*, October 25, 1964.

Sherrill, Robert. "Looking at America." *New York Times*, September 14, 1980.

Sidey, Hugh, "Sad Song of the Delta." *Time*, June 24, 1991.

Smith, Vern. "Showdown." *The Crisis*, July-August 2004.

Stricherz, Mark. "King David's Legacy." *America: The National Catholic Weekly*, September 22, 2008.

Sturgeon, Kelso. "Freedom Party Makes Plans for Challenge at Convention." *Jackson Daily News*, August 7, 1964.

Texas Observer, June 10,1960.

"The Least of These." *Austin Chronicle*, March 10, 2003.

"The Rev. Ed King." *Jackson Free Press*, October 30, 2003.

"The Southern Manifesto." *Congressional Record*, 84th Congress Second Session, v. 102, pt. 4. Government Printing Office, Washington DC, March 12, 1956.

Tisdale, David. "Peggy Jean Connor: A Pioneer in Mississippi Civil Rights." *Southern Quarterly*, July 1, 2000

"Tougaloo College." We Shall Overcome: Historic Places in the Civil Rights Movement. National Park Service. http://www.nps.gov/history/nr/travel/civilrights/mi1.htm.

"Victoria Gray Adams, Civil Rights Advocate." *Washington Post*, September 9, 2006.

Watson, Bruce. "The Summer of Our Discontent." *American Heritage*, Summer 2010.

Wicker, Tom. "Mississippi Delegates Withdraw, Rejecting a Seating Compromise; Convention Then Approves Plan." *New York Times*, August 26, 1964.

Zeitz, Joshua. "Democratic Debacle." *American Heritage*, June/July 2004.

_____. "1964: The Year the Sixties Began." *American Heritage*, October 2006.

Index

Adams, Victoria Gray 12, 21, 77, 166, 167, 189
Adams, Victorine 122
Agnew, Spiro 191
Algebra Project 182
Allen, Louis 12, 27
American Baptist Theological Seminary 17
American Heritage 173
Atlanta Daily World 73

Bailey, John 99, 114, 115, 185
Baines, Joseph Wilson 41
Baker, Ella 66
Baker, Howard 175
Baltimore Orioles 112
"Banana Boat Song" 92
Barkley, Alben 13
Barnett, Ross 27, 73
Bay of Pigs 70
Bayh, Birch 114, 148, 185
Baylor University 41
Beatles 11, 79, 112
Beittel, Adam 75–76, 189
Belafonte, Harry 78, 92, 93
Belfrage, Sally 149
Berea College 35
Berlin Wall 70
Billboard 11
"Black Power" 169, 183, 188
Blackwell, Unita 76, 77, 80, 147, 165–166, 190–191
Blair, Ezell, Jr. 17
Bond, James 11
Booth, John Wilkes 5
Boyle, Tony 184
Bradlee, Benjamin 48
Brandon, Henry 136

Brinkley, David 129
Brown, Edmund "Pat" 100, 114, 154, 158
Brown, Linda 14
Brown, R. Jess 36
Brown v. Board of Education 14
Buchanan, James P. 45
Buffalo Bills 112
Bunning, Jim 55
Bush, Dorothy V. 130
Bush, George 181
Byrd, Harry 15, 51–53
Byrd, Robert 181

Califano, Joseph 2, 3, 87, 90
Cameron, John 39
Canson, Verna 114, 122
"Can't Buy Me Love" 11
Carmichael, Stokely 66, 78, 92, 145, 169, 182
Carter, Jimmy 165, 174, 181, 182, 188
Central Intelligence Agency 175
Chafee, Lois 76
Chaney, James 7, 39, 57, 58, 62, 64, 66, 77, 80, 86, 95
Channing, Carol 162
Chicago Defender 73
Chicago White Sox 55, 112
Church, Frank 175, 176, 188
Civil Rights Act of 1957 22
Civil Rights Act of 1964 63, 67, 82, 86, 131, 132, 139, 160, 167, 173, 186
Clay, Cassius 11
Cleveland Call and Post 72
Clifford, Clark 126, 129, 162
Clinton, Bill 181, 184
Cobb, Charlie 33
Cochran, Thad 191
Collier, Clinton 78

Collins, E.K. 107, 108, 113, 192
Congress of Racial Equality (CORE) 12, 16, 18, 23, 31, 32, 35, 56, 85, 90, 107, 169
Connally, John 106, 111, 158
Connor, Theophilus "Bull" 19, 148
Conscience of a Conservative 68
Cornell University 56
Council of Federated Organizations (COFO) 31, 33, 35, 38, 92
"Crazy Guggenheim" 55
Credentials Committee 2, 7, 79, 80, 81, 91, 92, 96, 98–106, 108, 113, 114, 115, 117, 119, 121, 123, 124, 126, 127, 134, 141, 143, 145, 146, 147, 148, 152, 165, 167, 169, 184, 190

Daley, Richard 99, 156–157, 163
Daniel, Price 15, 117, 121, 128, 134
Dardin, C.R. 77–78
Declaration of Independence 5
DeLoach, Cartha "Deke" 65, 83–86, 92, 177, 178, 187
Delta Algebra Project 182
Democratic National Committee 18, 130
Dennis, David 32
Devine, Annie 77, 121, 149, 152, 189
Dewey, Thomas 159
Dexter Avenue Baptist Church 17
Diggs, Charles 114, 117, 124, 146
Dirksen, Everett 63, 70
Disraeli, Benjamin 1
"Dixie" 73
Dixiecrats 13
Doar, John 36
Dodd, Thomas 129, 154–155
Dodds, William 132
"Domestic Marshall Plan" 16
Donaldson, Ivanhoe 12, 32
Douglas, Paul 47
Drake University 37, 38, 187
Ducksworth, Roman 12–13, 21, 63

Eastland, James 15, 24–25, 62, 73, 76, 104, 121, 122–123, 189, 191–192
Ebeneezer Baptist Church 17
Economic Opportunity Act 95
Ed Sullivan Show 55
Edison, Thomas 5
Edwards, Willie, Jr. 13
Eisenhower, Dwight 22, 23, 68
Eisenhower, Milton 72
"11 and 8" 80, 96
Ellender, Allen 15

Ervin, Sam 15
Evans, Rowland 48
Evers, Medgar 20, 21, 36, 189
Eyes on the Prize 3

Fair Employment Practices Commission 47
Farmer, James 12, 16, 23, 35, 85, 90, 107
Federal Bureau of Investigation (FBI) 8, 65, 83, 84, 107, 175, 187
Ferraro, Geraldine 181
Finch, Cliff 191
Finney, Tom 138, 142
Fleming, George 72
Fong, Hiram 70
Fontaine, Frank 55
Ford, Gerald 192
Forman, James 92, 151, 152, 166
Fortas, Abe 45, 49, 126, 129, 162
Frady, Marshall 48
Freedom Houses 31, 57, 65
Freedom Riders 18
Freedom Schools 31, 32, 35, 39, 57, 65, 76
Freedom Summer 37, 38, 54, 56, 57, 62, 110, 132, 187
Freeman, Orville 128
Frost, Robert 5
Fulbright, J. William 15

Galbreath, John Kenneth 72
Garner, John Nance 129
George, Walter F. 15
Gleason, Jackie 55, 112
"Go Tell It on the Mountain" 104, 109
Goldfinger 11
Goldwater, Barry 11, 67–73, 80, 91, 95, 119, 124, 127, 128, 132, 136, 160, 170, 175, 179, 186–187
Goodman, Andrew 7, 57, 58, 62, 64, 66, 77, 80, 86, 95
Goodwin, Doris Kearns 44, 47, 50, 173
Goralski, Robert 106
Gore, Albert Sr. 15
Graham, Katharine 48
The Grapes of Wrath 131
Gray, Victoria 39, 152
Green, Edith 114, 116, 118, 124, 165, 181, 185–186
Green Compromise 115, 125
Greenfield, Meg 48
Greensboro sit-in 17, 26, 66
Gridiron Dinner 51, 53
Gulf of Tonkin Resolution 65, 86, 87

Guyot, Lawrence 32, 66, 78, 166, 188–189

Haggar, Joe 50
Hamer, Fannie Lou 7, 32, 35, 39, 53, 66, 75, 102–106, 108, 109, 110, 113, 114, 115, 124, 125, 141, 145, 146, 149, 152, 154, 165, 183–184, 188, 189, 191
Hamer, Perry "Pap" 103
Hamilton College 26
Harriman, Averill 128
Hart, Gary 175
Hart, Philip 175
"Hello, Dolly" 162
Henry, Aaron 32, 39, 53, 75, 80, 101, 104, 108, 109, 113, 114, 115, 117, 119, 124, 128, 139, 140, 141, 142, 143, 144, 146, 149, 151, 152, 154, 165, 170, 184, 188
Heston, Charlton 93
Hill, Lister 15
Hitchcock, Alfred 112
Hodges, Luther 128
Holland, Spessard 15
Hollywood Bowl 112
Hoover, J. Edgar 8, 58, 59, 60, 61, 84, 90, 187
Horace Mann High School 26
Houston, John 39
Houston Post 162
Howard University 16
Huddleston, Walter 175
Hudson, Winson 76, 190
Hughes, Richard 114, 130
Humphrey, Hubert 6, 7, 13, 14, 30, 47, 51, 53, 85, 86, 91, 96, 117, 119, 121, 123, 124, 125, 127, 128, 129, 132, 134, 138–139, 140, 141, 142, 143, 144, 146, 151–158, 160, 164–165, 169–170, 180–181
Humphrey, Muriel 156, 157
Huntley, Chet 129, 160
Hurst, E.H. 75

"I Want to Hold Your Hand" 11
Inouye, Daniel 129

Jackson, Jesse 183
Jackson Clarion Ledger 113
Jackson Daily News 113
Jackson State University 191
Jefferson, Thomas 5, 13
Jeffrey, Mildred 132
Jenkins, Walter 84, 100, 111, 114, 115, 127, 128, 136, 153, 177–178, 187
Jeopardy television program 11
"Joe Glotz" 85, 90, 140, 173, 174

John Birch Society 69
John F. Kennedy Presidential Library and Museum 3
Johnson, "Lady Bird" 51, 52, 131, 136, 137, 138
Johnson, Lynda Bird 84
Johnson, Lyndon B. 2, 3, 6, 7, 8, 11, 14, 15, 16, 22, 23, 25, 34–35, 40, 41–54, 56, 58, 61, 62, 64, 65, 69, 71, 80 — 87, 90, 92, 94, 95, 98, 99, 106, 110, 111, 114, 115, 117, 121, 125, 126, 129, 131, 132, 133, 134, 135, 137, 144, 146, 147, 150, 152–153, 157, 158, 160–162, 164–165, 173–174, 177, 178, 179–180
Johnson, Paul 27–28, 32, 35, 62, 64, 86, 106, 192
Johnson, Rebekah 41
Johnson, Sam 41
"Johnson Treatment" 48–53, 91, 132
Johnston, Olin 15
Jones, Parnelli 112
Judd, Walter 70

Kaler, Irving 117
Kansas City Call 16
Kastenmeier, Robert 114, 124
Katzenbach, Nicholas 61, 62, 77, 90
Keating, Kenneth 111
Kefauver, Estes 15
Kennedy, Edward "Ted" 56, 159
Kennedy, Jacqueline 22, 159
Kennedy, John F. 6, 11, 15, 18, 19, 20, 21, 22, 23, 41, 63, 68, 82, 99, 129, 131, 157, 159, 160, 165
Kennedy, Robert F. 8, 18, 51, 53, 58, 61, 84, 110, 111, 127, 129, 153, 159–160, 177, 180
Kennedy, Rose 159
Kerr, Robert 47
King, Corretta Scott 18
King, Ed 32, 53, 76, 78, 103, 104, 108, 114, 115, 119, 124, 125, 138, 139, 140, 141, 142, 146, 149, 190
King, Marjorie 114 .
King, Martin Luther, Jr. 8, 12, 17–18, 19, 33, 34, 35, 58, 66, 80, 85, 90, 92, 94, 95, 107, 110, 113, 114, 119, 121, 124, 125, 126, 127, 128, 132, 138, 139, 140, 141, 142, 146, 151, 152, 154, 169, 177, 180, 182–183, 187
Kleberg, Richard 43
Kotz, Nick 15, 43, 45
Ku Klux Klan 1, 13, 16, 28, 33, 56, 57, 58, 60, 62, 69, 92, 140

"Landslide Lyndon" 46
Lawrence, David 68, 91, 99, 100, 103,
    108, 115, 117, 121, 122, 123, 127, 128,
    134, 138, 141, 142, 143, 148, 169, 184–
    185
Lee, George 12
Lee, Herbert 12, 21, 27, 63, 75, 80
Lewis, David Levering 35
Lewis, John 17, 18, 28–29, 33, 34, 35, 36,
    39, 62, 66, 80, 85, 145, 147, 151, 167–
    169, 183
Lincoln, Abraham 5, 24, 136, 138
Lindsey, Merrill 78
Liston, Sonny 11
Lodge, Henry Cabot 68, 70
Long, Huey 43–44, 47
Long, Russell 15, 47
Lowenstein, Allard 29–30, 35, 124, 125
Lyndon Baines Johnson Library and
    Museum 3, 8

MacGregor, Clark 181
USS Maddox 64
Mansfield, Mike 154
March on Washington 12, 33, 90, 131
Mark Hopkins Hotel 69
Markman, Sherwin 117, 121, 134, 141,
    142, 143
Marshall, Burke 60, 62
McCain, Francis 17
McCarthy, Eugene 129, 153–154, 179
McClellan, John 15
McCormack, John 60, 61, 148
McDonald's restaurant 11
McFarland, Ernest 68
McGhee, Silas 78, 92
McGovern, George 181
McGrory, Mary 153
McLaurin, Charles 74, 191
McLemore, Leslie 101, 166, 191
McMathias, Charles 175
McNamara, Robert 2, 3, 86–88, 90, 154,
    156
McNeil, Joseph 17
Meet the Press 114
Meredith, James 36, 108
Merrill, Robert 130
Middleton, W.G. 78
Miles, Kay 34
Miller, Bill 71
Miller, Michael 145
Miller, Patti 3, 37–39, 170–171, 187
Mink, Patsy 185
Miss America 79

Mississippi: The Closed Society 34
Mississippi Freedom Democratic Party
    2, 6, 34, 39, 40, 43, 65, 80, 81, 84, 85,
    86, 87, 90, 92, 95, 96, 97, 98, 101, 108,
    109, 113, 114, 119, 121, 125, 126, 132,
    140, 142, 143, 145, 149, 152, 162, 163,
    164, 169, 170, 189
Mondale, Walter 3, 6, 109, 117, 119, 120,
    123, 128, 134, 138, 141, 141, 143, 165,
    167, 175, 181
Moody, Anne 21
Moore, Amzie 26–27
Moore, William Lewis 13
Morgan, Robert 175
Morse, Wayne 115, 151
Moses, Donna 114
Moses, Robert 1, 7, 25, 26, 27, 28, 29, 30,
    31, 32, 35, 36, 39, 53, 54, 56, 62, 65,
    75, 78, 80, 95, 103, 114, 119, 121, 122,
    125, 132, 138, 140, 145, 151, 166, 182
Moursund, A.W. 135
Moyers, Bill 153, 173
Mozart, Wolfgang 5

National Association for the Advance-
    ment of Colored People (NAACP) 8,
    12, 16, 27, 31, 32, 35, 107
National Civil Liberties Clearinghouse
    30
National Council of Churches 151
National Urban League 16
National Youth Administration 44
New York Mets 55
New York Times 95, 99, 113, 128, 149, 192
New York World's Fair 11, 31
New York Yankees 55, 112
Newman, Edwin 106
Newsweek 48
Nixon, Richard 18, 68, 174, 175, 180, 186
North Carolina A&T University 17
North Carolina State University 30
Novak, Robert 48

Oakland Raiders 112
O'Daniel, Wilbert "Pappy" 45
O'Donnell, Kenneth 91
Olson, Lynne 79
Oregon Education Association 115

Parker, Mack Charles 12, 36, 63
Parks, Rosa 14
Pastore, John 130–131, 133
Patton, Jim 128
Pearl Harbor 5

"Pepsi Generation" 55
Philadelphia Democratic Executive
 Committee 157
Philadelphia Inquirer 136
Philadelphia Phillies 55
Phillips, Rubel 32
Picasso, Pablo 5
Pittman, Jack 150
"Please, Please Me" 11
Poitier, Sidney 78, 92, 93
Pratt, Jack 151
Price, Cecil 57–58, 95
Princeton University 182
Public Broadcasting System (PBS) 3

Queens College 57

Randolph, A. Philip 92, 169
Rauh, Joseph 7, 30, 31, 33, 60, 66, 80, 81,
 82, 86, 91, 97, 98, 100, 101, 103, 106,
 107, 108, 113, 114, 115, 119, 124, 125,
 132, 134, 140, 141, 142, 143, 144, 145,
 147, 149, 151, 154, 169, 184
Ray, James Earl 183
Rayburn, Sam 47
Reagan, Ronald 181, 186
Reagon, Bernice Johnson 77
Reedy, George 72, 135, 136, 150, 162–163
Reese, John Earl 13
"Regular Democrats" 2, 34, 66, 100, 125,
 150
Reid, Ogden 60, 61
Republican Senatorial Campaign Com-
 mittee 68
Reston, James 128
Reuther, May 185
Reuther, Victor 131
Reuther, Walter 7, 60, 82, 86, 98, 125,
 126, 129, 131, 133, 134, 138, 140, 141,
 142, 144, 185
Richmond, David 17
Rich's department store 17
Robertson, A. Willis 15
Robinson, Jackie 72–73
Rockefeller, Nelson 68, 69, 70, 72
Romney, George 70
Roosevelt, Eleanor 84
Roosevelt, Franklin D. 44, 45, 82, 84,
 98, 136, 138
Roosevelt, Franklin D., Jr. 96
Rowe, James 153
Rusk, Dean 156
Russell, Richard 15, 22, 34, 47, 91, 100,
 126, 127, 134–135, 138

Rustin, Bayard 89, 90, 92, 110, 138, 140,
 147, 151, 169
Rutgers University 189
Ryan, William 60, 61

Sanders, Carl 147–148
Savas, Ted 4
Schweiker, Richard 175
Schwerner, Mickey 7, 56, 58, 62, 64, 66,
 77, 80, 86, 95
Schwerner, Rita 56, 106
Scott, W. Kerr 15
Scrabble 48
Scranton, William 68, 70, 72
Secret Service 84
"Segregation Forever" 13
Sellers, Cleveland 29
Shapp, Milton 185
Shaw University 17
"She Loves Me" 11
Shea Stadium 11
Sheppard, Morris 45
Shriver, Sargent 87
Siegenthaler, John 18
Silver, James W. 34
Skelton, Red 112
Smathers, George 15
Smith, Francis 157
Smith, Lamar 12
Smith, Margaret Chase 70
Smith, R.L.T. 78
Southern Christian Leadership Confer-
 ence 8, 12, 17, 31, 90, 131, 151, 177, 187
"Southern Manifesto" 14, 15
Southwest Texas State Teachers College
 42
Sparkman, John 15
Spike, Bob 151
Stahl, Norman 148
Stanford University 30
Steinbeck, Elaine 131
Steinbeck, John 131
Stennis, John 15, 23, 25, 62, 104,.191, 192
Steptoe, E.W. 75
Stevenson, Coke 45, 46
Streamline Bar 74
Student Nonviolent Coordinating Com-
 mittee (SNCC) 8, 17, 18, 26, 27, 28,
 29, 31, 35, 36, 37, 57, 58, 66, 74, 78,
 85, 90, 103, 145, 169, 177, 182, 183
Sutherland, Elizabeth 170

Texas State University-St.Marcos 42
"This Little Light of Mine" 75, 104

Thomas, Arthur 151
Thoreau, Henry David 5
Thurmond, Strom 13, 14, 15, 73
USS *Ticonderoga* 64
Till, Emmett 12, 21, 63, 124
Tougaloo College 21, 32, 75, 76, 188,
  189, 190
Tower, John 175
Travis, Jimmy 78
Truman, Harry 5, 13, 136, 138, 180
Turnbow, Hartman 75, 80
Turnbow, "Sweets" 80
USS *Turner* Joy 64
"Twist and Shout" 11

Ulman, Al 114, 115
United Auto Workers 7, 60, 82, 86, 131
United States Commission on Civil
  Rights 16
University of Arizona 67
University of Minnesota 16, 117
University of Mississippi 36
University of North Carolina 30
Unruh, Jesse 100

Valenti, Jack 154
Van Dyke, Vonda 79
Vanocur, Sander 100
The Vantage Point 180

Wagner, Robert 153
Wallace, George 19, 174
War on Poverty 54, 87, 186
Washington, George 5
Washington Post 48

Washington Star 153
Watergate 175
Watkins, Hollis 33, 166
Watson, Bruce 64
Watson, Marvin 149
"We Shall Overcome" 66, 73, 75, 78, 149
Wellstone, Paul 181
Wesley Foundation 37
Western College for Women 35
What's My Line 55
White, Theodore 37, 53, 71, 104, 149,
  164, 187
White Citizens Council 16, 62
Wicker, Tom 149, 150
Wiley College 16
Wilkins, Roy 8, 12, 16, 72, 90, 92, 107,
  119, 125, 144, 145, 146, 147, 188
Williams, Harrison 114
Winn, Doug 127
Wirtz, Willard 138
Woods, Randall Bennett 169
Wright, Frank Lloyd 5
Wright, Orville 5
Wright, Wilbur 5
Wright, Zephyr 23

Yablonski, Jake 184
Yarmolinsky, Adam 3, 87, 95, 186
Yoseloff, Martin 4
Young, Andrew 147
Young, George 72
Young, Whitney 16

Zeitz, Joshua 173